Teaching and Learning Portuguese in Canada:
Multidisciplinary Contributions to SLA Research and Practice

Inês Cardoso & Vander Tavares

Copyright © 2020 Boavista Press

All rights reserved.

ISBN: 1944676995
ISBN-13: 978-1944676995

Roosevelt, NJ

We would like to acknowledge the contribution made by the Scientific Committee in the form of a blind peer review, whose insights helped collaboratively produce a rigorous and innovative volume:

Adriana Fischer
Fundação Universidade Regional de Blumenau (FURB) – Blumenau, Brazil
Cátia Martins
York University, Canada
Fatiha Dechicha Parahyba
Universidade Federal de Pernambuco, Brazil
Luísa Álvares Pereira
Jubilee from Universidade de Aveiro, Portugal
Micaela Ramon
Universidade do Minho, Portugal
Naomi Nagy
University of Toronto, Canada
Pedro de Moraes Garcez
Universidade Federal do Rio Grande do Sul (UFRGS), Brazil
Philipp Sebastian Angermeyer
York University, Canada
Sílvia Melo-Pfeifer,
University of Hamburg, Germany
Vera Lúcia Cristóvão
Universidade Estadual de Londrina, Brazil

CONTENTS

Acknowledgments — vii

Contributing Authors — ix

Preface — xiii
Inês Cardoso
Vander Tavares

SECTION I. UNDERSTANDING THE DEMOGRAPHICS AND SOCIOLINGUISTIC CONTEXTS OF PORTUGUESE INSTRUCTION

1 Teaching Portuguese in Canada: Situation, Changes and Challenges — 3
Ana Paula Ribeiro
Universidade Aberta

2 Teaching Portuguese as a Heritage Language in Montreal — 20
Fabio Scetti
Université Paul Valéry Montpellier III

3 The Values Attached to Speaking Portuguese among Brazilian Migrant Families in Toronto: Pride and Profit — 35
Pedro de Moraes Garcez
Cecília Fischer Dias
Giana Bess
Universidade Federal do Rio Grande do Sul

4 Portuguese in Toronto: Identity, Attitudes and Linguistic Variation — 55
Michol F. Hoffman
James A. Walker
York University & La Trobe University

5 *Portinglês* Use in Toronto — 71
Joe Correia
York University

6   A Reflection on the Challenges of Language   86
    Acquisition Outside the Portuguese Classroom
    Evandro Rodrigues
    University of Toronto

SECTION II. DESCRIBING PRAXEOLOGICAL APPROACHES – PROGRAM DEVELOPMENTS AND PEDAGOGICAL DEVICES

7   The Role of Linguistics in the Additional Language   101
    University Classroom: The Case of the Undergraduate
    Portuguese Program at the University of Toronto
    Anabela Rato
    Suzi Lima
    Natália Rinaldi
    University of Toronto

8   A Personal Writing Device, with Heritage Language   122
    Speakers, at the University of Toronto
    Luciana Graça
    Camões, Instituto da Cooperação e da Língua, I. P.
    University of Toronto

9   Teaching Portuguese Language and Lusophone   142
    Literatures at York University: Innovating Curriculum
    and Enhancing the Student Experience
    Inês Cardoso
    University of Aveiro, CIDTFF & Polytechnic of Leiria
    Maria João Dodman
    York University

10 Challenging Cultural Stereotypes in the Pluricentric 164
    Portuguese as a Foreign Language Classroom
    Vander Tavares
    York University

Cover by Morgan Rogers, Co & Co, Halifax, NS

ACKNOWLEDGMENTS

As the Editors, in addition to recognizing the invaluable contribution made by the Scientific Committee, we would like to acknowledge our deep appreciation to the authors of this volume for their hard work and continuous patience as we worked to materialize this project. The current pandemic has made our lives more challenging than usual, and it was only through the support we received from each contributing author that we were able to reach the end, *together*. Thank you for being a part of this project and believing in it as much as we did. Your unique contributions have helped us better understand the relationship between Canada and the Portuguese language.

Muito obrigado,
Inês Cardoso & Vander Tavares.

Contributing Authors

Giana Bess holds a degree in Portuguese and English teaching from Universidade Federal do Rio Grande do Sul (UFRGS), Brazil, where she was a Brazilian National Council for Scientific and Technological Development (CNPq) research initiation grantee.

Inês Cardoso is Assistant Professor at the University of Aveiro and the Polytechnic of Leiria (School of Education and Social Sciences), Portugal. From 2013 to 2019, she was Sessional Assistant Professor, from Camões, Instituto da Cooperação e da Língua, at York University. She holds a PhD in Didactics and is also part of "CIDTFF – Research Centre on Didactics and Technology in the Education of Trainers". She coordinates the group "ProTextos – Ensino e Aprendizagem da Escrita de Textos."

Joe Correia is an educator at the Toronto Catholic District School Board, specializing in Portuguese language acquisition. He holds a Master of Arts degree in Linguistics at York University from 2015, where he completed his Major Research Paper entitled "Portinglês Use in the Greater Toronto Area." He interprets in the healthcare industry for patients that suffer from mental health illnesses, as well as patients with other issues such as neuro-cognitive, neuro-stroke and chronic pain.

Cecília Fischer Dias holds a degree in Translation (English–Portuguese) from Universidade Federal do Rio Grande do Sul (UFRGS), Brazil, where she was a Brazilian National Council for Scientific and Technological Development (CNPq) research initiation grantee.

Maria João Dodman is Associate Professor at York University where she teaches Lusophone cultures and Literatures in the department of Languages, Literatures & Linguistics. She holds a PhD from the University of Toronto. Her research interests and publication record include early modern Portuguese and Spanish literature, colonial encounters, Portuguese island culture and literary production and the Brazilian Northeast Novel.

Luciana Graça is a Portuguese Language Lecturer of Camões, Instituto da Cooperação e da Língua, in the Department of Spanish and Portuguese at the University of Toronto. She holds a PhD in Didactics and is also part of "CIDTFF – Research Centre on Didactics and Technology in the Education of Trainers." She is part of the research group "ProTextos – Ensino e Aprendizagem da Escrita de Textos."

Michol Hoffman is Associate Professor in the Department of Languages, Literatures and Linguistics at York University.

Suzi Lima is an Assistant Professor in the Department of Linguistics at the University of Toronto. She works on the documentation and description of Indigenous languages spoken in Brazil. She has also published about semantic aspects of Brazilian Portuguese. Her research interests include language acquisition, language documentation, linguistic typology and description, language revitalization, and semantics.

Pedro de Moraes Garcez is Professor of Applied Linguistics at Universidade Federal do Rio Grande do Sul (UFRGS), Brazil, and a CNPq (Brazilian National Council for Scientific and Technological Development) scholar. He received his PhD in Education, Culture and Society from the University of Pennsylvania. As a CNPq grantee, he was a visiting scholar at the University of Toronto's Ontario Institute for Studies in Education during the 2015-2016 academic year. He serves as associate editor of the *Journal of Sociolinguistics*.

Anabela Rato is an Assistant Professor in the Department of Spanish and Portuguese at the University of Toronto, Canada. She holds a PhD in Language Sciences from the University of Minho, Portugal. Her research interests include Second Language Speech Learning, Heritage Language Acquisition, and Applied Phonetics. She is also the President of the Canadian Association of Teachers of Portuguese (CATPor).

Ana Paula Ribeiro has been teaching Portuguese as a foreign language since 1985. From 2010 to 2018, she was the Coordinator of the Portuguese Language Program in Canada, representing Camões, Instituto da Cooperação e da Língua. She holds a PhD in Education and Interculturality from the Universidade Aberta and is the author of several Portuguese language teaching books for international students, including "Português XXI" and "Avançar em Português."

Natalia Rinaldi is a PhD candidate in Hispanic Linguistics at the University of Toronto. She is interested in language acquisition, language variation and psycholinguistics, and works on the acquisition of morphosyntactic and semantic features by monolingual children. Natalia's dissertation investigates how children acquire meaning relying on syntactic cues in Brazilian Portuguese modal verbs.

Evandro Rodrigues is an instructor at the School of Continuing Studies at the University of Toronto, Canada, where he was honored with excellence in teaching in 2014 and 2019 for his successful engagement with his students in learning Portuguese and Translation. As a TESL teacher, he has also provided language support for multinational companies from Brazil, USA and Canada. Additional activities include Portuguese language teaching at *Instituto Camões Toronto* with lessons aimed at promoting self-confidence and fluency in learners.

Fabio Scetti is Associated Lecturer at Université Paul-Valéry Montpellier III / DIPRALANG, France and Associated Researcher at CIRM / McGill University, Montreal, Canada. He holds a PhD in Linguistics and his research interests are: Sociolinguistics, Language Contact, Language Practices, Language, Identity and Migration. He participates in two groups of research in Lexicography of Endangered Minority Languages (VOLF and VVV).

Vander Tavares is an instructor of academic and professional communication skills in the Faculty of Humanities and Social Sciences at Sheridan College in Mississauga, Canada. He holds a PhD in Linguistics and Applied Linguistics from York University, Toronto, Canada. He also teaches courses in Portuguese as a Foreign Language (PFL) and English as a Second Language (ESL). He is the author of *International Students in Higher Education: Language, Identity and Experience from a Holistic Perspective* (Lexington Books/Rowman & Littlefield, 2021).

James A. Walker is Professor of Language Diversity in the Department of Languages and Linguistics at La Trobe University, Melbourne, Australia. From 2000 to 2017 he was at York University, Toronto. He holds a PhD in Linguistics from the University of Ottawa and is the author of *Variation in Linguistic Systems* (Routledge, 2010), *Bequia Talk* (Battlebridge Press, 2013, with Miriam Meyerhoff) and *Canadian English: A Sociolinguistic Perspective* (Routledge, 2015) and editor of *Aspect in Grammatical Variation* (John Benjamins, 2010), *Regional Chinese in Contact* (special issue of *Asia Pacific Language Variation*, 2019) and *Advancing Socio-Grammatical Variation and Change* (Routledge, with Karen Beaman, Isabelle Buchstaller and Sue Fox,

Preface

The development of the Canadian Association of Teachers of Portuguese (CATPOR, http://www.catpor.ca), founded in 2018, has represented an important milestone for the advancement of the teaching of Portuguese in Canada. In addition to the essential role the association has played in fostering a dialogue among teachers with respect to pedagogy, we believe that it would be of great value to now bring together multidisciplinary, scholarly perspectives to the broader theme of teaching and learning Portuguese in Canada. This impetus has led us to the collection of contributions stemming from all education levels that come to uniquely constitute this volume.

The teaching of Portuguese across the vast Canadian territory, characterized by one particular variety at times or through a dynamic convergence of both Portuguese and Brazilian varieties at others, has attracted primarily learners for whom Portuguese may be considered a heritage language. However, the number of learners from non-Lusophone backgrounds in the Portuguese language classroom continues to grow–a trend fueled by motivations as diverse as the learners' profiles.

Both teachers and learners contribute to the multi-dimensional diversity that the teaching and learning experience represents. Teachers and learners, from distinct ethno- and sociolinguistic backgrounds, come together in the classroom to cultivate and celebrate their personally unique–yet interconnected–relationship with the Portuguese language. However, considering that Portuguese in Canada is always taught and learned in a minority language context, teachers and learners' plurilingual and intercultural competencies are more-often-than-not left unacknowledged and unexplored, despite the Portuguese language classroom's rich multilingual and multicultural nature.

In light of these and other factors, this volume has been conceptualised with the objective of bringing scholars and teachers together to promote the sharing of knowledge and to foster a critical reflection relevant to the teaching and learning of Portuguese in Canada, simultaneously informing a holistic mapping of its current expansiveness. Hence, this work presents two main sections:

I. Understanding the Demographics and Sociolinguistic Contexts of Portuguese Instruction;

II. **Describing Praxeological Approaches – Program Developments and Pedagogical Devices.**

We introduce *Section I* beginning with a chapter that contextualizes the "Teaching [of] Portuguese in Canada: situation, changes and challenges," by **Ana Paula Ribeiro**, the former coordinator of the Portuguese language teaching in Canada financed by the Camões Institute/Portuguese Foreign Affairs Ministry of Portugal. Ribeiro held this position between 2010 and 2018, and here she provides an in-depth analysis of the broader instruction of Portuguese in Canada originating from her PhD thesis on this subject. Her study was informed by classroom observations and questionnaires distributed to students from 9 to 18 years old, teachers, and parents of students from 4 to 6 years old in relation to their profiles, motivations, practices, and difficulties concerning Portuguese language teaching and learning. Ribeiro identifies areas requiring special intervention in terms of professional development for the teachers, such as differentiated teaching; critical engagement in the creation of didactic resources in a more collaborative and reflexive environment among teachers; and the use of technologies in the classroom and online.

Secondly, **Fabio Scetti** focuses on the teaching and learning of Portuguese as a Heritage Language (PHL) in Montreal through an ethnographic approach. As PHL faces a decreasing trend in enrolment, Scetti identifies new discourses among the Portuguese-speaking community presenting Portuguese not only as "the language of our families" but also as a language for the inter-connected future, highlighting its global power. The unity of this presumed "international language" is sometimes questioned as the diversity of the language is visible right from within the "Lusophone Community," mainly because of the co-existence of Portuguese and Brazilian nationals within the "same" space. "Authenticity" and "purity," language and identity are topics of a pertinent discussion for a Lusophone collective who locally claims its place internationally, yet locally is still figuring out how to accommodate this intralinguistic diversity and make it a source of strength rather than division.

The third chapter explores "The values attached to speaking Portuguese among Brazilian migrant families in Toronto: Pride and profit," by **Pedro de Moraes Garcez, Cecília Fischer Dias, and Giana Bess**. In a multilingual environment and in the city with the greatest number of Portuguese-speaking people in Canada, interviews informed by an ethnographic approach were conducted with educators, community leaders, and consulate staff, as well as members of more than 30 Brazilian migrant families. Plans and motivations for maintaining Portuguese are analyzed via samples of this dataset configuring speeches of "pride" and/or of "profit." Whether Portuguese is the language of family ties or a language for the job market, these discourses co-exist and provide relevant information regarding foreign language policies and teaching. In fact, this contribution aligns with the previous as both suggest that the potential for the power in Portuguese might be more appealing if language promoters go beyond the realms of heritage and target the "value" of Portuguese in the labor market as well. In a similar vein to the first chapter—in which Ribeiro concludes that there is a noticeable difficulty attracting high school students to learn Portuguese, and foresees its teaching as an accredited foreign language course—such language ideologies, presented now by Garcez, Dias and Bess, point out that the value of language skills for "profit" might be of great use for achieving a wider promotion of Portuguese.

In the fourth chapter, **Michol F. Hoffman and James A. Walker** explore the attitudes of young Torontonian residents of Portuguese descent toward their ethnic and linguistic identities and how these affect their spoken (Canadian) English. Hoffman and Walker also examine the speakers' perceptions in comparison with those of speakers from other communities in the city in terms of their use of linguistic features that define Canadian English. How youth manage the tension between maintaining their family's language and culture while assimilating to the mainstream language and culture is a key question to which the authors respond with illustrative examples. These tensions are coped with in many diverse and complex ways, a discussion which instructors of Portuguese will highly benefit from since one cannot ignore the factors which shape students' personal relationships with the language while teaching the target language. In the case of these Portuguese-Canadians, these relationships are contextualized by code-switching that emerges from the co-existence of geographical, social, and situational varieties of Portuguese in the same city. Accommodating students' experiences with the Portuguese language, without stigmatizing this linguistic hybridity, is only one of many ways in which identity (re)construction can be respected and promoted.

A more in-depth description of this language hybridity is provided by **Joe Correia** in the second-to-last chapter of *Section I*. From a synergy between research conducted for his Master's thesis and his own experience as a Portuguese-Canadian and a high school teacher of Portuguese, Correia defines and describes what *Portinglês* means in the context of Toronto, and how this English-Portuguese blend has functioned as an expression of the Portuguese community assimilation experience to the host society while also preserving some of its ethnolinguistic features. Correia focuses his investigation on the use of *Portinglês* with an attention to the speakers' age and gender and the relationship of these to the frequency in use of *Portinglês*. He also presents a list of keywords that helps further construct the lexical repertoire of *Portinglês* speakers.

We conclude *Section I* with a chapter that takes a reflexive approach to teaching Portuguese in the classroom. **Evandro Rodrigues**, an instructor of Portuguese with enormous experience in online and classroom-based teaching, shares a thoughtful synthesis and a personal report on some useful tools he has adopted in his practice to direct students to a language learning experience beyond the classroom. He also acknowledges the contribution of the Portuguese-speaking communities in Canada for their potential to provide contexts of diverse, naturalistic language use.

Comprising *Section II: Praxeological Approaches – program developments and pedagogical devices* – are four contributions originating from the Portuguese language classroom specifically in the university context. The first two belong to the pioneer university program of Portuguese in Canada, housed at the University of Toronto, while the last two contributions are authored by senior and young researchers at York University, the second of the only two programs of Portuguese at the university level in Canada.

Anabela Rato, Suzi Lima, and Natália Rinaldi present "The role of linguistics in the second language university classroom: The case of the undergraduate Portuguese program at the University of Toronto." Describing the design of five linguistics research-based courses, the authors depart from the assumption that language learning benefits, mainly at an adult age, from metalinguistic knowledge on the part of learners. The authors subsequently demonstrate how this metalinguistic knowledge has been promoted in the courses together with what they refer to as "scientific-linguistic" thinking and research skills. With a range of examples from the areas of phonetics, phonology, syntax, and semantics, pedagogical paths are described showing how the learning of Portuguese in this university context has been anchored in linguistic concepts, aimed to promote critical thinking and cross-disciplinary research skills in the students.

Still at the University of Toronto, **Luciana Graça** explains the use of a personal writing device with heritage language (HL) speakers within an academic language development course. Based on pedagogical and didactic perspectives which value the proficiency already acquired by students in HL and their cultural experiences, as well as a humanized and personalized approach that continuously allows the students' relationship with the language to be taken into consideration, Graça outlines possible writing interventions in the context of the production of personal texts. Topics emerging in *Section I*, such as identity (conflict), culture, and language hybridity have their place now in students' voices through a writing process facilitated by the instructor. Graça demonstrates clearly how both writing processes and skills are being developed, but above all how identities are welcome in their diversity in an environment where the instructor safely stimulates the crossing of boundaries.

The creation and evolution of Portuguese and Luso-Brazilian Studies at York University is described by **Inês Cardoso and Maria João Dodman**. The authors provide insightful information about the university's context, namely the Lusophone-research "friendly" environment, given York University is the home of projects, associations, and centres focused on the Lusophone world; the student population, and the language (on its diversity); and Portuguese-speaking literatures teaching approaches that have been adopted. Informed by multidisciplinary research, pedagogic devices are presented and linked to experiential education opportunities - noting the role of Portuguese-speaking communities and partnerships - student-centred teaching and learning strategies, the development of research and cross-cultural skills, community engagement, and finally cultural sensitivity and global citizenship.

Vander Tavares superbly concludes the volume with a critical analysis of an in-class activity in the context of an advanced-level undergraduate Portuguese-as-a-foreign language classroom at York University. Challenging cultural stereotypes in this pluricentric language context was the main objective of this activity which afforded students an opportunity to reflect on stereotypes of others and of the self in relation to language, culture, and nationalities (including, but not restricted to those of Portuguese-speaking countries). As the students share their reflections with their peers in Portuguese, they imagine themselves as both producers and recipients of cultural stereotypes. Evident in this chapter are first an awareness of cultural images by the students and of the broader consequences of cultural images for intercultural interaction, and second the potential of this kind of activity to foster deep reflection and critical understanding of overgeneralised images of others.

We believe this volume presents novel contributions in a well-balanced, informative, and formative manner, with a clear and relevant connection to *praxis*. As we have summarized, this volume stands for the teaching of Portuguese that accommodates its varieties for Lusophone and non-Lusophone audiences alike. In alignment with this, pedagogical practices are challenged or equated to reflect a transnational and pluricentric approach and to adjust to the relationship of students toward the Portuguese language and Lusophone cultures. Uniquely, this volume offers a significant presentation of the teaching of Portuguese in Canada and of the only Portuguese language learning university programs in Canada. This portrait does not neglect the multilingual context where Portuguese is taught, namely that of the sociocultural contact of Portuguese with

English- and French-speaking Canada. One must note there is a higher presence of researchers and university professors in this volume, hoping that, in future volumes of this kind, there will be more signs of collaborative work among teachers of different levels.

We hope this volume will be useful and illuminating for present and future researchers, teacher trainers, and teachers of Portuguese. With it, we would like to pay homage to all – students, teachers, families, their communities, and all others interested in the teaching-learning of Portuguese – whose contributions to sustaining the life of Portuguese in Canada have now inspired us to recognize and respond to the need for such a volume.

The editors,
Inês Cardoso
Vander Tavares
Summer, 2020

SECTION I
UNDERSTANDING THE DEMOGRAPHICS AND SOCIOLINGUISTIC CONTEXTS OF PORTUGUESE INSTRUCTION

1
Teaching Portuguese in Canada: Situation, Changes and Challenges

Ana Paula Ribeiro
Universidade Aberta

Being a land of immigrants, 21.9% of Canada's current resident population was born outside the country, as stated in the 2016 Census (Statistics Canada, 2017). According to Garnett (2010), 75% of the country's population lives in Ontario, British Columbia, and Quebec. The Canadian people, with their diverse origins, try to preserve the cultural, linguistic, religious, ethical and obviously ethnic diversity brought to the country, which, in turn, defines Canada. Diversity is visible and felt everywhere. Canada's official policy promotes multiculturalism by encouraging the various ethnic groups to preserve their own identity, which gives rise to the cultural mosaic that shapes and defines this country. However, this policy ultimately encourages the development of relatively homogeneous ethnic communities, which, according to Da Silva (2011), facilitates the management and control of ethnic, linguistic, religious and other differences.

Among the diverse communities that make up Canada the way it is today, there is the Portuguese community, estimated to be composed of more than 450,000 inhabitants, spread throughout the country, but with the highest concentration in the province of Ontario (around 300,000 of Portuguese origin). The official and legal Portuguese emigration to Canada began in 1953 and the number of Portuguese immigrants gradually increased, mainly from the Azores, reaching its highest level between 1970 and 1974. This is a community that is already mostly in its second and third generations, with many mixed marriages and a good integration in their host societies; this has caused a measure of distancing from their Portuguese origins and consequently a greater resistance towards the preservation of the Portuguese language and culture. However, and according to our observation, we have to emphasize the important role that Portuguese grandparents and community associations have played in this process of preservation in such a multicultural and intercultural environment.

Considering the multicultural and multilingual character of the Canadian population, many studies were conducted in the time of Pierre Trudeau, Canadian Prime Minister between 1968 to 1984, reflecting the desire of various ethnic groups to preserve their mother language. Following the results of those studies, the Canadian federal government created, in 1977, the *Cultural Enrichment Program,* with the purpose of supporting the teaching of different origin languages and the preservation of the cultural heritage of the different communities. This program, later called the *Heritage Language Program*, is now the *International Language Program* offered by the different Boards of Education. The teaching of these International Languages has been carried out according to three different models, depending on the number of students enrolled and the options of each School Board: i) after the regular school hours; ii) on Saturday morning; iii) integrated during school hours for all school students. The weekly teaching of the international language is, in general, for two and a half hours . In Toronto alone, the number of students involved in this program exceeds 60,000. Although the Canadian federal government is still aware of the importance of learning a foreign language and of preserving heritage languages in a multicultural and multilingual country composed of diversity, Pierre Trudeau's ideals and his policies to support bilingualism and multiculturalism have gradually been affected, in particular in Toronto, where the International Language Program during the day was offered in the past in more schools than nowadays.

In a country of such a great geographical size, the Portuguese community is specially present in and around Toronto and in Montreal, but also in other cities like Ottawa, Winnipeg, Edmonton, Calgary, Vancouver, Cambridge, Kitchener, Kingston and London. The fact that the community is already in its second and third generation and that the existence of many mixed marriages within the community have made Canada's population of Portuguese descent open to other cultures and exposed to more than one second language, in most cases, has reinforced the use of English or French at home. These two official languages are, in fact, the most usual languages of communication for these Portuguese descendents, with the exception of some occasions when this communication takes place with the grandparents. There are also some families who occasionally communicate at home in both languages, although the children's ability to understand Portuguese is usually higher than to speak it.

In this new context, teaching and learning the Portuguese language as a mother tongue, like it was done in the first decades after a Portuguese massive emigration, is no longer adequate. Portuguese has become a heritage language, although in some cases the students only inherit cultural references and no longer have proficiency in the language. It was time for a change with a new approach, new programs, new resources and new methodologies. These changes have involved teachers who, for the most part, have another full-time job, and often in areas with no relation to teaching, and who have dedicated most of their extra time to the preservation of the Portuguese language and culture in Canada, teaching sometimes more than one generation of students in community schools and for the different school boards. These teachers are highly dedicated, but they are also very heterogeneous regarding their academic qualifications, their teaching experience, their professional occupation in Canada and even their availability and motivation.

The Portuguese language is taught throughout the country, especially in areas where Portuguese-speaking communities are more concentrated, not only by different school boards, in the context of the International Language Program, like mentioned above, but also by Portuguese community associations and private schools, which have played a fundamental role in the preservation of the language. In 2017, the Portuguese program offered by the school boards, mostly in Ontario, affected approximately 5,400 students, 3,600 of which in the city of Toronto.

Many Portuguese community schools have been facing a significant drop in the number of students who once attended their classes and many were even forced to close, due to the natural and gradual integration of the immigrant community in Canadian society, and, to the decrease of immigrants coming from Portugal. In fact, the number of students enrolled in the Portuguese language program offered by the school boards, especially by the different catholic boards, is much higher than the number of Portuguese students attending community schools. This program is active in many schools in Ontario (Toronto, Mississauga, Oakville, Milton, Hamilton, Windsor, Chatham, Wallaceburg, London, Harrow, West Lorne, Kingston, Cambridge, Kitchener, Ottawa), but also in Montreal, Quebec, and in Winnipeg, in the province of Manitoba.

In the province of Ontario and in the cities of Montreal, Edmonton, Winnipeg, and Vancouver, secondary school students can earn credits with their Portuguese classes that can be used also for university access. This also happens with classes offered by some community and private schools, provided that they are taught by recognized Canadian secondary teachers. This recognition for teachers arriving in Canada with qualifications from Portugal is a long and expensive process. According to the numbers we have, there are not many students attending Portuguese classes at the secondary level, probably due to the fact that, in Canada, most students start attending a Portuguese language class between 4 and 7 years of age although the majority of these students leave the Portuguese classes when they start the secondary level. An important factor is probably the huge and flexible variety of subjects offered by the secondary school curricula. Their selection of subjects in the secondary school is often advised by counsellors and according to many students most of these counsellors consider the study of languages less important for the students' academic curricula. Moreover, during our study, we could understand that the students over 12 years old do not feel so dependent on their parents' wishes and there are many extracurricular activities much more attractive than Portuguese classes on a Saturday morning.

In 2017, around 7,200 students who were enrolled in kindergarten, elementary and secondary schools attended Portuguese classes. Unfortunately, there are some cities where, in spite of a relevant interest in learning Portuguese, there are no teachers with academic background and linguistic proficiency to ensure the teaching of the language.

The presence of Camões, Instituto da Cooperação e da Língua (Instituto Camões) through the Department of Coordination of the Portuguese Language Studies in Canada (CEPE-Canada), as of 2010, was a turning point in Portuguese language teaching and learning in Canada. We were responsible for this department between 2010 and 2018 and, in the beginning, we realized that most of the teachers were teaching Portuguese as a mother language to the students, who belonged already to the second or third generation of the Portuguese community or did not have any relationship with the Portuguese community. A whole different program was proposed to the Portuguese schools, school boards and Portuguese language teachers, in a collaborative process, putting into practice the main objectives of that Portuguese institution, among them: to support and to ensure the quality of the Portuguese language teaching abroad, specially as a second or foreign language, to promote the Portuguese language and culture and to develop appropriate mechanisms for teachers' training.

In Canada, this department is looked after by the coordinator, without the support of any teaching staff or assistants, and its office is located at the Consulate General of Portugal in Toronto. The coordinator works together with the different diplomatic missions in Canada and with the University Professors from Instituto Camões present in four universities, at least between September 2010 and September 2018: University of Toronto, York University, University of Ottawa, and the University of Montreal.

Bearing in mind that there has never been a network of teachers at the level of elementary and secondary education in Canada supported by the Portuguese government, the work of CEPE-Canada, since 2010 on behalf of Instituto Camões, has always required a supervision based on collaboration, negotiation and diplomacy, regarding all those who are involved in this process: teachers, learners, parents, Portuguese community, Portuguese diplomats present in the country, different Canadian and Portuguese-Canadian institutions and lately other Lusophone emigrants, considering more recent substantive emigration from Brazil, Angola, Mozambique.

In the beginning, in September 2010, the new CEPE-Canada tried to understand the situation of the Portuguese language teaching and learning and the profile of both students and teachers, in order to develop a plan that met their needs. At that time, most of the students were still studying Portuguese as if it was their mother language with resources that were not adequate to the new context of the Portuguese community. This situation was causing increasing discouragement and gradual disinterest from the students.

In view of these difficulties and aware of the significant Portuguese community integrated in the Canadian multicultural context, it became clear that it would be important to act in different areas: i) to plan an effective professional training for the Portuguese teachers, who frequently have students with different ages and diverse levels of proficiency in Portuguese in the same class; ii) to have more online courses for both teachers and students; iii) to offer new Portuguese language teaching books appropriate to the profile of the students (Portuguese as a second language); iv) to offer more initiatives to encourage the reading in Portuguese; v) to promote the Portuguese language and culture. All this was important for the young generation to preserve their Portuguese roots and their pride of being Portuguese descendants.

It was also urgent to follow a new strategy to promote and disseminate Portuguese as an important international language, underlining its economic potential in a country with such a large Portuguese community. This new strategy outlined by CEPE-Canada has included: i) a closer contact with the Portuguese community; (ii) more frequent teacher training sessions, more adapted to the context and needs of the teachers and their students; iii) strengthening of the relationship with the different school boards that offer a program of Portuguese language classes, so that it may be preserved or even extended, improving its quality and diversifying the available resources; iv) encouragement to read in Portuguese among the younger ones, without ignoring the adult audience; v) the promotion of the Portuguese language and the Lusophone cultures among the different Portuguese-speaking communities and the Canadian population in general; vi) participation in the certification process of the Portuguese language proficiency, operated by the Portuguese State. This is a global certificate jointly managed by the Portuguese Ministry of Education and the Ministry of Foreign Affairs (through Instituto Camões) and it enables evaluation and full appreciation, recognition and accreditation of students' abilities in Portuguese, in a communicative perspective, regardless of where they live outside Portugal.

It was considered a priority to start a teacher training plan in order to promote a new approach for teaching Portuguese as a second or foreign language, according to the levels of linguistic proficiency established by the Common European Framework of Reference for Languages (Council of Europe, 2018), and to the guidelines and programs proposed by Instituto Camões. This new approach brings new methodologies and interactive activities, the use of new language teaching resources, with a strong focus on the development of communication and interaction. The teachers' training program which has been proposed in recent years has taken into account the profile and needs of the teachers and also the profile of the students. The teachers training program in Canada have always been planned for a maximum of four hours because of their already full schedules.

The training program sessions should take into account not only the knowledge of the teaching and learning context, but also the results of a previous analysis of the training needs of these particular teachers and the knowledge of the profile of both students and teachers, their difficulties, their interests, expectations, methodologies and practices and their resources. Being aware of these facts, we decided to proceed with the present study.

The Study

The study had the following research question: *How can a deeper understanding of the Portuguese teaching and learning context in Canada contribute to a plan for teachers training appropriate to their needs?* In view of this same question, we defined the following research objectives:

i. to understand the context of the Portuguese language teaching and learning in Canada in non-formal, parallel courses, offered mostly by community schools on Saturday morning or, in the case of Ottawa, under the responsibility of a Catholic School Board;

ii. to understand some difficulties, motivations, expectations and needs of students and teachers;

iii. to take some conclusions about the needs of the teachers, depending on the results achieved; and

iv. to contribute toward a plan of teacher training adapted to this particular context and to the needs of students and teachers.

The study was divided into two different stages. Between 2011 and 2014, there was close contact with the teachers and some classes were observed in 12 schools from different cities, with the purpose of obtaining a real knowledge of their context, of the teaching practices and methodologies, the resources used in class and the existing interaction between teachers and students. According to Reis (2011), "observation plays a key role in improving the quality of teaching and learning, providing a strong inspiration and motivation and a strong catalyst for change at school" (p. 11). Observation allowed conclusions to be drawn, before providing some feedback to the teachers themselves during a brief discussion on the observed aspects. More specifically, it was an informal observation, on a short-term visit (about 15 minutes in each classroom), "with an essentially formative character, focused on the individual and collective development of teachers and on improving the quality of teaching and learning." (Reis, 2011, p. 12).

On a second stage, already with an overview of the situation in Canada, and after a collaborative work with some teachers, based on advising and proposing strategies and changes that we felt appropriate to the different contexts, we prepared different questionnaire surveys according to four groups of participants involved in this whole process of teaching and learning the Portuguese language. The participants in this study were teachers, parents of pupils aged between 4 and 6 and students of the following age groups: 9-12 years and 15-18 years old. Eight schools were selected, most of them community-based, that offered a Portuguese language program in the different regions where there is a more significant presence of the Portuguese community: Toronto (2 schools), Ottawa, Montreal, Edmonton, Winnipeg, and Vancouver (2 schools).

Finally, the questionnaires were sent by email, with the close collaboration of the directors of each school and, after a predetermined period of time, the completed questionnaires were collected and sent back by mail. This study was possible because of the good relationship that we could establish with the directors and the teachers of the different schools.

The number of questionnaires collected in relation to the universe of the study is in the following table:

Table 1
Number of questionnaires collected

Target- public (Parents of:)	Questionnaires received	Universe of the study
Students between 4 and 6 years old	**50**	90
Students between 9 and 12 years old	**116**	190
Students between the ages of 15 and 18	**45**	75
Teachers	**36**	59

The four different questionnaires had the same three categories of questions, although some were more complete. They were prepared so that we could understand better: the profile of each public (birthplace, nationality, age, studies, first language, language(s) spoken at home, family in Portugal, etc.); the students (reasons to learn Portuguese; other activities in Portuguese, etc.); the Portuguese classes (methodology, activities practiced, preferences, language used in class, etc.). The questionnaire sent to the teachers was more elaborated and had an extra category related to the professional development they had already had, their real needs and difficulties.

These questionnaires were sent halfway through the school year of 2014-2015, after a considerable period of time used to understand: (i) the Portuguese language teaching and learning context, (ii) the different existing teaching systems and the different institutions that offer Portuguese classes in Canada, (iii) and the Portuguese and Portuguese-speaking communities.

Results of the Study

Most of the students in this study are second or third Portuguese generation and have Portuguese as a heritage language, although Portuguese is rarely the language of communication at home. According to their answers, the majority confirmed that they have family living in Portugal (94%) and they visit that country quite often (only 26% said that they had rarely or never visited Portugal).

As mentioned by Valdés (2005), a heritage language speaker is considered to be someone who grows up in a family whose origin is different from the country where he or she resides and who has been exposed to a language that is also different from the official language and the language at school. This situation gives them some developed bilingual skills, which is the case for these students. Lachman (2003) makes reference to a multilingual competence, which comes from this mutual influence among all the languages to which these students are exposed: the language of schooling, the second language (in the case of Canada) or foreign language included in the school curriculum, and their heritage language (sometimes more than one).

According to the data obtained through the different questionnaires, we know that the first language of most of these students is one of the official languages of Canada (English or French). In the Portuguese language classes, most Portuguese heritage language students are revisiting a language they have learned or were exposed to during their childhood (Melo-Pfeifer & Schmidt, 2016). In fact, although 20% say that Portuguese is the language of communication at home, there are many cases of bilingual communication in which the parents speak Portuguese and the children answer in the official language of the country, which is their first language. There is often the influence of the grandparents, whose presence still promotes the use of the Portuguese language. In fact, 78% of the students answered that they were learning Portuguese to communicate with their grandparents and 88% said it was also to communicate with the family in Portugal. The form of communication that Garcia (2009) calls "translanguaging" is very characteristic of heritage language speakers and it is the result of the influence of the language of schooling and socialization on the language used at home, especially in the case of the second and third generation, in which the discursive practices are gradually moving away from what is considered the norm. When we consider teachers' perception of this issue, we find that, according to 48% of respondents, students do not use Portuguese outside the classroom. The competence of these students in their heritage language cannot be the same as that of a child growing in their country of origin, nor can it be expected to be (Flores & Melo-Pfeifer, 2016).

Although most of the students involved in this study were born in Canada, there is a small group who has recently arrived in this country from different parts of Portugal and who eventually joined classes where Portuguese is taught as a second language. We clearly understand then that the proficiency of these students is much different when compared to second and third generation students. One of the characteristics of heritage language speakers, referred by Melo-Pfeifer and Schmidt (2016), is precisely their heterogeneity in the Portuguese language competence, due to the different conditions of its acquisition.

Many heritage language students, who do not speak the language, feel culturally connected to it. The results of the different questionnaires about their motivations for learning the Portuguese language show that, in general, the reasons mentioned are mostly emotional, either because their parents want them to learn it (82%), or to be able to communicate with their grandparents (78%) or with their family when they visit Portugal (88%). This is the most important motivation mentioned by all the different groups of respondents, parents, students, as well as teachers. Their learning and linguistic development and the way they are related to their roots are strongly dependent on all the oral interactions between them and many other parties involved, including close or more distant relatives, friends, but also colleagues and teachers like mentioned in other studies (He, 2010; Pinho, 2016). It should also be stressed that many students consider Portuguese as an important language in the world (79%), which leads us to believe in the future of Portuguese language teaching in Canada, with the progressive recognition of our language as a language of communication with an important economic value, and not only taking into account the preservation of the Portuguese language among the new generations of our diaspora.

Another aspect that we consider relevant, as a conclusion to be drawn from the data of the questionnaires answered by the students of the two different age groups (9 to12 and 15 to 18 years old), and which surprised us a great deal, is related to the importance that community associations and media in Portuguese (in particular television and radio) have in the preservation of the heritage language. In fact, according to the answers of these students, these are the activities in Portuguese, besides the classes, most referred by them (21% referred the media and 28,5% the Portuguese associations), although it is often thought that the associations and the means of communication are directed to an adult audience.

It is also relevant that a significant majority of the students start learning Portuguese in a school when they are between 4 and 6 years old. We have noticed that when they start learning the language there is a general intention to go on studying Portuguese until the end of their secondary education, which, however, does not end up happening. In fact, according to our numbers, in the school year 2016-2017, about 4,000 students from pre-school to grade 4 were learning Portuguese in Canada, and this number drops to 2,900 between grades 5 and 8, and finally there were only around 320 students in the secondary level, despite the possibility of obtaining credits with these classes. This small number of students, despite the approximately 7,200 who study Portuguese between the ages of 4 and 18 in Canada, is difficult to understand, especially when, according to the results of the questionnaires, the vast majority of respondents from the four target groups, including teachers (more than 90% of the total), consider that students learn a lot in the Portuguese classes and like to attend them. If we look at the results of the teacher surveys, we can also confirm that, according to their responses, only 9% say they have high school students in their classes. It will be important to reflect on this strong decrease in the demand for Portuguese language classes as students reach the secondary level, although we have already mentioned some of the factors that may contribute to this situation.

With regard to the aspects or activities practiced in the classroom that the students of the two age groups most appreciate, these are the most important: being with colleagues and friends, the teachers, learning, in general, and, in particular, History and Geography of Portugal, and interactive activities, whether they are debates, games and interdisciplinary or group work. As for what they least enjoy in class, the answers are also very coincidental, including the fact, mentioned by both groups, of having Saturday classes, as well as doing homework, studying grammar, doing individual work, writing compositions, having tests and exams.

The activities most practiced by teachers in the classes, according to the students of both groups, are: the correction of pronunciation, writing, listening to the teacher, correcting the homework and studying History and Geography of Portugal.

We could also confirm that in the Portuguese classes, the computer, the internet and other information technologies, in general, are rarely used. Instead, there is a more traditional teaching methodology which may be considered less interactive. It is regrettable that there is not a stronger promotion of learning in a more interactive environment, taking advantage of the predisposition of young people to the digital media, in an era marked by a digital culture, as Ilharco (2008) points out. After all, in order for these students to learn their heritage language we must try to diversify the resources used, through an "involvement with their roots and cultural identity," as Silva and Lamas (2016, p. 111) refer, so that they feel more motivated to learn. However, it should be noted that many schools do not have access to these resources, and besides, there are some teachers who are still not used to the use of the digital *media* and the training in this area has not yet been offered by CEPE.

As for teachers, we found out that 75% of the respondents were born in Portugal or in another Portuguese-speaking country and 68% completed their academic education in Portugal. Most of the teachers visit Portugal with some regularity (every two or three years), considering the distance between Canada and Portugal and the costs that these trips entail.

We are, therefore, talking about a group of teachers mostly from the first generation, 94% of them considering Portuguese as their mother tongue. When questioned about their profession, only 61% have claimed that teaching is their main professional occupation. In fact, as we have already mentioned, only a few teachers in Toronto have the possibility of teaching Portuguese as a full-time job, since only in this city, and especially in some schools of the catholic school board, the teaching of the Portuguese language is integrated in the students schedule, which allows the hiring of full-time teachers. The other teachers teach Portuguese as an extracurricular course after school hours or on Saturday morning, although, among these there are some full-time teachers of other subjects in different school boards. Regarding the academic education of the Portuguese teachers who participated in this survey, the data shows that 70% finished University, either at the undergraduate (56%) or masters' level (14%); on the other hand, only 50% admit having specific training in teaching the Portuguese language and also 50% have more than 10 years of experience teaching Portuguese in Canada. We can conclude that, according to the results of the study, we have a majority of teachers with a good academic background, although not necessarily in the Portuguese language teaching, with a good proficiency in Portuguese. A significant number of teachers have been teaching their mother language as a mission (sometimes carried out with great effort), in order to preserve their roots and the Portuguese language and culture in Canada, a country that, for many different reasons, received them in their quest for a better life standard.

During the first period of our class observation, in different schools and diverse geographic areas of Canada, we have noticed that sometimes there was an excessive use of English in class. Therefore, there has always been some insistence about the benefits of using Portuguese right from the very beginning of the learning process, trying to create a language immersion environment. The teachers' responses to this question, however, indicate that about 93% consider that they use only or mostly Portuguese in their classes. This number, although very positive, does not refer to the language most students use in the Portuguese classes. In fact, in the observation that we continued to make during our visits to classes, we have found that the main language of communication among students and often when they address the teacher is still English. It should be noted that in this respect there is a different reality in Escola Santa Cruz, in Montreal, where the classes of the students between 4 and 6 years old focus exclusively on oral communication. This school is the only one to introduce writing in Portuguese only in the classes of students who are older than 7 years, when their literacy in the language of schooling is already complete.

When the teachers were asked about their approach for teaching the Portuguese language in their classes, we found that most of them consider that they teach Portuguese as a second or heritage language, although the number of teachers who chose the option "Portuguese as a foreign language" is also significant. The complexity and ambiguity of the criteria considered for the definition of these concepts, as Faneca (2016, p. 136) points out, may in part contribute to an apparent disparity in the responses to this question. However, these different approaches referred to by the teachers may reflect the diversity of the students who sometimes are in the same class. The newcomers from Portugal, who have Portuguese as their mother language, have a very different profile from those students from a second or third generation, whose families, fully integrated in the Canadian community, most of the time already have a linguistic and cultural diversity, often originated by mixed marriages. This diversity in terms of the student profile, their linguistic proficiency and the frequency of use of the Portuguese language outside the classroom will certainly require different approaches within the same class of students.

The different proficiency levels in the language is, moreover, the difficulty most mentioned by the teachers, followed by the lack of motivation on the part of the students, the lack of adequate resources and the different level of ages of the students within the same classroom. This heterogeneity of students' profiles in the same classroom, regarding their linguistic proficiency, their motivations, the frequency of use of the language outside the classroom and, sometimes, the age level, is also a very usual feature in the teaching and learning of a heritage language. This is, in fact, a problem which hinders the work of the teachers and requires some training sessions within the scope of differentiated teaching practices.

Regarding the resources used in the class, it is noted that, according to the results, many teachers still preferred, in 2015, to use the old teaching books, their own materials or even a collection of "Portuguese Booklets" prepared by a group of teachers from the catholic school board of Toronto for different levels, from pre-school to grade 8, and distributed throughout the country at very low costs. All these resources followed a mother language teaching perspective, with many drawing or coloring activities and exercises to complete, literacy and numeracy exercises, traditional texts followed by questions to get the classic written responses, and many grammar exercises. The new school books which gradually started coming from Portugal, in the school year 2012-2013, were offered by Instituto Camões and distributed by CEPE, although for financial reasons they could not cover all the students. These new resources introduced a new teaching and learning approach. They were meant for Portuguese as a second language, with a very playful and interactive character, but at the same time much more demanding for the teacher in terms of the time spent in preparing the lessons and adapting to a new rhythm, new programs, a different posture and a new methodology that took into account a new context and the profile of the students today. There was some resistance to a change of practice, which is referred to by Burns & Shadonian-Gersing (2010) as a challenge to be overcome. In fact, it was noticed during our collaborative work with the teachers that there was a progressive adaptation to the new approach proposed by CEPE-Canada / Instituto Camões and the new resources were more and more appreciated, valued and used in the classroom.

In order to plan a professional development for teachers, one must take into account the teaching situation, in general, but also the profile of both teachers and students, and their real needs, expectations, motivations and problems. Our classroom observation allowed us to collect information, work closely with the teachers of each school and it was a very important starting point for the training plan that we have been drawing. The information we were getting allowed us to start planning the content of the training sessions according to the teacher's availability (from 3 to 4 hours).

By 2015, 22% of the teachers surveyed said that they had never participated in any training, a fact that we can understand, due to the frequent mobility of many teachers mainly for professional reasons, and the difficulty to reconcile their teaching activity with another full-time job and their personal and family life. However, 90% of the teachers considered the training offered by CEPE useful or very useful. The most significant training areas, according to the teachers surveyed in the study were: teaching pedagogy, use of new technologies, use and creation of resources, dealing with diversity within a class and the dynamic of collaborative work. It has to be underlined that this information was very useful for the planning of the following training sessions and the results were very good, according to the general feedback that we had from the teachers.

When asked about their opinion about the support received from Instituto Camões, through CEPE, 82% of the teachers who participated in this study considered it useful or very useful, which is a very positive indicator of the institution's work on the ground, with the human and budget resources available.

Conclusions

Clearly, there is still much to be done at many levels, although, to a large extent, it will depend on political wills and budget constraints. It will be necessary a more productive and intervening action in this country with a community of about half a million Portuguese and "luso-descendentes," not to mention the communities of other Portuguese-speaking countries living in Canada. The current policy for the promotion of the Portuguese language in the world by Instituto Camões has been changing into a vision of an international language of communication with an unquestionable economic power.

From the survey, we could confirm that the main motivations for parents and students to learn Portuguese are related to emotional reasons, although we may already realize that there is some awareness of the importance of the Portuguese language in the world. We also noticed that, according to the answers, in general, the students like the Portuguese classes, although there is a demand for a more interactive approach in the class with the purpose of developing a communicative and intercultural competence. There is also a need to improve the collaborative work among the teachers, who will benefit from sharing and cooperating in order to overcome the impact of the distance both from Portugal and from each other.

The results also confirm that it will be necessary a greater intervention by the Portuguese institutions, namely by Instituto Camões and the different Portuguese diplomatic representatives in Canada, in promoting the teaching of the Portuguese language at the secondary level. This will require a more intense negotiation with the different school boards of the various cities and at a provincial and federal level. That will also depend on the existence of more teachers with academic qualifications recognized by the Ministry of Education of each province, which is an essential requirement for teaching the Portuguese language in this level of education. It will also be essential to promote the awareness of the relevance of the Portuguese language in Canada, not only as a heritage language but as a more valued curricular subject available in more secondary schools.

We also emphasize promoting the use of new technologies in the class, which would require specific training in this area for teachers and a special financial support from the Portuguese government in order to make these resources available in most community schools in this country. The Portuguese classes would certainly benefit from the use of these technologies and from all the possible interactive activities available. These students belong to a digital generation and there are numerous interesting and interactive activities which are very useful in a language class. The teachers should also be encouraged to take advantage of the distance learning courses offered by Instituto Camões, in a country such as Canada, with such a vast geographical dimension. However, we think that those online training sessions should be offered with no costs to the teachers in Canada, since these sessions would not bring any formal professional progression and we are aware that they have very little availability for any extra commitment. It would depend exclusively on their personal will and interest in improving their knowledge in their teaching practices, and the Portuguese language would certainly benefit from their extra effort.

In summary, Canada, with its approximately 450,000 Portuguese and Portuguese descendants, and a growing general interest in Portugal and in Portuguese as a language of international communication, requires a more efficient involvement of the Portuguese government, both in terms of financial and human resources. The language policy followed by the Portuguese government has to include Canada as an important target country. The Portuguese community deserves it, and the new generations will be prouder of their roots if the promotion of the Portuguese language and culture is more visible and open to Canadians, in general.

It is also essential, in terms of the teachers training, to promote collaborative practices among teachers of the various schools that offer Portuguese language teaching in the different cities and provinces, but also with the teachers who teach Portuguese in other countries. We hope that CATPor - *Canadian Association of Teachers of Portuguese*, formally presented on April 28, 2018, at the University of Toronto, will contribute to a (more) effective union and a more collaborative atmosphere among teachers, not only from Portugal but also from other Portuguese-speaking countries.

As for training methodologies, the results of our study, together with our knowledge of the Portuguese teaching and learning context in Canada and of the teacher training needs, lead us to propose training plans based on a balanced relationship between theoretical deepening, interactive practices and reflection, in a truly collaborative environment. The training sessions were planned according to the results of the study and were always adapted to the needs and contexts of the different areas of the country.

We hope that our study can contribute to the promotion of teaching and learning of the Portuguese language in Canada, taking into account the evolution of the Portuguese community and the growing general interest in the Portuguese language and culture, for a variety of reasons, including for its economic potential.

Portugal will also have to broaden its view of Canada, considering it as a country of interest, not only because of the Portuguese-speaking community, which is already moving towards a fourth generation of Luso-descendants, mostly already integrated in the Canadian society, but also in order to promote the full economic potential of Portuguese, an important international language.

References

Council of Europe (2018). Common European framework of reference for languages: Learning, teaching, assessment - Companion volume with new descriptors (provisional edition). Retirado de https://rm.coe.int/common-european-framework-of-reference-for-languages-learning-teaching/168074a4e2

Burns, T., & Shadoian-Gersing, V. (2010). The importance of effective teacher education for diversity. In Organisation for Economic Cooperation and Development, *Educating Teachers for Diversity – Meeting the Challenge* (pp. 19–40). Paris: OECD.

Da Silva, E. (2011). *Sociolinguistic (re)constructions of diaspora portugueseness: Portuguese-Canadian youth in Toronto*. Ph.D. dissertation. Canada: University of Toronto.

Faneca, R. (2016). Aprendizagem e representações do português língua de herança em França. In S. Melo-Pfeifer (Coord.), *Didática do português língua de herança* (pp. 132-151). Lisboa: Lidel.

Flores, C., & Melo-Pfeifer, S. (2016). «Em casa mais português, mas também alemão»: Perspectivas da linguística e da didática de línguas sobre narrativas de uso da língua de herança. In S. Melo-Pfeifer (Coord.), *Didática do português língua de herança* (pp. 41-72). Lisboa: Lidel.

García, O. (2009) *Bilingual education in the 21st century: a global perspective.* Oxford: Malden, MA and Oxford: Basil/Blackwell.

Garnett, B. (2010). Diversity in education: The importance of disaggregating data. In Organization for Economic Cooperation

and Development, *Educating Teachers for Diversity. Meeting the Challenge* (pp. 93-116). Paris: OECD.
He, A. (2010). The heart of heritage: sociocultural dimensions of heritage language learning. *Annual Review of Applied Linguistics, 30*, 66-82.
Ilharco, F. (2008). Interculturalidade e novas tecnologias. In M. Lages, & T. Matos (Orgs.), *Portugal: Percursos de interculturalidade* (volume V, pp. 141-184). Lisboa: Alto Comissariado para a Imigração e Minorias Étnicas.
Lachman, K. M. (2003). Defining mother tongue education in plurilingual contexts. *Language Policy*, 2 (3), 239-254.
Melo-Pfeifer, S., & Schmidt, A. (2016). Português língua de herança na Alemanha: Imagens dos professores e da comunidade portuguesa. Implicações pedagógico-didáticas. In S. Melo-Pfeifer (Coord.), *Didática do Português Língua de Herança* (pp. 88-106). Lisboa: Lidel.
Pinho, A. S. (2016). Português língua de herança: vozes de professores em contexto e reptos à formação de professores. In S. Melo-Pfeifer (Coord.), *Didática do português língua de herança* (pp. 219-244). Lisboa: Lidel.
Reis, P. (2011). *Observação de aulas e avaliação do desempenho docente*. Lisboa: Ministério da Educação - Conselho Científico para a Avaliação de Professores. Retirado de https://pt.scribd.com/doc/57866194/Observacao-de-aulas-e-avaliacao-do-desempenho-docente.
Silva, F. & Lamas, E. (2016). Para uma pedagogia diferenciada no ensino do português língua de herança: Contributos etnográficos e psicossociais. In S. Melo-Pfeifer (Coord.), *Didática do português língua de herança* (pp. 109-130). Lisboa: Lidel.
Statistics Canada. (2017). *Focus on geography series, 2016 Census*. Statistics Canada Catalogue no. 98-404-X2016001. Ottawa, Ontario.
Valdés, G. (2005). Bilingualism, heritage language learners, and SLA research: opportunities lost or seized? *The Modern Language Journal, 89*(3), 410-426.

2
Teaching Portuguese as a Heritage Language in Montreal
Fabio Scetti
Université Paul-Valéry Montpellier III
McGill University

In a context of globalization where languages are regarded as an added value in economic terms (Duchêne & Heller, 2012), the Portuguese language is presently reinforcing its position internationally, leading its historical dominion over the five continents. In fact, a study conducted in Portugal about the economic potential of Portuguese, underlines the importance of Portuguese in the world as it is currently spoken by around 250 million speakers, or 3.7% of the world's population (Reto, 2012). Meanwhile, in terms of communication, Portuguese is the fifth most used language on the Internet (Statistics ITU, 2016) and the language may become a real tool for business in the future, which reinforces its presence in terms of education, from school to universities, in Portuguese-speaking countries as well as in non-Portuguese-speaking countries.

In East Asia, for instance, the promotion of Portuguese in education has increased (Matos, 2016; Araújo, 2008). In fact, institutions such as *Instituto Camões*, IPOR or IILP within the actions of CPLP, together with public and private institutions such as language schools and universities, have played an important role in promoting the Portuguese language and culture abroad. Since 2005, QuaREPE (*Quadro de Referência para o Ensino do Português no Estrangeiro*) (Grosso & al., 2011) was created in order to consider the diversity of contexts and learners where Portuguese is taught (Silva, 2016).

Considering this phenomenon, it is important to highlight how Portuguese is taught within migrant communities of the diaspora, envisioning for their members the maintenance of the identity of these communities through time. I suggest that in order to describe how Portuguese, being a Heritage Language (HL), is maintained and promoted in Montreal through the impulse of the local community, it is necessary to explain how the economic and commercial environment of our globalized era has influenced its spread. Furthermore, in analysing discourses about language, its status within the group, its position and practices, I aim to show the commodification of national identities, in the form of the marketing of authenticity (Duchêne & Heller, 2012).

In these terms, it is important to consider the influence of such discourses for the process of construction of linguistic ideologies, referring to "the situated, partial, and interested character of conceptions and uses of language" (Errington, 2001, p. 110). These linguistic ideologies consist of representations, through discourses, of the perceptions and beliefs about the language and its positions constructed in the interest of the speakers, who may be seen as members of a certain group (Woolard, 1998). These representations may influence language attitudes, intended as evaluative reactions of speakers within the group, as well as the status given to languages in discourse. Language becomes an element of power, competitiveness, and this opens the reflections on the challenges of the Portuguese language today in our context of study: the Portuguese language reaching the position of "global", while it was at first "communitarian" within the community of Montreal.

For that purpose, it is in our interest to analyse linguistic policies as well, since their mechanism impacts the structure, function, use, or acquisition of language (Johnson, 2013). According to Johnson (2013), linguistic policy is not only a product, but a process that is implemented by linguistic ideologies woven and circulating inside the given context, being both urban, communitarian and in relation to the Portuguese diaspora. These ideologies were seldom reproduced and applied in the context of diaspora, their influence "end up by trying to impose a certain orthodoxy in the way the language and communities are thought" (Ferreira & Melo-Pfeifer, 2018, p. 240). The relationship between language and identity arose then, where members questioned the position of the language within the given community, not only how the language is transmitted and maintained, but also in terms of strategies used by some members of the community to defend their HL. When we speak of teaching a HL, "the target group refers primarily to students who have either learned the language as their home language or who have some form of family or 'heritage' connection to the language (e.g., second and third generation immigrants)" (Cummins, 2005, p. 2).

In this chapter, the context of Montreal is illustrated, firstly, by describing which institutions offer Portuguese language classes at different levels, i.e. universities, schools and private schools. Secondly, I present the Portuguese community in Montreal and the evolution of the construction of the local communitarian school, *Missão Santa Cruz*, the institution responsible for the education in Portuguese of young members of the group. Then, I analyse discourses about learners' motivations and engagement into the language courses offered at *Missão Santa Cruz*, supporting linguistic policies from a macro (state, province) to a micro level (community and families), reflecting on the question of varieties, considering the pluricentric position of the Portuguese language (Clyne, 2012), with two dominant varieties: European Portuguese (EP) and Brazilian Portuguese (BP).

Teaching and Learning Portuguese in Montreal and Canada

Besides the fact that the Portuguese language may have an economic potential in the future (Reto, 2012), its development in terms of education within the Canadian system appears slow. In Montreal, in fact, in terms of schools in general, universities and language schools, it seems that finding Portuguese language classes today is a real *'desafio'* (challenge).

Thankfully, the Government of Quebec instituted the *Programme d'Enseignement des Langues d'Origine* (PELO), which aimed to improve the students' (with an immigrant background) evolution at school by learning their HL (Gouvernement du Québec, 1998). For that reason, various schools within the urban area of Montreal offer Portuguese support lessons, i.e. *École au Pied-de-la-Montagne* and *École Saint-Enfant-Jésus*.

At the university level, the *Université de Montréal* (UdM) – *Centre de Langues* offers classes of different levels allowing students to develop skills such as oral comprehension, oral expression, reading and writing, altogether needed to master any language. There is also the possibility to continue to register for a minor or module in Portuguese language and culture in Portuguese-speaking countries. UdM also signed a procedure of cooperation with the *Camões Institute, Instituto da Cooperação e da Língua* to open a lectureship such as in other main universities of the country: Queen's University in Kingston, the University of Ottawa, the University of Toronto and York University, in Toronto. However, in another main university of the city, McGill University, Portuguese courses are unavailable, even though the Department of Languages, Literatures, and Cultures, within their Hispanic Studies curriculum, "offers the option to study of all aspects of the literature, intellectual history, and culture of Spain and Latin America, as well as the Spanish and Portuguese languages". Concordia University does not offer Portuguese either. However, it offers an immersion program for language, culture, and traditions of the Lusophone world within the *Concordia Language Village*. Finally, Portuguese language courses are available at the *Université du Québec à Montréal* (UQAM). However, the local *École des Langues* promotes courses of Portuguese focusing only on the Brazilian variety. To strengthen the promotion of this language, the program offers weekly lunches organized by the *Centre d'Étude et de Recherche sur le Brésil* (CERB) within the university, and a preparation for a long stay in Brazil, considering that UQAM maintains bilateral and international agreements with many universities in Brazil.

In terms of private language schools, the availability of Portuguese language classes is different and wider. Portuguese is offered by the main schools in the city, namely YMCA, Berlitz and CILM, where the decision of the variety taught is seldom the responsibility of the teacher. Additionally, there are private schools geared for adults such as *Portugais Sans Limites*.

Otherwise, the local communitarian school, *Missão Santa Cruz* (MSC), is the only institution administering courses in Portuguese language today for children (descendants of Portuguese immigrants), in primary and secondary school; and for non-native Lusophone adult learners, with or without a direct connection to a native Portuguese language speaker (spouse, extended family members, neighbours, etc.). MSC is an example of a communitarian school founded by the Portuguese in Canada, together with the *Escola Portuguesa do Laval*, located in the province of Quebec. Today, according to the *Coordenação do Ensino do Português* (CEPE), there are 12 communitarian schools that are still active in the in Canada, from the west to the east coast: in British Columbia, the *Escola Portuguesa Nossa Senhora de Fátima* in Vancouver and the *Escola Portuguesa Santíssima Trindade* in Maple Ridge; in Alberta, the *Escola Portuguesa Gil Vicente* (St. Cecilia Junior High School) in Edmonton and the *Escola Portuguesa de Calgary*; in Manitoba, the *Escola Portuguesa de Manitoba*, located in Winnipeg and finally, in the province of Ontario, we find the majority of them, the *Escola First Portuguese* and the *Escola Portuguesa Novos Horizontes* in Toronto, the *Centro Cultural de Mississauga* and the *Clube Cultural Português de Vaughan* in the surroundings, and another school located in Hamilton, the *Escola Portuguesa de Hamilton*. These schools are complementary to the system of each province and are normally only open on Saturdays.

It is important to underline that nowadays the promotion of education in Portuguese, in relation to Portuguese communities of the diaspora, have a much wider public due to increased immigration to Canada (Grosso & al., 2011). The development of these Portuguese language and culture courses within these communities aimed to foster the connection between learners and their 'heritage' (Silva, 2016). To achieve this, the language has been, at the same time, the goal and the means.

The Portuguese Community, in the Heart of Montreal

Montreal is a modern multicultural city where different 'islands', due to the process of immigration, have been settled through time. The Portuguese community, also called *a comunidade* in Portuguese, which describes both members of the group and the geographical district, flourishes in its core. It is located in the central district of Saint-Louis along Boulevard Saint-Laurent, the central axe that for centuries has welcomed and established different communities. Chinatown, Little Portugal, *La Petite-Italie*, Mile-

End and *Parc-Extension* for the Greek and Jewish communities, all help paint a colourful image of the city's diversity.

According to Canadian statistics, in 2016, the Portuguese community in the urban area of Montreal reached around 76,000 Portuguese and their descendants (Statistics Canada, 2016). This community has been the main topic of an ethnographic study conducted between 2011 and 2016 (Scetti, 2016, 2019). This research in sociolinguistics provides insights into the evolution of oral practices in Portuguese within the group and the effects of those practices in representations of Portugueseness and identity. The methodology of research included questionnaires, observations, and semi-structured interviews, and data collection explored day-to-day language practices in Portuguese and language mixing or hybrid practices. Interviews were conducted with speakers of different age, sex, occupation, educational level and origins. In addition, a selection of 8 speakers for each generation was elaborated in order to observe diverse oral practices and uses in accordance with the context and situation. The generational categorization was organized considering a 1st generation (Portuguese who immigrated in adulthood), a 2nd generation (descendants born in Montreal to parents who immigrated as adults) and a 3rd generation (descendants having at least one grand-parent of Portuguese background).

The analysis focused on the relation between oral practices and discourses on identity. At first, I could highlight oral practices in Portuguese and mixed or hybrid practices, between Portuguese and both French and English. Finally, I combined this linguistic analysis to a discourse analysis interpreting some elements related to ideologies and representations of languages in the process of construction of a collective identity, even though this diasporic identity remains imagined and ideological (Rosa & Trivedi, 2017).

The first Portuguese community was settled in the 1950s (Moura & Soares, 2003) because of the immigration process from continental Portugal, Azores, and Madeira Islands. The notion of origin is still important today, in terms of language transmission as well as for the process of creating a collective identity within the group. In fact, being *continental* (from continental Portugal) or *ilhão* (islander) is still very important today, in terms of recognition within the group. In addition, speaking a different variety of Portuguese is a mark of identity representation (Scetti, 2017).

However, despite the fact that the community could be regarded as divided and fragmented over time, the Portuguese community is generally an example of linguistic integration within the particular context of Montreal, where both French and English dominate the linguistic landscape, in a context of *double majorité* (Anctil, 1984). Findings from the study (Scetti, 2016) contextualise the dynamics of the Portuguese language spoken within the group, demonstrating the many ways speakers of different generations use this language in diverse contexts and situations. Even though its uses are more confined to private and familiar situations, Portuguese is maintained as a semi-public language spoken all around this neighbourhood. Portuguese is still present on a day-to-day experience in the city: it can be heard around Saint-Louis, read on local signs, and in Portuguese businesses, such as restaurants, bars, and shops where customers are still mainly of a Portuguese background and speak Portuguese (Teixeira & Da Rosa, 2009).

Finally, this sociolinguistics research delineates the evolution of the Portuguese language in context, in which some points of "weakness" of its practice have been analysed. This process of language attrition (Scetti, 2016) is the consequence of the situation of language contact with the two dominant languages. Moreover, by combining the linguistic analysis with a discourse analysis, this research shows how the Portuguese language and its representations may contribute to the understanding of the complex process of defining the group's identity through language practices. The main objective is to observe how the urban context of Montreal is favourable to HL transmission and the maintenance of Portuguese over time (Scetti, 2016). However, because of the decreasing immigration flow from Portugal since the 1980s – 1986 being the date of the entry of Portugal into the EEC at the time – some institutions and members of the community are facing the problematic loss of speakers: "*A comunidade está a ficar velha*" explained Maria, a Portuguese woman born in 1951 in Northern Portugal, while stressing the need to find ways to extend the use of 'their' language in the future.

The Need for Teaching and Learning Portuguese

The Portuguese community in Montreal is well known within the city for their local identity and their famous summer festivals, where Portuguese specialities such as *sardinhas, frango assado* and *pastéis de nata* (sardines, roast chicken and custard tarts) are sold at the community's square between the Portuguese church *Santa Cruz* and the *Associação Portuguesa do Canadá* (APC), surrounded by the sound of local *Fado* singers and musicians.

The communitarian centre of *Missão Santa Cruz* (MSC) is the institution in the district responsible for the religious dimension of community life, *Igreja Santa Cruz* and education in Portuguese of young descendants of this immigration today. MSC reunified the *Escola Santa Cruz* (the first primary school created in 1971), teaching children from 6 to 12 years old; and the school *Lusitana* (secondary school created in 1975 by Professor José de Barros), teaching children from 12 to 18 years old. Both schools run every Saturday morning, and 15 teachers, all originally from continental Portugal, teach classes of Portuguese language, literature, and other subjects such as geography, history, and mathematics. Classes are only delivered in Portuguese. According to some members of the community, Portuguese classes were already taught before the foundation of the school. In fact, during the 60s, the Consulate of Portugal in Montreal used to organise classes for young descendants, like Helena, born in 1955, a 2nd generation descendant now living in Portugal, who attended those classes, reported: "*tenho uma foto, teria uns 7, 8 anos, e portanto estaríamos em 1962/63. Um dos professores era um fundador do jornal Voz de Portugal*".

MSC is also responsible for the creation of *Universidade dos Tempos Livres* (UTL), founded in 1999, which oversees the education of senior citizens within the community, offering them a large variety of courses: dance and music, IT, history, religion and morality, cooking and handicrafts. English and French language classes are also offered for those people who lacked the time, desire, or the need to learn those languages before. With the exception of these two courses, all courses are delivered in Portuguese. The UTL is also known outside the community, and all Montrealers who are interested in Portuguese language and culture can join Portuguese classes for adults.

MSC is the only Portuguese communitarian school still open in Montreal; *Escola Português do Atlântico* (1972) closed down due to the decreasing number of admissions. Other schools outside Montreal were created, in Brossard and Laval, meeting the increasing demand of Portuguese families in those areas in the 1970s and 1980s. Today, *Escola Portuguesa do Laval* is still functioning while the *Escola Portuguesa de Brossard* closed down in 2013. In Laval, we still find a good example of a communitarian school even though it proved difficult to remain in operation. Established in 1976 by priest António Araújo, the school rented the local space of the *École Saint-Martin*, at first, in the neighbourhood of Chomedey. Then, the municipality of Laval offered the school to move to a communitarian centre, a property of the city. The school still functions there, but "*o problema que se põe ano após ano é a tremenda falta de alunos?*", underlines Raul, a member of the school's commission for 20 years. In fact, this school which provided, at the beginning, only classes of the first and second cycles of primary school, later opened classes to the *9.º ano* (14 years old – *Ensino Básico*). The highest number of students reached 90 children and numbers were maintained of around 70 children for decades. However, because of the lack of emigration flows and the lack of interest by some members of the community, the number of enrolments decreased steadily and today only approximately 30 children remain enrolled, divided in 6 classes – the other levels ceased to function.

Since the 2000s, MSC has been similarly facing a drop in the school's enrolments (Eusébio, 2001) – only around 300 students in the last school year of 2017/18. The question of who will be sustaining the use of

Portuguese in Montreal in the future is recurrent. For that reason, discourses within the community and mainly promoted by some members have been changing through time.

In fact, Portuguese is promoted today, not only as a HL and language of the past, but also as a language of the future. Its position as a strong language in business and its presence internationally and on the internet are seldom vectors of local discourses within the neighbourhood and among the community members. "*O português é a sétima língua mais falada do mundo*" explains Jaime, a young student born in 1995 whose grandparents are originally from Minho, in Northern Portugal. He is a former student of the communitarian school MSC and knows the importance of speaking Portuguese at home and for his future. Lurdes, now a grand-mother, born in 1951 in Northern Portugal, defends the importance of speaking Portuguese to her children and grand-children: "*porque o português é uma língua muito falada no mundo*". She explains how Portuguese is important on an international dimension. In fact, in terms of profession, the use of Portuguese or another language is an asset along with the two dominant languages spoken in Montreal and this is a recurrent discourse between young students at MSC. For example, Katherine, a young student born in 1998, argues: "*quando quer um trabalho, ser capaz de falar mais que duas, ou só uma língua, seria melhor*". And finally, in terms of leisure, the fact that Portuguese is spoken in many countries all over the five continents provides an opportunity for travel and discovery. According to Elizabeth, a 2nd generation young mother born in 1980 to Azorean parents, speaking Portuguese can afford the opportunity to travel more easily around the world. She highlights its importance for her own travel experience, during a journey in Brazil: "*fomos ao Brasil há dois anos […], graças à língua portuguesa consegui sentir muito mais o povo brasileiro*".

These comments illustrated the different discourses promoted and disseminated by the major actors of schools, such as teachers and members of the management body, which are then reproduced by students and parents. These discourses convey ideologies about the 'power' of a language, in terms of large numbers of speakers, but also concerning international rankings in business and uses (i.e. internet, publication, etc.). This kind of discourse is frequent within the community nowadays. MSC members want to improve annual admissions, and they fear the tragic destiny of other Portuguese communitarian schools in the urban region of Montreal, such as *Escola Português do Atlântico* and recently the *Escola Portuguesa de Brossard*. Thus, Portuguese is commodified as a tool for the future of the young members of the community, and an important element to add to and through which to evaluate their professional life, a proper 'skill' (see Urciuoli, 2008; Vigouroux, 2017). This perspective of value might be more important than that of the transmission of the language for identity recognition. The position of the Portuguese language within the community of Montreal is changing from a marker of group identity to a marker of internationalization, that members "need" in order to be more 'global' then 'local', in their "confined" community.

The need to promote the Portuguese language in this context of immigration is incorporated today in a contemporary era of globalization where a language becomes fundamental for the achievement of an international status. Over the years, the question of variety has also evolved within the *comunidade*, in Montreal. In fact, even though there is more concern about linguistic varieties on dictionaries today, non-dominant varieties of Portuguese spoken in Montreal, mainly from Madeira island, the Azores, and Northern regions of Portugal (see Scetti, 2017), still experience stigmatization and are diminished in relation to the dominant *norma-padrão* (standard) of EP, and are seldom valorised in the context of the diaspora (Ferreira & Melo-Pfeifer, 2018). Language variation within Portugal, but moreover among different countries, could be taken into account to better understand the diversity of the Portuguese language and the challenges this diversity poses to the "Portuguese linguistic market," where different Portuguese-speaking/Lusophone communities interact, and also in the context of education. However, by considering Portuguese as a pluricentric language with two dominant centres, one being Portugal and the other Brazil, the only issue that persists relates to the dominance and supremacy, as in prestige, of one of these two over all other varieties.

The Question of Varieties

The contemporary situation in which I situated the promotion of the Portuguese language worldwide has been accelerated by some efforts toward disseminating one of the two main dominant varieties: European Portuguese (EP) and Brazilian Portuguese (BP). For instance, the *Acordo Ortográfico da Língua Portuguesa* of 1990 (AO90) is a very interesting example of linguistic policy largely debated in the last years (see Oliveira, 2013).

Considering that Brazil and Portugal have always been in competition to promote their own standards for the Portuguese language (da Silva & Gunnenwiek, 1992) and have a protracted trajectory of unilateral and bilateral actions (Mendes, 2018), it is still problematic to assert that only EP and BP are recognized and characterized as "normative varieties" (Bagno, 2018), besides the large variety of norms that may be found in other contexts. Moreover, the relation between these two norms of power is challenged today; the thesis being that EP and BP are two languages related to each other rather than the notion of being two varieties of Portuguese (Bagno, 2018).

For that reason, the more recent Brazilian immigration to Montreal (see Almeida, 2014; Barbosa, 2009) can be interpreted both as a new opportunity to revitalize the Portuguese language in this special urban context or as a threat to the European norm in favour of BP. A study published in 2015 on the presence of Brazilians in Montreal (Almeida, 2015) showed how the two groups were not interconnected, and that the presence and participation of Brazilians in MSC was rare. Today, the situation has changed slightly and a statue of *Nossa Senhora Aparecida* has been placed inside the church of MSC not far from the *Nossa Senhora de Fátima*, representing Portugal. However, despite the fact that more Catholic Brazilians may attend the local mass in Portuguese at MSC, there is an absence of students of Brazilian background at the school. There is not a communitarian school for the Brazilian community, and MSC may be the only reference of communitarian school for them, with the purpose to improve the education in Portuguese of young children from Brazilian origins in Montreal.

Meanwhile, it is also relevant to consider how difficult is to enter the 'fortress' of the EP norm, where other varieties, from continental Portugal or the islands, which are widely spoken within the community, still suffer stigmatization (Scetti, 2017). According to the statistics of the school, most of the students enrolled during the 2000s had parents and grandparents originally from mainland Portugal, also called *continentais* (Eusébio, 2001). Additionally, during the decade of the 1990s, according to a collaboration project with the Consulate of Brazil in Montreal, a group of Brazilian teachers had the opportunity to teach language courses for free at MSC. At that time, this could be understood as "a solution to expand Lusophony in this part of Canada" (Eusébio, 2001, p. 84). However, this action did not appeal to a lot of students. This factor related to parents' place of origin and the fact that all teachers were also originally from continental Portugal, which helps explain why many descendants of Azorean immigrants do not attend the communitarian school, even today.

While considering the question of norms and varieties, it is also important to refer to the question of authenticity, not only in terms of geographical varieties, but also based on the ideology of the "older-speaker purism" (Dorian, 1994). This ideology refers to the fact that older speakers within the group have a better knowledge of the 'good' Portuguese. "*Os jovens não falam muito bem*" argues Maria, a woman born in 1951 in Northern Portugal, while speaking about young Portuguese descendants. This is a common representation of young speakers within the community that may discourage these learners from engaging in learning Portuguese. Young Portuguese descendants may also challenge their personal and familiar motivations and question their practices in terms of identity representations. Some heritage speakers, in fact, "must constantly choose, construct, and perform their social identities vis-à-vis the different groups of people with whom they interact" (Hornberger & Wang, 2008, p. 5).

Older members within the community may question this social identity and speaking Portuguese can be an element to be observed and judged.

The absence of students from Brazilian origins enrolled at MSC today shows the distance between these two groups of immigrants in Montreal. However, the situation may change in the future. Firstly, because there is a better conception of the existence of both groups in the city. Secondly, because there are more official discourses promoting Portuguese as a common and singular language (Ferreira & Melo-Pfeifer, 2018), "*a mesma língua*", as Vítor, a 1st generation man born in central Portugal in 1952, defends. However, I observed that there is still a kind of logical contradiction, mainly while talking about television: "*bom, português e brasileiro, a língua é a mesma, mas (há) programas em português e brasileiro*". And finally, because there is a need to create a new connection between these two communities. Sílvia, for example, a young 2nd generation lady, born to Portuguese parents, and member of the folkloric group within *Clube Portugal de Montreal*, affirmed that in Montreal: "*vamos fazer mais portugueses e brasileiros misturados, somos todos juntos, ou açorianos e madeirenses. Uma grande festa*", while highlighting the vivacity of the community (parties, festivities, *rancho*, etc.). This may be an indicator of change, as may be the launch of new social groups created by young people of different Lusophone backgrounds with the aim of speaking Portuguese, such as the *Montreal Brazilian-Portuguese Meetup Group*.

Conclusion

This contribution explored the evolution around the importance of the promotion of Portuguese within the Portuguese community in Montreal and in the context of diaspora in general. I focused on discourses and linguistic ideologies, emerged in interaction and grounded in practices (Krostrity, 2004), that helped illustrate the situation today, contributing to the consolidation of the Portuguese roots of Portuguese descendants together with internationalization.

At first, I recognize the need for young members of the immigrant generation to preserve the use of Portuguese within the community. Discourses analyzed from interviews and observations, show how this choice of maintaining Portuguese within the group is more related to its use and its commercial position as 'international,', as well as a 'skill' for the future of the young generation, than as the HL of the group (Scetti, 2015). In fact, the actors within MSC, considering pupils, parents (parents' commission), teachers, and members of the school management (priest, secretaries) are agents in the processes of maintenance and promotion. Their social actions support the claim that decisions regarding the use and the importance of Portuguese in Montreal are not only taken at the institutional level (macro), but also at the family (meso) and individual (micro) levels (King & al., 2008).

Secondly, the promotion efforts made by MSC are essential for the understanding of how Portuguese is disseminated abroad. A homogenization of how Portuguese is taught may be observed, which takes place because different didactical approaches adapted to each system (country, province, region) and elaborated for different learners are not taken into consideration (Ferreira & Melo-Pfeifer, 2018).

Indeed, the example of how Portuguese is still promoted at MSC today is interesting because it allows us to observe how the language has been shaping its position from HL to a commercial language, to be ranked in a proper "market of languages" (Calvet, 2002). According to rankings and official discourses, Portuguese is then promoted as a "singular, as well as, a global and international language" (Ferreira & Melo-Pfeifer, 2018, p. 252), as Jaime, a young 3rd generation student at MSC, born in 1995, proposes: "*as ex-colónias da Angola, o Moçambique, mesmo agora o Brasil, daqui a vinte ou trinta anos vão ser superpotências, então eu acho que o português vai ser uma grande língua no futuro, então eu acho que não há nenhuma desvantagem de 'tar aqui a estudar a cultura e a língua portuguesa*". It seems to refer to the "*Quinto Império*" (the Fifth Empire), a concept of a global Portuguese empire popularized by Fernando Pessoa in the 20th century with the publication of *Mensagem* in 1934.

Finally, we observe the relation between the Portuguese language and Lusophone identities and cultures, where the concept of Lusophony is taking importance (Faraco, 2012). The 'power' of the Portuguese language may be expressed as a 'power of many,' a potential position of a new global, international, and transnational language (Mendes, 2018). This may confirm that some discourses officially stated and disseminated through institutions, such as those through the MSC in Montreal, hold the power to format linguistic ideologies and promote linguistic policies from the macro to the micro level within a given context.

References

Almeida, E. (2014). La citoyenneté au-delà des frontières nationales: La politique étrangère brésilienne et les Brésiliens au Québec. *RITA*, 7.

Almeida, E. (2015). *Les immigrés brésiliens au Québec: Une diaspora sélectionnée en territoire francophone*. (Unpublished PhD dissertation). Université Paris Descartes, France.

Anctil, P. (1984). Double majorité et multiplicité interculturelle à Montréal. *Recherches Sociographiques*, *3*(25), 441-456.

Araújo, G. A. (2008). A língua portuguesa no Japão: Um panorama. In G.A. de Araújo & P. Aires (Eds.), *A língua portuguesa no Japão* (pp. 9-24). São Paulo: Paulistana Editora.

Bagno M. (2018). Duas línguas. Quantas políticas? In P. Feytor Pinto & S. Melo-Pfeifer (Eds.), *Políticas linguísticas em Português* (pp. 24-40). Lisboa: LIDEL.

Barbosa, R. (2009). Brazilian immigration to Canada, *Canadian Ethnic Studies, 41*(1-2), 215-225.

Calvet, L. J. (2002). *Le marché aux langues: Les effets linguistiques de la mondialisation.* Paris: Plon.

Clyne, M. (2012). Pluricentric Languages. Introduction. In M. Clyne (Ed.), *Pluricentric languages* (pp. 1-10). Berlin: De Gruyter Mouton.

Cummins, J. (2005). A proposal for action: strategies for recognizing heritage language competence as a learning resource within the mainstream classroom. *The Modern Language Journal, 89*, 585-592.

da Silva, J. F. & Gunnenwiek, K. (1992). Portuguese and Brazilian efforts to spread Portuguese. *International Journal of Sociology of Language, 95*, 71-92.

Dorian, N. C. (1994). Purism vs. compromise in language revitalization and language revival. *Language in Society, 23*, 479-494.

Duchêne, A., & Heller, M. (Eds.) (2012). *Language in late capitalism: Pride and profit.* New York: Routledge.

Errington, J. (2001). Ideology. In A. Duranti (Ed.), *Key terms in language and culture* (pp. 110-112). Malden, MA: Blackwell.

Eusébio, J. (2001). *Falando Português em Montreal.* Montreal: Quebec World.

Faraco, C. A. (2012). Lusofonia: utopia ou quimera? Língua, história e política. In T. Lobo & al. (Eds.), *ROSAE. Linguística histórica, história das línguas e outras histórias* (pp. 31-50). Salvador: Editora da Universidade Federal da Bahia.

Ferreira, T. S., & Melo-Pfeifer, S. (2018). Política linguística e ensino de português para a Diáspora. In P. Feytor Pinto & S. Melo-Pfeifer (Eds.), *Políticas linguísticas em português* (pp. 240-258). Lisboa: LIDEL.

García, O., & Wei, L. (2014). *Translanguaging: Language, bilingualism and education.* New York: Palgrave Macmillan.

Giles, H., Bourhis, R.Y., & Taylor, D.M. (1977). Towards a theory of language in ethnic group relations. In H. Giles (Ed.), *Language, ethnicity and intergroup relations* (pp. 307-348). London: Academic Press.

Gouvernement du Québec, Ministère de l'Éducation du Québec et Ministère des Relations avec les Citoyens et de l'Immigration

(1998). *Une école d'avenir. Politique d'intégration scolaire et d'éducation interculturelle*. Québec: Gouvernement du Québec.

Grosso, M. J., Soares, A., Sousa F., & Pascoal, J. (2011). *QuaREPE - Quadro de Referência para o Ensino Português no Estrangeiro – documento orientador*. Lisboa: Ministério da Educação – DGIDC.

Hornberger, N. H., & Wang, S. (2008). Who are our heritage language learners? Identity and biliteracy in heritage language education in the United States. In D. M. Brinton, O. Kagan & S. Bauckus (Eds.), *Heritage language education: a new field emerging* (pp. 3-35). New York: Routledge.

Johnson, D. C. (2013). *Language policy*. Basingstoke: Palgrave Macmillan.

King, K.A., Fogle, L., & Logan-Terry, A. (2008). Family language policy. *Linguistics and Language Compass, 2*(5), 907-922.

Kroskrity, P. V. (2004). Language ideologies. In A. Duranti (Ed.), *A companion to linguistic anthropology* (pp. 496-517). Malden, MA: Blackwell.

Lauerman, J. (2011, August 30). Mandarin Chinese most useful business language after English. *Bloomberg Business*, https://www.bloomberg.com/news/articles/2011-08-30/mandarin-chinese-most-useful-business-language-after-english-1-.

Matos, A. Soeiro. (2016). O ensino de Português na Ásia Oriental: De quem para quem. *Forum Sociológico, 28*. Retrieved from http://journals.openedition.org/sociologico/1436.

Mendes, E. (2018). Política linguística do Brasil no exterior: Entre o isolamento e a cooperação. In P. Feytor Pinto & S. Melo-Pfeifer (Eds.), *Políticas linguísticas em português* (pp. 210-239). Lisboa: LIDEL.

Moura, M. de Almeida, & Soares, I. (2003). *Pionniers. L'avant-garde de l'Immigration Portugaise, Canada 1953*. Montreal: Direcção Geral dos Assuntos Consulares e Comunidades Portuguesas.

Oliveira, G. M. (2013). Política linguística e internacionalização: A língua portuguesa no mundo globalizado do século XXI. *Trabalhos em Linguística Aplicada, 52*(2), 409-433.

Outeiro, A. (2011). *25° Aniversário da igreja Santa Cruz, 1986-2011: Respigos e Retalhos*. Outremont: Les Éditions du Passage.

Reto, L. (2012). *Potencial económico da língua portuguesa*. Alfragide: Texto.

Rosa, J., & Trivedi, S. (2017). Diaspora and language. In S. Canagarajah (Ed.), *The Routledge handbook on migration and language* (pp. 330-346). New York: Routledge.

Scetti, F. (2015). "O português não é só a língua do passado e dos avós, mas é também uma nova língua do futuro!". In *Atas do XII CONLAB, 1° congresso da Associação Internacional de Ciências Sociais e*

Humanas em Língua Portuguesa (pp. 6443-6451). Lisboa: FCSH – Universidade Nova de Lisboa.

Scetti, F. (2016). *Évolution de la langue portugaise dans sa dynamique de transmission au sein de la « communauté portugaise » de Montréal.* (Unpublished PhD dissertation). Université Paris Descartes, France.

Scetti, F. (2017). Variation dialectale du portugais parlé au sein de la communauté de Montréal. *Géolinguistique, 17*, 151-175.

Scetti, F. (2019). *La communauté portugaise de Montréal: Langue et identité.* Québec: PUL.

Silva, F. (2016). *O ensino do português no estrangeiro – O resgate de uma língua. Contributo para a identificação da identidade linguística e cultural de alunos lusodescendentes.* (Unpublished PhD dissertation). Universidad de Santiago de Compostela, Spain.

Statistics Canada. (2016). *Census of Canada 2011: Immigration and ethnocultural diversity.* Retrieved from http://www.12.statcan.ca.

Statistics ITU (2016). Geneva: International telecommunication union, http://www.itu.int/en/ITU-D/Statistics/Documents/facts/ICTFactsFigures2016.pdf

Teixeira, C., & da Rosa, V. M. (2009). *The Portuguese in Canada: Diasporic challenges and adjustment.* Toronto: University of Toronto Press.

Urciuoli, B. (2008). « Skills and selves in the new work place ». *American Ethnologist, 35*(2), 211-228.

Vidigal, I. (2018). Entradas de portugueses no Canadá diminui em 2017. *Observatório da Emigração.* Retrieved from http://observatorioemigracao.pt/np4/6356.html.

Vigouroux, C. B. (2017). Rethinking (un)skilled migrants: Whose skills, what skills, for what, and for whom?. In A. S. Canagarajah (Ed.), *The Routledge handbook of migration and language* (pp. 312-329). London/New York: Routledge.

Woolard, K. (1998). Introduction: Language ideology as a field of inquiry. In B. Schieffelin, K. Woolard, & P. V. Kroskrity (Eds.), *Language ideologies* (pp. 3-47). New York: Oxford University.

Wortham, S. (2001). Language ideology and educational research. *Linguistics and Education, 12*(2), 253-259.

3
The Values Attached to Speaking Portuguese among Brazilian Migrant Families in Toronto: Pride and Profit[1]

Pedro de Moraes Garcez
Cecília Fischer Dias
Giana Bess
Universidade Federal do Rio Grande do Sul

Linguistic Diversity and the New Globalized Political Economy: Mobility Rules

Recent developments in sociolinguistics have emphasized that studies of language in contemporary societies must consider the new dynamics in the flows of people, money, products, information and discourses brought about by globalization (Canagarajah, 2016; Del Percio, Flubacher, & Duchêne, 2016; Kelly-Holmes, 2016). As De Fina and Perrino (2013) pointed out, the unprecedented nature of current global flows complicates previously dualistic distinctions of "micro-macro" dynamics, which now operate in various scales. In this frame, language diversity must be examined in tandem with mobility, and languages cannot be seen as intrinsically bound to specific spaces or people. Instead, a focus on real-life, often mobile speakers' perspectives is called for to unravel how they frame their understandings regarding their own uses of language in specific social milieux. To this end, the concept of language ideologies has become

---

[1] We thank the participants, for their time and trust, as well the many people in Toronto who introduced us to them. We are also grateful to Monica Heller and everyone at CREFO/OISE/UofT for their generous support. The research reported here was also made possible through PQ, PDE and IC scholarships granted to the authors by CNPq and Propesq/UFRGS.

central to understanding language practices from the actors' own perspectives.

This chapter thus examines language ideologies in reports of language practices by members of a set of Brazilian migrant families with school-age children in Toronto. Stressing contextual singularities, we move away from the idea of migrants as indistinct and uniform groups (Britain, 2016) as we seek to describe and discuss the values these families attach to Portuguese as a key item in their multilingual repertoires. We draw special attention to the children's own discourse as well as their parents' accounts of plans for maintaining Portuguese in their family's next generation. While they all affirm – in general terms – that the language is needed to keep ties with family and community, we point out many also invoke more specific reasons associated with perceived advantages of multilingualism – locally or globally – with Portuguese being a language that is already present in their lives. Few see a need to cultivate Portuguese language skills specifically through formal language education. We thus raise the possibility that language teaching programs framed primarily as heritage language education may be unappealing to these representative potential targets for Portuguese language education in Canada, especially those adopting contemporary language ideologies valuing language skills for their worth in labor markets.

Brazilians as Speakers of Portuguese in Toronto
Since the 1950's, Toronto has been an important destination for Portuguese migrants (Teixeira & Murdie, 2009), who have been joined more recently by Brazilians and, in lesser numbers, migrants from elsewhere in the Lusophone world. Brasch (2007) and Sega (2013) trace the beginning of significant migration of Brazilians to the area back to a period of political and economic instability in Brazil in the 1980's. Even though it was not a main choice destination, Canada became a viable option as visas to the United States became more difficult to obtain, and Canada did not require them of Brazilians at the time. Some also entered Canada by claiming refugee status. Many in these early migrant waves remained in the country illegally and occupied low-skills jobs (Brasch, 2007).

The 2000's saw a change in the profile of the Brazilian migrants headed to Canada, with skilled workers and professionals seeking better work conditions. Sega (2013) highlights the strengthening of social networks established in Canada and Canadian policies to recruit skilled labor as factors that attracted Brazilian migrants in this period. The 2016 census identified 29,315 Brazilians living in Canada, 50% of whom were living in Ontario, 36% of them in Toronto (Statistics Canada, 2017).

These more recently arrived Portuguese-speaking migrants from Brazil may benefit from resources available in and to the established Portuguese community. Diverse themselves, however, they may not share or sustain the dominant ideology of Portuguese culture and language in the city, that celebrates an image of one culture, one language and one history – the one from mainland Portugal (Silva, 2015). Their presence brings complexity to what constitutes "the Portuguese" in Toronto.

A significant aspect of this complexity comes to the fore in the conception of "Portuguese-speaking students", a category often employed by educational agents in Toronto in association with poor academic performance to refer at times to all speakers of the language, but mostly as "a proxy for Luso-Canadians" (Presley & Brown, 2011, p. 1). According to this same School Board report, in 2010, 12% of their Portuguese-speaking students were born in Brazil, 5% in Portugal and 4% in Angola. As summarized in a news magazine article:

It's Portuguese who, according to a 2006 Toronto District School Board report, have the highest [dropout] rate in the city: 42.5 percent. (Another report puts the number at 34 percent, but these estimates vary wildly over time, and the historical mean is closer to 40 percent.) That's nearly 20 percent higher than the municipal average, and almost four times the rate for Chinese students. The Toronto Catholic District School Board doesn't keep track of dropout rates by language group, but, according to a source in the TCDSB, their Portuguese students have the same problem. (Andrew-Gee, 2012)

As the numbers of "Portuguese-speaking students" in Toronto schools remained large – Brown, Newton and Tam (2015) reported 1,426 in the Toronto District School Board, and a report from the Toronto Catholic District School Board (2014) mentioned 3,946 students whose parents informed having Portuguese as language spoken at home (4,3% of the total amount of students enrolled in the board) –, this has been an issue of discussion and concern to schools boards across the area.

Based on the same dataset examined in this chapter, Garcez (2018) identified "different socioeconomic profiles, as indicated by the regions of residence and the occupations of parents" among "children of Brazilian migrant families in Toronto ... indiscriminately identified as Portuguese-speaking students" (p. 749). Looking at samples of the interviewees' discourse in each profile, he found signs that the less skilled migrants indexed closer ties to the Portuguese in the city than the more affluent skilled migrants, and that families in each profile displayed slightly contrasting language ideologies about the value of speaking Portuguese.

As we report below, all participants in the study valued the language, in generic terms, around discourses of pride, but some also made reference to specific advantages of maintaining Portuguese premised on discourses of profit. One family reported concerted efforts to cultivate the language. Before we focus on the language practices these families reported, the next section provides more details about the study and the data to be examined.

A Sociolinguistic Ethnography of Brazilian Migrant Families with School-Age Children in Toronto

The data we report on here was generated in a multi-sited sociolinguistic ethnography carried out by the first author during the 2015-2016 academic year. Brazilian migrant families who had children enrolled in Toronto schools and specialists in areas related to the research topic were contacted for interviews through seven entry sites, three of which are relevant to what we present here. Conversa com Qualidade, a monthly lecture-series gathering Brazilian migrants around invited guest-lecturers, was the entry site for interviews with 17 families. A second entry site was Ready, Set, Learn (pseudonym borrowed from Kwiczala and Kutsyuruba, 2012) – a tutoring program for Portuguese- and Spanish-speaking students in elementary and high school offered by a community organization – through which seven students and their families were interviewed. Finally, through fieldwork at one Secondary School, seven other students were interviewed. Below we analyze samples of a representative section of this dataset: one interview with Marita, mother of Emily, who attends Ready, Set, Learn; one with Anrel, a student at the Secondary School; and three with families contacted through Conversa com Qualidade. These five interviews will guide this chapter as we try to understand how these Brazilian migrant families' views on language relate to their perspectives on the value of speaking Portuguese.

Pride and Profit

We understand the families' positions regarding language as situated in late capitalism in terms of *pride* and *profit* as proposed by Heller and Duchêne (2012). According to these authors, in the historical context of industrial capitalism, when the modern nation-state was conceived as a means to regulate national markets, states had to validate themselves through homogeneity as well as through boundaries and social stratification. Language would play an important role as a criterion of membership in or exclusion from states and their markets: "If you don't speak the language of the nation, and speak it properly, you show that you lack the ability to reason and the strength to prevail that citizenship requires; you therefore can't claim access to political and economic power" (p. 5). To be a full participant in the market regulated by states, to have access to the rights of citizenship to one's nationality, one had to be a member of the nation-state, and this required speaking the language of the state. This created an identity relation towards language which is seen in discourses of "pride".

The national markets established in industrial capitalism eventually *saturate*, which is the first of five processes characteristic of the shift to late capitalism as described by Heller and Duchêne (2012), along with *expansion, distinction, tertiarization* and *flexibilization*. In late capitalism, the tertiary sector becomes central, with main activities involving information, services and symbolic goods. Combined with the three first processes, *tertiarization* leads to *flexibilization*, the most relevant process for our discussion: "As markets grow and are increasingly integrated, and as it becomes more difficult and more important to find new ways to source cheap goods or labor, niche markets, or sources of distinction, it becomes more important to be able to change any of these modes quickly" (Heller & Duchêne, 2012, p. 9). Companies close and move much faster, which demands a flexible worker, who must be ready to move to different places, and who must rely not only on hard technical skills, but also be able to display as many soft skills as possible, to the point where an employable person must be a "bundle of skills" (Urciuoli, 2008). In this context of mobility and of prominence of the tertiary sector, language ability becomes a relevant soft skill, a distinctive aspect one can display in one's portfolio. Therefore, an economic relation towards language is established, and this can be seen in discourses of "profit".

As Heller and Duchêne (2012) point out, however, no clear-cut distinction exists between these two discourse domains. When language is used to confer authenticity to a product that is being marketed as connected to national identity, or to a person who is promoting a soft skill, "the trope of 'profit' appropriates the trope of 'pride'" (p. 10). Identity values legitimize economic values in terms of authenticity. We therefore do not expect the families to present either one type of discourse or the other as we try to understand their experience as Brazilian migrants in Toronto.

Migration has, of course, long been an important socioeconomic phenomenon. The difference in late capitalism is perhaps the intensity and scale of the flows, and the ease of communication via new technologies. In the superdiverse (see Blommaert & Rampton, 2011) landscape of Toronto where they now find themselves, Brazilian migrant families are sensitive to a complex interplay of variables involving diversity and mobility. Moreover, these families have to deal with the various language repertoires in this multilingual urban setting and are often led to consider their own language practices; they demonstrate their language ideologies through the discourses apparent in their reported actions.

Language Ideologies

To approach the speakers' perspectives on language, we draw on the concept of language ideologies as defined by Irvine and Gal (2000): "ideas with which participants and observers frame their understandings of linguistic varieties and map those understandings onto people, events and activities that are significant to them" (p. 35). Gal (2016) adds that the concept "labels a form of reflexivity: it is metacommunication, participants' talk about talk, or their reflections, signals, and presuppositions about linguistic forms and their uses" (p. 116). These reflections can be explicitly formulated or appear in implicit comments made by the participants.

By focusing on language ideologies, we avoid assuming that "there is a 'view from nowhere' that would allow investigators to determine what are the important variables existent in a population" (Gal, 2016, p. 131). We seek to analyze speakers' statements and how they interpret them in a specific social context and historical process. In this sense, the interviewees' identities as speakers of Portuguese are not simply revealed by the act of speaking what is recognized as the Portuguese language, but by how they produce discourses and interactions, and how these are related to attributed identities and qualities.

As we study the participants' perceptions of language practices in a context of transnational migration in Toronto, we highlight our view that any social value attributed to language practices is not fixed, but, rather, it varies in different social milieux and in where it is placed in space and time. This means that each local, regional, national or global index may signal different meanings, values and status for different codes (see Prinsloo, 2017). In this view, "in multilingual settings every variety of language can be used on one or a number of scales: no language dominates all scales and there isn't a single variety that can be used in every situation with all people in that setting" (p. 365). In their mobility, migrants have to evaluate and re-evaluate their language practices in different scales.

Therefore, we seek to understand the language ideologies in the interviewees' perceptions, understandings, attitudes and interpretations in different scales and in a context of late capitalism and globalization. In the next section, we analyze how participants frame their language practices as Portuguese speakers. We identify their discourses of "pride" and "profit", pointing to how they navigate through attitudes towards Portuguese and their perspectives for maintaining the language or not.

What Some Brazilian Migrants Tell Us About the Value of Speaking Portuguese
Marita and César
We first introduce you to Marita and César, who share a family history of migration in their own parents' generation, while still keeping many singularities.

Marita, 49, is a cashier at a department store. As mentioned before, her daughter, Emily, attends Ready, Set, Learn. Marita was born in Mozambique to a Chinese father and a Chinese-Mozambican mother who eventually migrated to Brazil, where Marita herself was raised. Marita shares a home with her sister, to whom she speaks Portuguese – or sometimes Cantonese when they don't want Emily to understand something. With her parents, who are in Brazil, Marita says she speaks a mixture of Cantonese and Portuguese; with Emily, she says she and her sister used to speak Portuguese, but the girl started to respond in English, and now they speak English mixed with Portuguese.

César, 46, a metrics analyst, and Adriana, 38, an artist, are Celeste's parents. César's parents emigrated from Japan to Brazil, where César was born and raised. He says he doesn't speak much Japanese in Toronto, only with his parents (remotely) and a friend. With Adriana and Celeste, he speaks Portuguese, but, like Emily, Celeste started to respond in English, so sometimes they speak English. He says, however, that Celeste has been "getting better" and is beginning to use some words in Portuguese in English sentences.

All three parents in both families report they want to keep speaking Portuguese at home, but point out their children often respond in English, which makes them tend to switch to English. This practice was reported by many families, especially as children start going to school. Emily was ten at the time of the interviews; Celeste was four and had been going to childcare for two and a half years. Emily has Portuguese language classes daily at school, where she says there are few other Portuguese speakers (Marita mentions two), but they interact with each other in English. Adriana had just recently found out that there was a boy in Celeste's school whose mother is Brazilian, but he only spoke English.

Both girls' parents say they think Portuguese is important for their daughters in terms of pride and of profit. However, they seem to set such values according to different scales. When asked if it is important for her that Emily should know Portuguese, Marita answers confidently that it would be important for Emily's future. When asked why, this is what she had to say:

    Pedro: por quê? assim, qual é o valor, por que que seria in-interessante pra ela?
    Marita: (a porque a e:-) o pai dela fala português, né, [e:]
    Pedro: [mhm]
    Marita: (eu não) falo muito bem inglês, então (.) é bom. e pros meus pa:is, pra tod- é, pra todo mundo, né, acho que futuro, um trabalho né, arrumar um trabalho bom também
    Pedro: a senhora acha que tem valor aqui, saber português?

Marita: é, claro, mhm
Pedro   como assim? se eu tivesse que explicar pra um
        brasileiro assim que não conhece aqui,
Marita: ah, [tipo] assim se nã-, se alguém não fala portug- não=
Pedro: [ahn]
Marita: =fala inglês, precisa de uma que ajuda, né, pra traduzir
        alguma coisa assim (.) é bom também pra ela, né

Pedro: why? I mean, what is the value, why would that be in-
       interesting for her?
Marita: (well because e:-) her father speaks Portuguese, right, [and:]
Pedro: [mhm]
Marita: (I don't) speak English very well, so (.) it's good and for my
        pa:rents, for everyo- it's, for everyone, right, I think the
        future, a job right, finding a good job also
Pedro: do you think it has value <u>here</u>, to know Portuguese?
Marita: yes, sure, mhm
        (.)
Pedro how so? if I had to explain it to a Brazilian who doesn't
       know it here,
Marita: oh, [like] I mean if someone doesn- doesn't speak=
Pedro: [uh]
Marita: =Portug- doesn't speak English and needs someone to help,
        right, to translate something like that (.) it's good also for
        her, right

The main reasons Marita points out for Emily to maintain Portuguese are communication with the family and, when pressed, the possibility of Portuguese being an advantage in the local labor market.

In César's discourse, we identify values of pride as well, but also of profit on a global scale. When asked what the relevance may be for Celeste to speak Portuguese, this is what César had to say:

César: eu acho que (.) uma segunda língua. eu ach:o também pra
       interagir com familiares
Pedro: mhm
César: eu acho que- a gente é- a gente acredita baseado em pesquisa
       e tudo (mais) ter mais de uma língua só beneficia em todos
       os aspectos. seja ele no futuro no mundo corporativo ou
       não, seja do lado social.
Pedro: mhm
César: e também ã pra exercitar.

César: I think that (.) a second language. I thi:nk also to interact
       with family members
Pedro: mhm

> César: I think that- we uh- we believe based on research and (all) having more than one language only brings you benefits in all aspects. be that in the future in the corporate world or not, be that on the social side,
> Pedro: mhm
> César: and also uh for practice.

When asked if he saw any advantages of speaking Portuguese for his daughter as a Canadian citizen, he replied: "absolutely. well unfortunately or fortunately we consider more the corporate world" ["totalmente. é (.) infelizmente ou felizmente a gente considera o mundo corporativo"]. He then mentioned Adriana's sister, who was offered a job in a big company in the US, as an example of advantages Celeste could have for speaking Portuguese.

Notice that, in addition to the usual importance of Portuguese for communication with the extended family, César immediately and voluntarily mentions advantages of multilingualism, with Portuguese being a value, not necessarily in and of itself, but as an additional language, an asset within the corporate world. This is emphasized when he is asked to think of Celeste as a Canadian citizen, with the example of her aunt as someone who has been offered "a great opportunity" [uma grande oportunidade] while living in North America due to her language skills in association with her knowledge of a regional world market area. Much louder than in Marita's interview, in what César had to say we thus hear echoes of the flexibilization that is typical of late capitalism.

These two parents also reported different plans for the girls to learn and cultivate Portuguese. When asked if there was a specific kind of Portuguese he would like Celeste to speak, César favored what he termed "grammatically correct Portuguese" ["correta gramaticalmente"] and went on to explain how they plan to achieve that:

> César: e uma das coisas que a gente tá pensando em fazer, bom, primeiro procurar professores né continuar lecionando em casa ao mesmo tempo quando der
> Pedro: mhm
> César: e: e possivelmente a gente tá tentando descobrir outras alternativas e- mesmo na TV. ahm onde possa ser bastante útil. a gente tem que encontrar maneiras e e assuntos e e métodos que atraem,
> Pedro: mhm
> César: que acho que é dessa forma que ela vai conseguir
> (...)
> César: a razão pela qual quando ela vai pro Brasil a gente: continua mantendo onde ela consiga ficar o tempo suficiente pra ela absorver a língua

> César: and one of the things we've been thinking of doing, well, first look for teachers right keep teaching at home at the same time when we can
> Pedro: mhm
> César: a:nd and possibly we're trying to find other alternatives and- even on TV. uh which may be very useful. we have to find ways and and subjects and and methods that are attractive,
> Pedro: mhm
> César: that I think that it is this way she's going to manage (...)
> César: the reason why when she goes to Brazil we: keep trying where she may stay long enough to absorb the language

Celeste's father, speaking in first-person plural, has established a goal for his child to learn proper Portuguese and an obstinate plan for her to get there. He mentions extracurricular classes, in addition to exposing her to Portuguese at home and during extended stays in Brazil as a way to compensate for eventually being remiss to speak Portuguese with her at home.

Marita's discourse differs. She does mention, when talking about languages spoken at home, that they have been going to Brazil, where Emily is able to grasp a few words. But after talking about the importance of Emily knowing Portuguese, she is asked if she has been doing anything for Emily to speak Portuguese or if going to Brazil is enough, and she does not address traveling.

> Pedro: e: e a senhora tem f- feito alguma coisa pra ela aprender português? ou a senhora acha que ela indo pro Brasil de vez em quando (.) ela vai aprender
> Marita: ah fi- financeira né a situação financeira não tá muito bom pra todo mundo né [ye]ah
> Pedro: [hm]
> (...)
> Marita: entã:o, é bom que ela aprenda né mas eu não tenho dinheiro pra pagar né. yeah.
> (.)
> Marita: e alguns tipo tr- ã aquel- que tem que pagar um pouquinho também é mais caro também tipo pra pr- aprender português né. yeah.
> Pedro: mas aí a senhora acha que: aprender português é fora de casa? não=
> Marita: =fora de casa yeah

Pedro: a:nd and have you been d- doing anything for her to learn
Portuguese? or do you think that by going to Brazil every
now and then (.) she will learn
Marita: oh fi- financial right the financial situation is not very good
now for anyone right [ye]ah
Pedro: [hm]
(...)
Marita: so:, it'd be good if she learned it right but I don't have the
money to pay right. yeah.
(.)
Marita: and some like w- uh tha- which one must pay a little more
also it's more expensive also like to l- learn Portuguese right.
yeah.
Pedro: but then you think tha:t learning Portuguese is outside
the home? not=
Marita: =outside the home yeah

    She goes on to talk about a teacher at Emily's school who offered private Portuguese classes after school. Some of Emily's classmates were attending those classes, but she said it was too expensive. She is then asked if speaking Portuguese at home wouldn't help with that, and that's the first time in the interview she says it is difficult to maintain Portuguese as a home language.

    Marita and César see some of the same possibilities for their daughters to learn Portuguese: traveling, private classes, speaking at home. However, while having the child pick up Portuguese while visiting family in Brazil is a possible plus in the case of Emily and Marita, for César this is a central goal of the trip for his daughter. Private classes are too expensive for Marita, while César plans to hire a teacher and look for other alternatives. And, when it comes to speaking at home, they have a similar situation, but César is looking for methods to make Portuguese attractive.

    These two parents, who share a similar family history of transcontinental migration from Asia to Brazil in their own parents' generation and report similar difficulties in enforcing a Portuguese language environment at home, both see membership and economic uses for Portuguese. However, they set these values in different scales, locally in the case of Marita, globally in the case of César. Accordingly, the ideas they have for their daughters to learn Portuguese suggest different degrees of determination and resolve. Like other participants who identify advantages of using Portuguese mostly at a local level, whether in terms of pride or profit, Marita does not set a *plan* to support the child to learn Portuguese. César, like other participants who identify advantages of multilingualism in the "corporate" world at large, formulates a goal for the child to speak proper Portuguese and an investment plan to help the child get there.

What about the youth themselves: what do they have to say about learning Portuguese and about the prospect of formal Portuguese language education? The next section brings a sample of their discourse and an array of language ideologies in that regard.

Anrel and Marcos

Anrel, 19, moved to Canada when he was 17 to live with his father, who had been living in Toronto for ten years working in construction. Anrel uses Portuguese to speak to his mother and other relatives in Brazil, and at home with his father, who does not speak English. At school, he hangs out with a group of about ten Brazilian students and has contact with other Portuguese-speaking students of Portuguese origin. Anrel is taking an extra year of secondary school in order to obtain the necessary credits for post-secondary education. He wants to become an electrician, and this plan came from talking to one of his father's coworkers.

> Pedro: e tu acha que pode ter alguma: alguma vantagem ser falante também de português aqui? nessa cidade?
> Anrel: trabalho. é sempre bom você ter dois idi- saber falar dois ou três idiomas em qualquer lugar do mundo.
> Pedro: mhm
> Anrel: acho que isso sempre ajuda saber falar dois ou três idiomas
> Pedro: mhm
> Anrel: trabalho. coloca no seu currículo eu sei falar português, espanhol e inglês, entendeu? acho que é isso. trabalho (...)
> Pedro: mhm. e- e pra conseguir emprego tu acha que pode ajudar ser falante de português? como eletricista?
> Anrel: ajuda. porque, trabalhador, de construção, aqui no Canadá, construção é muito forte no- na área dos portugueses, como eu disse, português gosta muito de trabalhar em construção
> Pedro: mhm
> Anrel: e como eletricista envolve construção, eu sabendo falar português, me ajuda a entrar numa empresa portuguesa, vamos dizer assim

> Pedro: and do you think there might be some: some advantage in being a speaker also of Portuguese here? in this city?
> Anrel: work. it's always good to have two langua- to know how to speak two or three languages anywhere in the world.
> Pedro: mhm

Anrel: I think this always helps to know how to speak two or three languages
Pedro: mhm
Anrel: work. you put that in your cv I can speak Portuguese, Spanish and English, you know? I think that's it, work (...)
Pedro: mhm an- and to find a job you think being a speaker of Portuguese might help? as an electrician?
Anrel: it does. because, a worker, in construction, here in Canada construction is big in the- among the Portuguese, as I said, the Portuguese really like to work in construction
Pedro: mhm
Anrel: and as an electrician is involved in construction, my knowing to speak Portuguese helps me join a Portuguese company, let's put it that way

Anrel clearly recognizes value in multilingualism for "work", "anywhere in the world". However, his life plans highlight the value of speaking Portuguese as rooted in the local scale of the Toronto area, where he can benefit from previously established social networks among speakers of Portuguese of various backgrounds.

We turn now to Marcos, 18, and his family, who had been living in Toronto for seven years, in a neighborhood far from the areas of concentration of Portuguese speakers in the city. His father, Antônio, 47, works with information technology in a multinational company, and his mother, Selene, 46, is an administrative assistant in an office. Marcos' sister, Marília, 13, is in grade 8. The parents report using Portuguese at home constantly, but Marcos and Marília speak English with each other. Antônio and Selene estimate that about 60% of their local friends are Brazilian, whose children also prefer to speak English or a mixture of English and Portuguese.

The school Marcos attended was part of the same board as the Secondary School Anrel attends. Differently from Anrel, however, Marcos and Marília reported no use of Portuguese nor contact with other Portuguese speakers at school. Marcos is now a university student majoring in computer science. When asked about the value of speaking Portuguese, three members of the family in a row referred to the added value of being a multilingual speaker:

Antônio: não só porque é uma língua adicional, que pode ajudá-los (.) no mercado profissional no futuro, empresas que (.) é precisam de falantes de português para interagir com parceiros no Brasil e essas coisas todas mas também para manter contato com a família
(...)

Marcos: agora (.) que eu estou entrando no mercado de trabalho então eu acho que é:: coisa boa saber um- outra língua, então eu quero continuar falando português, mas eu não quero (.) ter que fazer nenhuma aula de português no futuro, então eu espero que eu consiga continuar a falar português
(...)
Marília: ajuda muito tipo a arrumar um trabalho se você fala mais línguas

Antônio: not only because it is an additional language, which can help them (.) in the professional market in the future, companies that (.) uh need speakers of Portuguese to interact with partners in Brazil and all that but also for contact with the family
(...)
Marcos: now (.) that I am about to join the job market so I think that it i::s good thing to know a- another language, so I want to keep speaking Portuguese, but I don't want to (.) have to take any Portuguese classes in the future, so I hope I can keep speaking Portuguese
(...)
Marília: it helps a lot to get a job if you speak more languages

Besides its importance for keeping in touch with family, Portuguese is stressed as a competitive advantage in "the professional market", echoing César's emphasis on "the corporate world". Differently from Anrel's perspective, therefore, the value of speaking Portuguese for Marcos and his family is not linked to the possibility of direct contact with other Portuguese speakers locally, in Toronto; instead it relates to the discourses of "profit" that value the ability of speaking a language as a soft skill, in a broader, global scale. The formulation of Marília's comment is particularly telling as it implies that what is valued is not necessarily Portuguese but the capacity to speak multiple languages. Since Portuguese is already part of their repertoire, it can be strategically mobilized as competitive advantage.

Although diverging about possible scales of use in the job market, one thing both Marco and Anrel have in common is their unwillingness to take Portuguese classes. When asked if he would like to have Portuguese classes in school, Anrel immediately said he wouldn't; and Marcos, as we can see above, hopes he can continue speaking Portuguese, but does not want to take any classes in the future. It seems that both are satisfied with their Portuguese as maintained through daily social practices; and both are confident that it can bring advantages in the future, whether locally or globally.

Cecília, Marco, Maria and Romeu

We turn finally to a family with a strict policy to both maintain and cultivate Portuguese among the children. Marco Antônio, 42, is a medical doctor; his wife Cecília, 41, an interior designer. Their children, Romeu, 9, and Maria, 6, both born in Canada, are enrolled in a university laboratory school where, like Marcos and Marília, they have few opportunities to speak Portuguese. The parents estimate that 50% to 60% of their circle of friends are Brazilian, but most of their daily interactions are held in English. At work, both parents report using Portuguese as a resource: Marco Antônio speaks the language with patients; and Cecília uses it with workers at construction sites. These parents say that Portuguese is important for their children so they can speak to their grandparents in Brazil, but also because it provides extra opportunities, in terms similar to those used by Marcos and his family. Marco Antônio and Cecília elaborate on how the language can be valued at both local or global scales:

Cecília: ((o Canadá)) é um país multicultur- a cidade é multicultural t- a comunidade portuguesa tá aí, tem várias coisas que acontecem então eu acho que é importante
(...)
Marco: então, e-eu acho que pra pra eles no futuro, não tenho dúvida que isso vai ser que vai facilitar. é:: que eles façam uma entrevista pra:: pra i- entrar numa empresa ah mas a empresa não tem tal não sei o quê e um dia ela abre uma sucursal no Brasil porque o Brasil tá:: [maravilhoso=
Cecília: [ou né sei lá (na)=
Marco: =tá não sei o quê]
Cecília: =Angola, na África, sei lá quê]
Marco: ou aí ele vai poder dizer assim não eu posso ir falar eu falo é eu vou tá (.) preparado pra é:: ap- aprender ou poder [me
Cecília: [ou mesmo se tiver que falar espa]nhol o português já tá
[é uma ajuda]
Marco: [já ajuda então] acho que vai facilitar pra eles

Cecília: ((Canada)) is a multicultur- the city is multicultural t- the Portuguese community is here, there are a number of things that happen so I think it is important
(...)
Marco: so, I- I think that for them in the future, I have no doubt that this will make things easier. uh:: for them to have a job interview to:: to g- join some company oh the company doesn't have such whatever and one day it starts operating in Brazil because Brazil i::s now [wonderful or=
Cecília: [or who knows in=
Marco: =whatever]

Cecília: =Angola in Africa whatever]
Marco: or then he can say hey I can go I can speak it I do speak it and I'm going to be (.) prepared to uh:: l- learn or be able to [communicate]
Cecília: [or even if speaking] Spanish is needed Portuguese is [of some help]
Marco: [it helps] so I think it will make things easier for them

Their rationale for maintaining Portuguese as a competitive edge related to mobility in a global job market extends to it being a stepping stone to other romance languages. Cecília also associates the ability to speak Portuguese with learning French, a key item in one's language repertoire in Canada: "Romeu and Maria do very well in French because of Portuguese" [inclusive o Romeu e a Marília vão muito bem no francês por causa do português."]. Cecília and Marco Antônio have taken action to make sure Portuguese will remain part of their children's repertoire by instituting a strict Portuguese-only policy within the home. They have also hired a full-time Brazilian maid and a private language tutor, a retired Portuguese teacher who uses the teaching material they brought back from Brazil. Like César and Adriana, they manage to have the kids take frequent trips to stay with their grandparents in Curitiba. In a separate interview, Romeu and Maria were happy to speak Portuguese, which they said they prefer over English or French, and raved about their visits to Brazil, which they like best, "because it is more fun" ["porque lá é mais divertido eu acho"].

The interview excerpts above thus indicate all participants value speaking Portuguese to maintain family ties and other social networks. We can also see that the discourse of multilingualism as an advantage in the job market also appears as a constant. However, different scales are evident in how discourse of "profit" are featured: while a local and immediate scope is suggested in Anrel's and Marita's perspectives; a broader, global scale looms in Marcos' and his family's views, as well as in Romeu and Maria's and César and Adriana's families, in which Portuguese is an asset to be preserved and also cultivated.

Portuguese Language Skills as an Asset

We hope to have provided a glimpse of the array of language ideologies that circulate among Brazilian migrant families that have settled in Toronto, especially in terms of their perspectives on the values associated with the Portuguese language in their repertoire and how that relates to the prospects for Portuguese language maintenance and cultivation through language education.

The interviews also suggest that maintaining Portuguese among the children requires some degree of effort, and perhaps planning and investment. A supply of formal Portuguese language education would most probably be welcome among these families. However, few of the participants highlight Portuguese language education as crucial. Some, like Emily's mother, neglect the available supply as effective, and consider other options to be too expensive; Anrel and Marco actually dismiss it as desirable. Celeste's father considers it among other alternatives, and only Romeu and Maria's parents report actual investment in cultivation.

We note that, while all of the parents mentioned it is important to keep the language for communication with the kids' extended families, no one produced strong statements about a larger group identity to be kept through heritage language maintenance. In contrast, all of the interviews featured here signal attentiveness to positive attitudes toward multilingualism, and of language skills as valuable assets now and in their children's futures. In other words, while we found discourses of pride, we distinctively heard discourses of profit from these participants, though in different scopes and projecting different scales, which we may relate to different strengths of resolve to keep the language and cultivate it. As suggested by findings reported in Garcez (2018), class positions may play a role here.

Marita and César, who share a background of transcontinental family migration, diverge in the scales in which they see value in Portuguese for their daughters, generic local in Marita's case; corporate global in César's. Accordingly, their planning for their children to learn Portuguese varies from a general, tentative one by Marita to a more specific, resolute one by César. The two young men we featured also display a similar contrast: while Anrel points to the value of Portuguese in the local job market, Marcos sees Portuguese as a good thing to keep as he is entering the labor market at large. Interestingly, both volunteered statements about not being interested in taking Portuguese classes. Marco Antônio and Cecília see a more global use for Portuguese and have devised and implemented a plan for their children to maintain and cultivate Portuguese, also as a path to an extended multilingual repertoire.

We thus notice that all participants attach identity and (global or local) economic values to Portuguese. Anrel and Marcos gave us an example of discourses of profit being legitimized by those of pride: they don't feel the need to make any further effort to learn Portuguese, but, since they have that soft skill at hand, as legitimate speakers of Portuguese, they shall use it to their favor. In terms of economic values, we notice a tendency among those pointing to local economic uses of Portuguese to have more generic planning for their kids to learn the language, and of those whose discourses point to a more global economic use for Portuguese to have more specific plans to make sure their children maintain it.

Considering the children of Brazilian migrant families as prospective recipients of formal Portuguese language education in Canada, despite the importance of identity relations between these youth and the language, we note our participants displayed considerable evidence that they regard Portuguese as equally valuable not in and of itself, but as a soft skill in contemporary political economies where multilingualism is an asset. Highlighting the potential value of developing instrumental skills for those who have Portuguese in their repertoire to some extent, even if only symbolically, may help make the language more attractive than insisting they should care for it because it is part of their (parents' or grandparents') "heritage". Attention to this may be key for Portuguese language teaching in Canada to reach this profile of students – and perhaps others in Toronto and in similar superdiverse settings as well. In any case, we hope to have contributed to highlighting the need to understand what youth and their families may be looking for in Portuguese language education.

Appendix: Transcription Conventions

,	more to come
.	final intonation
i:s	lengthening of preceding sound
<u>here</u>	emphatic stress
Eng-	cut-off
(.)	pause
[uh]	overlapping talk
=	contiguous utterances
(text)	transcription doubt
((text))	contextual information
(…)	intervening material omitted

References

Andrew-Gee, E. (2012). What's eating Little Portugal? *Maisonneuve, 45* (Fall 2012).

Blommaert, J., & Rampton, B. (2011). Language and superdiversity. *Diversities, 13*(2), 1-21.

Brasch, K. (2007). *Finding their place in the world: Brazilian migrant identities in an interconnected world.* (Unpublished doctoral dissertation). Ontario Institute for Studies in Education, University of Toronto.

Britain, D. (2016). Sedentarism and nomadism in the sociolinguistic of dialect. In N. Coupland (Ed.), *Sociolinguistics: Theoretical debates* (pp. 217-241). Cambridge: Cambridge University Press.

Brown, R., Newton, L., & Tam, G. (2015). *The Toronto District School Board's student group overviews: Aboriginal heritage, Afghan, Portuguese-speaking, Somali-speaking, and Spanish-speaking students.* (Research Report No. 14/15-31). Toronto: Toronto District School Board.

Canagarajah, S. (Ed.). (2017). *The Routledge handbook of migration and language.* Oxon, UK/New York: Routledge.

De Fina, A., & Perrino, S. (2013). Transnational identities. *Applied Linguistics, 34*(5), 509-515.

Del Percio, A., Flubacher, M., & Duchêne, A. (2016). Language and political economy. In O. Garcia, N. Flores, & M. Spotti (Eds.), *Oxford handbook of language in society* (pp. 55–75). New York: Oxford University Press.

Gal, S. (2016). Linguistic differentiation. In N. Coupland (Ed.), *Sociolinguistics: Theoretical debates* (pp. 113-135). Cambridge: Cambridge University Press.

Garcez, P. M. (2018). Quem é "estudante falante de português" em famílias de origem brasileira em Toronto, Canadá? Questões de classe. *Linguagem em (Dis)curso, 18*(3), 729-749.

Heller, M., & Duchêne, A. (2012). Pride and profit: Changing discourses of language, capital and nation-state. In A. Duchêne & M. Heller (Eds.), *Language in late capitalism: Pride and profit* (pp. 1-21). New York: Routledge.

Irvine, J. T., & Gal, S. (2000). Language ideology and linguistic differentiation. In P. V Kroskrity (Ed.), *Regimes of language: Ideologies, polities, and identities* (pp. 35-84). Santa Fe, NM, EUA: School of American Research Press.

Kelly-Holmes, H. (2016). Theorising the market in sociolinguistics. In N. Coupland (Ed.), *Sociolinguistics: Theoretical debates* (pp. 157-172). Cambridge: Cambridge University Press.

Kwiczala, C., & Kutsyuruba, B. (2012). A case study of a community-based tutoring and mentoring program for Portuguese-Canadians students. *Portuguese Studies, 20*(2), 79-100.

Presley, A., & Brown, R. S. (2011) *Portuguese-speaking students in the TDSB: An overview.* Toronto: Toronto District School Board – TDSB. Retrieved from http://www.tdsb.on.ca/Portals/0/AboutUs/Research/Portuguese-speakingStudentsInTheTDSBOverview.pdf.

Prinsloo, M. (2017). Spatiotemporal scales and the study of mobility. In S. Canagarajah (Ed.), *The Routledge handbook of migration and language* (pp. 364-380). London/New York: Routledge.

Sega, R. F. (2013). *Projeto Canadá: seletividades e redes de imigrantes brasileiros qualificados em Toronto.* (Unpublished master's thesis). Graduate

Program in Sociology, Universidade Federal de São Carlos, SP, Brazil.

Silva, E. (2015). Sociolinguistic tensions in the Portuguese/Lusophone community of Toronto, Canada. In L. P. Moita Lopes (Ed.), *Global Portuguese: Linguistic ideologies in late modernity* (pp. 124-143). London: Routledge.

Statistics Canada. (2017). *Immigration and Ethnocultural Diversity Highlight Tables*. Retrieved from http://www12.statcan.gc.ca/census-recensement/2016/dp-pd/hlt-fst/imm/Table.cfm?Lang=E&T=21&Geo=01, http://www12.statcan.gc.ca/census-recensement/2016/dp-pd/hlt fst/imm/Table.cfm?Lang=E&T=21&Geo=35 and http://www12.statcan.gc.ca/census-recensement/2016/dp-pd/hlt-fst/imm/Table.cfm?Lang=E&T=22&Geo=535.

Teixeira, C., & Murdie, R. A. (2009). On the move: The Portuguese in Toronto. In C. Teixeira & V. M. P. Da Rosa (Eds.), *The Portuguese in Canada: Diasporic challenges and adjustment*. (2nd. ed.) (pp. 191-208). Toronto: University of Toronto Press.

Toronto Catholic District School Board. (2014). *Annual report of the Portuguese-speaking committee. Toronto: Toronto Catholic District School Board*. Retrieved from https://www.tcdsb.org/Board/TrusteesoftheBoard/Committees/AgendaDocs/Student%20Achievement%20Committee/September%2011,%202014/Annual%20Report%20on%20the%20Portuguese%20Speaking%20Committee.pdf.

Urciuoli, B. (2008). Skills and selves in the new workplace. *American Ethnologist, 35*(2), 211-228.

4
Portuguese in Toronto: Identity, Attitudes and Linguistic Variation

Michol F. Hoffman
James A. Walker
York University & La Trobe University

Introduction

Toronto has been home to the largest Portuguese community in Canada since the 1950s (Rocha-Trindade, 2009; Teixeira & Murdie, 2009; Troper, 2003). The Portuguese co-exist with a wide array of other ethnic and linguistic groups in a densely populated urban centre, with English as the majority language and the language in which most children are schooled. For young people of Portuguese background, growing up in Toronto presents a tension between maintaining the Portuguese language and culture and assimilating to the language and culture of the majority. How do Portuguese youth manage this tension? What consequences do their choices hold for how they view themselves, whether and how they use Portuguese? Do they express these attitudes and choices in the way that they speak English?

In this chapter, we explore the attitudes of young residents of Toronto of Portuguese descent toward their ethnic and linguistic identity and how this affects their spoken English. As part of a larger ongoing project investigating the ethnolinguistic landscape of the city, we have conducted and recorded sociolinguistic interviews with a small sample of residents of Toronto of Portuguese background. This interview, which is intended to provide a sample of spoken English for analysis, also includes a questionnaire on the participant's self-identification and attitudes towards their background language and culture. We begin by providing some historical and demographic background on the formation and status of the Portuguese community in Toronto before detailing the speakers included in this study and how data were collected. We present the results of their responses to the questionnaire, both qualitatively and quantitatively, before examining the distribution of several linguistic variables of Canadian

English, comparing their results to those of other participants of the same age-group but different ethnolinguistic background. Our goal is to understand how young Portuguese residents of Toronto position themselves in relation to other communities in the city in terms of their use of linguistic features that define Canadian English and its ongoing changes.

Portuguese in Toronto: History and Demographics
Portugal has been characterized by emigration since the early 16th century (Rocha-Trindade, 2009), but for most of this time the destination of this migration was not Canada but instead was focused along existing Portuguese trade routes and colonies. The east coast of what is now Canada (specifically, Newfoundland and Labrador) was frequented for a time by Portuguese fishermen, but they never established permanent settlements there. Canada only became a destination for Portuguese migration and settlement in the middle of the 20th century (Rocha-Trindade, 2009; Teixeira & Murdie, 2009). A Portuguese community was established in Toronto in 1953, located first in Kensington Market and Alexandra Park (Teixeira & Murdie, 2009), then moving northwest into the areas along Dundas and College Streets, now recognized by locals as "little Portugal." Immigration to Canada by speakers of Portuguese has come primarily from Europe (rather than from Brazil or other Portuguese colonies), with the vast majority (60-70%) from the Azores (Rocha-Trindade, 2009). According to the 2016 census, 324,930 Canadian citizens and 160,000 permanent residents claim Portuguese ethnic origin, with 210,425 (65%) with citizenship in Toronto, making it home to the largest Portuguese community in the country (Rocha-Trindade, 2009). Portuguese is claimed as a mother tongue by 104,305 residents of Toronto, making it one of the top 10 languages in the city (Statistics Canada 2016). However, since only 3.5% of the city claims Portuguese ethnic background and only 1.7% claim Portuguese as a mother tongue, the Portuguese are a small minority who co-exist with people of dozens of other ethnolinguistic backgrounds, against the backdrop of an English-speaking majority in a historically Anglo-Saxon city. Our hypothesis is that this sociolinguistic context affects the way that Canadians of Portuguese background view themselves, the role that the Portuguese language plays in their lives, and is reflected in their use of English.

'Contact in the City'
As part of an investigation into Toronto's diverse ethnolinguistic landscape, we have been engaged in an ongoing large-scale project, entitled 'Contact in the City' (Hoffman & Walker 2010). The goals of this project

are to obtain recordings of naturalistic spoken English from a representative sample of people from different ethnolinguistic groups in the city, along with a 'control group' of Toronto's old-line British/Irish-background ('Anglo') population.

Table 1 shows our stratification of participants along three dimensions: ethnic background, sex and generation or age-group. The ethnic groups we have chosen to investigate represent the groups with the largest demographic representation in the city, and many of them have communities recognized by their public signage and use of heritage languages. The division by generation is intended to contrast immigrants with people who were born and raised in the city: first-generation participants arrived in Toronto as adults (aged 18 or over) and lived there for at least 20 years prior to being interviewed (older British/Irish speakers are matched in age but were born and raised in Toronto), while second/third-generation participants were born and raised in Toronto (or arrived before the age of 5). Dividing by generation allows us to distinguish between second-language speakers of English (first generation), who may exhibit transfer from their first language, from younger speakers (second/third generation) who are bilingual to various degrees but acquired English as children.

Table 1
Stratification of participants in the "Contact in the City" project by ethnolinguistic background, generation/age-group and sex

	British/Irish		Chinese		Filipino		Greek		Italian		Portuguese		Punjabi	
	F	M	F	M	F	M	F	M	F	M	F	M	F	M
1st (Older)	8	6	5	4	5	2	4	2	6	4	5	1	4	3
2nd/3rd (Younger)	6	6	11	11	7	9	1	3	10	8	4	2	13	13
Total:	14	12	16	15	12	11	5	5	16	12	9	3	17	16
Ethnicity total:	26		31		23		10		28		12		33	
Grand total:	163													

Participants were recruited by student research assistants at York University who were themselves members of the relevant ethnic group. These assistants, who made use of their extended social and family networks in identifying and recruiting participants, were trained in the techniques of conducting and recording sociolinguistic interviews, as well as the ethical protocols of the project (see Hoffman & Walker (2010) for details about methods and fieldwork). Other research assistants transcribed the interviews into time-aligned files to enable automated location and measurement of linguistic features.

As the final component of each recorded interview, the research assistants elicited participant responses to an 'ethnic orientation' (EO) questionnaire, which included questions related to their language proficiency and use (English and e.g., Portuguese), their connections to their ethnolinguistic community and their perceptions of identity (see the appendix to Hoffman & Walker (2010) for a sample questionnaire). We quantified the responses to the questionnaire to compare the relationship between linguistic variation and EO across different groups. In the following section, we first offer qualitative summaries of younger Portuguese participants' attitudes towards their heritage, language and identity before providing quantitative summaries of these responses, in comparison with those of other groups.

As shown in Table 1, the project currently holds interviews with 12 Portuguese Canadians (6 first-generation, 6 second/third-generation), but here we focus on the younger participants, who were born and raised in Toronto.

Ethnic Orientation and Portuguese Youth

Ethnicity is a notoriously complex social construct, pertaining to issues of descent, physical/racial characteristics and the perception of difference (both by in-group and out-group members) (e.g. Buchignani & Letkemann, 1994; Le Page & Tabouret-Keller, 1985). Ethnic identity is also complex, especially in a diverse context such as Toronto, a city of immigrants, 50% of whose population was born overseas (Statistics Canada, 2016). A comparable proportion of the city's residents claim a mother tongue other than English, which is the majority language (and the official language of the province of Ontario and one of the two official federal languages of Canada). Since multiculturalism was adopted as official federal government policy in 1969, it has become more common to take pride in one's ethnic background. Although this topic provokes discomfort in many parts of the world, in Toronto residents commonly ask people about their ethnic background. A noticeable feature of the linguistic landscape of the city, both in ethnic enclaves (where particular communities are concentrated) and during events devoted to particular communities, is the prevalence of flags and the use of other languages in signage. For example, during the FIFA World Cup games, Torontonians fly the flags of their countries of descent on their houses and cars (e.g., Armstrong, 2018). In this context, Portuguese flags are among the most popular and visible.

However, while Torontonians are generally open to discussing their ethnic background, identification can be nuanced and fraught with stereotypes and association with particular social values (good and bad). For communities whose members are not identifiable by their physical/racial characteristics, accent has been identified as a common source of discrimination in employment and housing (Statistics Canada, 2003).

In this section, we first discuss these considerations as they arose from the responses of participants in our project to the ethnic orientation questionnaire, before comparing the quantitative ethnic orientation scores across different communities and among young Portuguese Canadians.

1.1. Ethnic Orientation: Qualitative Discussion

The EO questionnaire begins by asking participants directly how they identify: as Portuguese, Canadian or Portuguese Canadian. While some speakers chose one of these options without hesitation, others offered more nuanced answers. All but one first generation speakers born in Portugal identify as both Portuguese and Canadian. For example, Speaker 87 (F, 57) begins by asserting her Canadian citizenship before identifying as Portuguese-Canadian, while Speaker 93 defines herself as Canadian Portuguese. Speaker 96 (F, 50) stated, "I'm a Portuguese lady [...] but I'm Canadian too. Uh, because this now- is my country." Only one of the older speakers (F, 53), identified as Portuguese only.

All of the second-generation participants also signaled both aspects of their identities. One speaker initially answered just "Canadian" but then corrected himself:

(1) Canadian just 'cause I was born in Canada ... I think [being Portuguese] defines me to some degree but you know and maybe that's not true. So maybe, you know, I'd have defined myself or said that I am Portuguese. (Speaker 77, M, 27)

Speaker 92's answer foregrounds the importance of place (and highlights the salience of ethnic background in Canada):

(2) Uhm, I would say Portuguese-Canadian but often times I think of myself more as Portuguese 'cause we're in Canada so usually there's a distinction between everyone. Like, "What are you? What's your background? ... I'm Spanish, I'm Italian, I'm Portuguese." So like in Canada, I feel like more Portuguese than actually Canadian. And like family-wise it's like all Portuguese traditions and (we) go to all the Portuguese festas and Portuguese music [...] yeah I think of myself more as Portuguese than Canadian but it's both, a bit of both. (92, F, 22)

Another section of the EO questionnaire gauges attitudes to maintaining Portuguese culture in Toronto, living in a Portuguese-dominant neighbourhood and choosing a partner of Portuguese descent. Here, we focus on the responses of the second-generation speakers, all of whom agreed that it is important for children in Toronto to learn Portuguese language and culture. A number of them aligned this view with the general importance of learning another language, as shown in excerpts (3)-(5).

(3) Being about to communicate in another language opens a lot of doors and it opens up your mind to thinking about things in different ways. (79, M, 28)

(4) You wanna be able to speak to those people and know the culture too because it's part of who you are. (78, F, 28)

(5) I think it's good to have that... 'cause you're already getting the Canadian culture here so it's always like a richness to get another culture. And especially Europe, the culture where you come from. So it's good to have both. (92, F, 22)

However, responses were mixed when it came to neighbourhood and partner. Four of the six younger participants favoured diversity over predominantly Portuguese neighbourhoods. When asked whether he wanted to live in a Portuguese neighbourhood, Speaker 79 (M, 28) said, "No, not now. I think it's limiting." Speaker 78 (F, 28) voiced a negative stereotype of her community: "No, I'd rather not actually, just 'cause some of them are pretty nosy." Two participants (both women, aged 22 and 18) did express a desire to live in a Portuguese neighbourhood, for example:

(6) I feel more at home when I'm surrounded by Portuguese people. (92, F, 22)

Only one participant (102, F, 18) believed that Portuguese should have Portuguese partners, while the others agreed that romantic partnerships should be guided by personal choice and that staying within communities is "old fashioned," as illustrated by the response in (7):

(7) I don't think you should force anyone to marry like someone just because they're Portuguese. Uhm, personally I would prefer to marry someone who's Portuguese just because I think they would understand me better and where I'm coming from and, like, be able to teach my kids like Portuguese and Portuguese customs. But like I'm not like closed off to other cultures 'cause it depends on who it is, right? If you really like the person then you can incorporate three cultures and even have more richness. (92, F, 22)

With regard to language practice, all of the younger participants reported learning Portuguese at home from their parents or grandparents, and a number of them lived with their grandparents during their childhood. However, responses to questions about language use were complicated. Almost all younger speakers reported that both Portuguese and Spanish are spoken at their family gatherings, and several noted a generational split:

(8) Uh, it's probably divided, like, the younger the people probably speak English. And some of my aunts speak some English, yeah. It- it's less flexible if- if the person in question is fifty and over, or forty-five and over. (79, M, 28)

Speaker 77 (M, 27) reported speaking to his girlfriend's mother in Portuguese but said he prefers English, which he described as his "first language" socially. He claimed to be able to read Portuguese but not well and to enjoy occasional Portuguese language shows from Brazil. Speakers 78 (F, 28) and 79 (M, 28) reported speaking Portuguese very well and using it on a daily basis with their immediate families and in 79's case, with customers in a Portuguese bakery owned by his family. Speaker 80 (F, 23) reported speaking Portuguese less than other participants, weekly with her grandparents, but not much outside of that interaction.

All speakers, except 78 and 92, said they prefer to speak English with their Portuguese friends, though they do code switch on occasion:

(9) Sometimes I slip in and out of Portuguese when I'm joking around or sometimes I say words that I can't remember how to stay in English for some reason. (78, F, 28)

Speaker 92 (F, 22) reflected more carefully on the contexts for her use of Portuguese with friends:

(10) Sometimes like when we're with like- yesterday with- when we were at the club and we were in the taxi and we wanted to talk about like how to divide the money, we talked in Portuguese so the guy wouldn't understand what we were saying. (92, F, 22)

Speaker 92 is the most linguistically aware and self-critical. She responded that using Portuguese is an important aspect of her identity and that she prefers to use it with other Portuguese speakers, although she lamented her lack of proficiency:

(11)   [I want to speak Portuguese] where everyone else speaks Portuguese so I don't wanna speak English 'cause I know how to speak Portuguese well, so I might as well, like, use it. Uhm, but sometimes like I want t-- even like at home when I'm trying [to] tell Ma or Pa something and I can't express it as well like in Portuguese. I'm trying to think of the right word and I think of it in English and I'm like- I get frustrated 'cause what I want to say would probably be better said in English then in Portuguese but I wanna say it in Portuguese so they can get what I mean and then I get frustrated 'cause my vocabulary is probably not as advanced. I need to read more. (92, F, 22)

She also reported her parents' critique of her proficiency:

(12)   Well actually when I'm angry usually more English comes out 'cause it's easier. Yeah. But like- I don't know. When I'm more calmer, I think I talk better Portuguese. Like when I'm angry like and I'm like yelling, like I say everything *trocado* [mixed] and I like, mix up the verbs and then my mom starts yelling about my vocabulary. (92, F, 22)

Overall the younger participants reported reading and writing little Portuguese if any, but they all watch some Portuguese TV and listen to Portuguese-language music to different degrees. While speakers did not comment on having been discriminated against in housing or employment, the young women mentioned negative stereotypes about the Portuguese community.

1.2. Ethnic Orientation: Quantitative Analysis

Each of the responses to the questions in the EO questionnaire was independently scored on a scale of 1 to 5 by the authors and two research assistants, with a score of 1 indicating a response of low orientation to ethnic background (e.g. identifying as "Canadian") and a score of 5 indicating the highest orientation (e.g. identifying as "Portuguese"). We averaged the quantified responses to all of the questions for each speaker in our sample to calculate a mean EO score. Table 2 shows mean EO scores for each ethnic group and generation in our sample, along with the standard deviation, which provides an indication of the amount of variance by individual in EO scores within each group.

Table 2
Mean ethnic orientation scores for five ethnic groups and two generations included in the 'Contact in the City' project

Ethnicity	Generation	Speakers	Mean EO	Standard Deviation
Chinese	1st	10	3.183	0.325
	2nd/3rd	21	2.661	0.542
Greek	1st	5	2.520	0.244
	2nd/3rd	4	2.269	0.512
Italian	1st	9	2.453	0.267
	2nd/3rd	17	1.830	0.449
Portuguese	1st	6	2.671	0.484
	2nd/3rd	6	2.104	0.490
Punjabi	1st	3	3.248	0.326
	2nd/3rd	26	2.494	0.346

All of the ethnic groups show two main differences between the first generation and the second/third generation: a decrease in their mean EO scores and an increase in the standard deviation. These differences indicate not only that second/third-generation Canadians on average have a lower degree of orientation to their ethnic background than do the first generation that arrived in Canada, but also that there is a wider range of ethnic orientation in the second/third generation.[2]

Table 2 shows that first-generation Portuguese have mean EO scores

---

[2] Although the quantified scores may be interpreted as representing the participants' (self-reported) orientation toward their ethnic background, we would not necessarily expect scores to cluster at either end of the scale (i.e. 5 or 1), since ethnic identity is not absolute in a diverse English-dominant context such as Toronto. In the larger sample of 139 speakers, from a variety of ethnic backgrounds, the highest EO score (a second-generation Chinese-Canadian woman (speaker 57)) is 3.7. Most speakers have scores ranging between 2 and 3, reflecting their complicated ethnic identity.

comparable to those of the Greeks and Italians, but lower than those of the Chinese and Punjabis. These differences may reflect the relative timelines of establishment of these communities: the Portuguese, Greeks and Italians all arrived in large numbers after the Second World War while the Chinese and Punjabis are more recent arrivals. The second/third generation Portuguese have relatively low mean EO scores, only higher than that of the Italians, but the standard deviation is rather high, suggesting a range of ethnic orientations within the group.

Table 3 provides a breakdown for the younger Portuguese Canadians, showing their individual EO scores as well as their sex and age. While there does not appear to be a correlation between age or sex with EO score, it is interesting to note that the two youngest speakers (92 and 102, both female), have the highest EO scores. A closer look at individual responses reveals that these two women have stronger Portuguese social networks in Toronto. Speaker 102 prefers speaking Portuguese and speaker 92, who studied Portuguese formally in school, also prefers speaking it, particularly in Portuguese neighbourhoods and shops. Participants with lower EO scores may express positive attitudes toward their ethnic background while not having high levels of proficiency in the language associated with that background. The EO scores will be useful in interpreting the speakers' use of English, which we turn to in the next section.

Table 3
Individual mean ethnic orientation scores for the six young Portuguese Canadians included in this study

Speaker	Sex	Age	Mean EO Score
92	Female	22	2.773
102	Female	19	2.586
79	Male	28	2.071
78	Female	28	1.968
77	Male	27	1.710
80	Female	23	1.516

Linguistic variation

Having reported on the results of responses to the ethnic orientation questionnaire, in this section we examine the linguistic behaviour of the young Portuguese Canadians in our sample compared with youth of other backgrounds, focusing on three phonetic features that define current Canadian English, before examining an ongoing change in the discourse system.

1.3. Canadian Raising

A classic defining feature of Canadian English phonetics, one that distinguishes it from American English, is the pronunciation of the diphthongs /ay/ and /aw/. When these vowels precede a voiceless consonant (as in *white* or *house* (noun)), the onset of the vowel is raised to a more central position than when the vowels precede a voiced consonant or occur word-finally (as in *wide* or *house* (verb) or *why* or *how*). This difference leads to the American perception that Canadians say "oot and aboot" instead of "out and about." While this type of raising, which reflects older stages of a vowel shift in English that first started in the 15th century, does occur in other varieties of English, the specific conditioning of the raising is considered to be uniquely Canadian (Chambers, 1973, 2006).

Using the FAVE suite of automated forced alignment and extraction (Rosenfelder et al., 2011), we located each occurrence of these diphthongs in the recorded interviews and measured the properties of the first part of the vowel on the basis of the first formant (F1, a measurement of height) and the second formant (F2, a measurement of frontness/backness). Figure 1 (based on 61,568 tokens from 73 speakers) plots the average realization of these vowels for each of the six younger Portuguese speakers in our sample as well as for all of the younger speakers in four other ethnic groups: British/Irish (Anglo), Chinese, Italian and Punjabi. The left side of Figure 1 shows the realizations of /ay/ and /ayT/ (preceding a voiceless consonant), while the right side shows realizations of /aw/ and /awT/. Plots are organized to resemble the relative place of articulation in the human mouth.

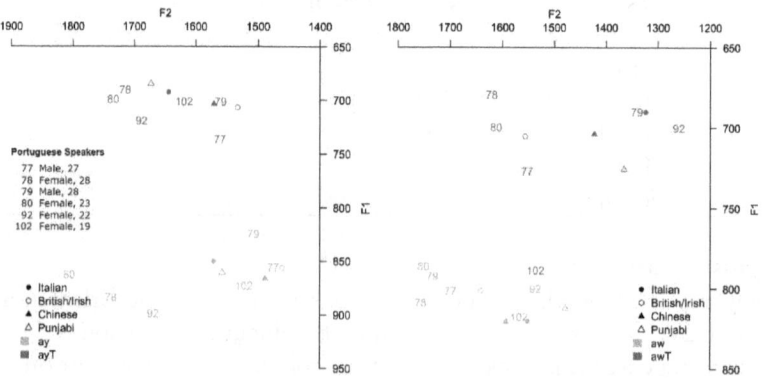

Figure 1: Plot of Canadian Raising for younger Canadian English speakers, by ethnic background

As Figure 1 shows, almost all younger speakers regardless of ethnic background maintain a distinction between diphthongs before a voiceless consonant (in which the onset is raised) and all other contexts, although the degree of raising varies slightly. The one exception to this pattern is Speaker 102, who shows little raising of /aw/, and who had one of the highest EO scores among young Portuguese speakers. Taken together, these findings suggest that she may be distancing herself from this stereotypical Canadian English feature because of her higher identification with her Portuguese background.

1.4. Canadian Vowel Shift

A second defining feature of the phonetics of Canadian English is the lowering and/or retraction of the lax front vowels /ɪ/, /ɛ/ and /æ/ (in words such as *bit*, *bet* and *bat*). This feature, which has received a great deal of attention since it was first identified by Clarke et al. (1995) and dubbed the Canadian Vowel Shift (CVS), has been identified as an ongoing change in Canadian English, with younger speakers featuring more lowered and/or retracted realizations of these vowels than older speakers (Boberg 2008; Hoffman, 2010; Hoffman & Walker, 2010; Kettig & Winter, 2017; Roeder & Jarmasz, 2010). Figure 2 (based on 77,103 tokens from 42 speakers) plots the realizations of all occurrences of the three front lax vowels in the interviews with younger Portuguese speakers in our sample, along with mean realizations for young speakers of four other ethnic groups: British/Irish (Anglo), Chinese, Italian and Punjabi.

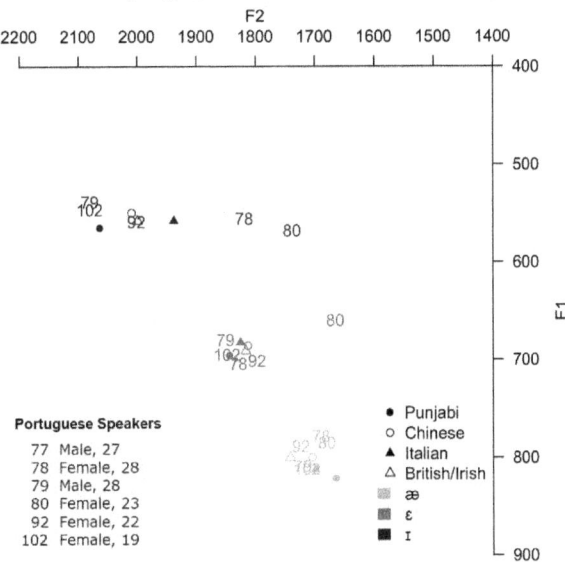

Figure 2: Plots of front lax vowels in younger Canadian English speakers, by ethnic background

All of the young speakers cluster together in their realizations of front lax vowels, with two exceptions. For /ɛ/-shifting, Speaker 80 has a much more retracted realization than all other speakers. For /ɪ/-shifting, Speakers 78 and 80 have much more retracted realizations. Recall from Table 3 that these speakers, both female, have the lowest EO scores in our sample.

1.5.   Back Vowel Fronting

Another ongoing change in the Canadian English vowel system is the fronting of the back vowels /u/ and /o/ (as in *boot* and *boat*) (e.g., Boberg, 2008, 2014). This change has been reported in many varieties of English worldwide (Baranowski, 2008; Fridland, 2006; Haddican et al., 2013). Using the methods outlined above, 14,123 tokens of /u/ (excluding following palatal glides) and 37,705 tokens of /o/ from 73 speakers were extracted and measured acoustically.

Figure 3 plots the mean realizations of these two vowels in the interviews of the six younger Portuguese speakers in our sample, along with the mean realizations for younger speakers from other ethnic groups: British/Irish (Anglo), Chinese, Italian and Punjabi.

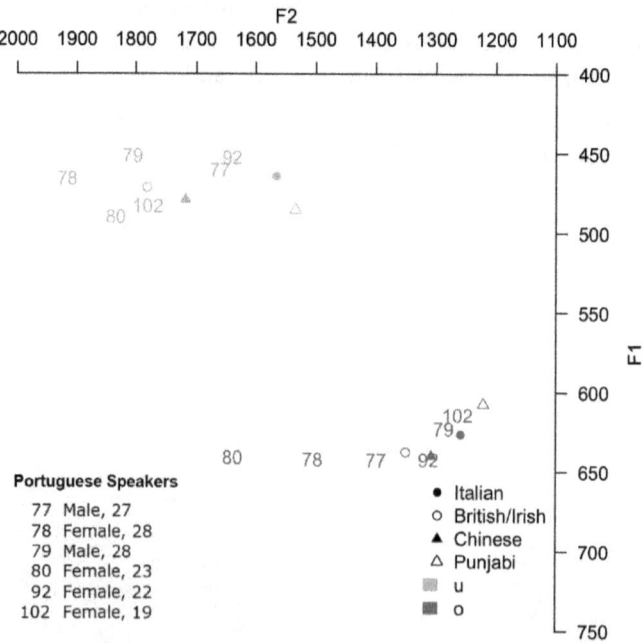

Figure 3: Plots of /o/ and /u/ in younger Toronto English speakers, by ethnic background

Most young Portuguese speakers are at the forefront of this shift for both /u/ and /o/, patterning with or more advanced than the British-Irish group. This pattern is similar to that of Canadian Raising, in which the young Portuguese also led fronting for /awT/ and /ayT/. As with the Canadian Vowel Shift, we also see Speakers 78 and 80 at the forefront of the change.

1.6. *Quotative* be like

The final linguistic variable we examine is a recent and spectacular change in the quotative system of English. When quoting speech, traditional *verba dicendi* such as *say*, illustrated in (13a), and other expressions of quotation, such as *go* (13b), are now being supplanted by constructions with *(be) like* (13c) (Tagliamonte, 2006; Tagliamonte & D'Arcy, 2004).

(13) a. I **said** to her, "I hope I don't have an ugly baby." (80, 46:36)
b. He **goes**, "That's what it is, the boulevard of broken dreams." (79, 36:28)
c. They**'re like**, "Hello, it's us, you're supposed to look good, come on." (102, 25:23)

Figure 4 (based on 1,801 tokens from 52 speakers) shows the rates of use of *(be) like* against the two other most common forms of quotation (*say* and *go*) for three ethnic groups: British/Irish, Chinese and Italian. For the young Portuguese, we show the results for each speaker. As Figure 4 shows, the Italian and British/Irish groups are behind in adopting this new quotative. The Chinese group is ahead, but it is the young Portuguese speakers who have adopted this feature most enthusiastically, with the lowest rate (Speaker 79, M, 28) matching that of the Chinese group. In contrast with the phonetic variables that we have examined, there does not appear to be any correlation between low- or high-EO speakers and participation in this ongoing change.

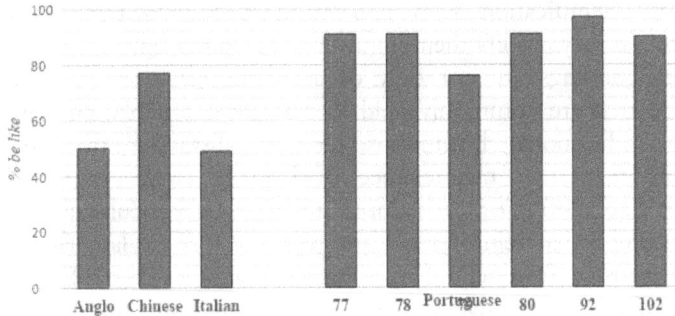

Figure 4: Rates of use of quotative (be) like (vs. say and go) in younger speakers of Toronto English, by ethnic background

Discussion

In this chapter, we have examined the self-identification and attitudes of a sample of young Portuguese Canadians and detailed their linguistic behaviour in their use of several English variables, comparing their behaviour to that of young speakers of different ethnic backgrounds.

Responses to a questionnaire on ethnic orientation revealed a range of identification with and attitudes toward Portuguese culture and language. This range was reflected in the quantitative analysis of responses, which showed a (slight) decrease in EO mean scores between first- and second/third-generation Portuguese Canadians, consistent with the patterns observed for other ethnic groups. A closer examination of the individual EO scores for the younger speakers showed the extent to which members of the same ethnolinguistic background may have very different degrees of identification with and attitudes toward their background and language.

The analysis of the responses to the ethnic orientation questionnaire served as the background for an examination of the realization of four linguistic features (three phonetic, one discourse-pragmatic) in the younger Portuguese speakers in comparison with their cohorts of other ethnolinguistic backgrounds. The results of these analyses showed that the young Portuguese speakers in our sample are participating enthusiastically in ongoing changes in Canadian English (the Canadian Vowel Shift, back vowel fronting and quotative (*be*) *like*) and exhibit adherence to a traditional feature of Canadian English (Canadian Raising). Exceptions to group behaviour, such as advanced participation in ongoing changes or lack of engagement with traditional Canadian English features, can mostly be linked to the speakers' EO scores. These results show that, while young Portuguese residents of Toronto are largely following trends observed in the English of other ethnic groups in the city, individual differences among speakers' identification with and attitudes toward their Portuguese background may modify their linguistic behaviour.

These findings are not only of academic relevance. Ideologies of language that are commonly held by the general public and promoted through educational institutions tend to disfavour multilingualism, fostering fears that maintenance of heritage languages will impede children's acquisition of the majority language. In particular, teachers may be concerned that reinforcing Portuguese as a home language through formal instruction in school may interfere with children's English. The results of our study suggest that such concerns are unfounded. While Canadians of Portuguese background may engage in linguistic behaviours that serve to mark their ethnic and linguistic background, related to their degree of identification with that background, the results of our research demonstrate that the English spoken by these speakers aligns more with their cohorts from other backgrounds than it does with the English spoken by their parents or grandparents. In other words, speaking a heritage language in an English-dominant context does not interfere with proficiency in English.

Conclusion
Portuguese youth in Toronto co-exist and interact with other young people from a wide array of other ethnolinguistic groups in a city where English is the common and majority language. They are faced with the challenge of negotiating an identity that allows them to participate in mainstream society while acknowledging their roots, and individuals arrive at different solutions to this challenge. Portuguese Canadians thus have complex relationships with their ethnic identity, expressed both in Portuguese and in English. Differences among individuals as to how they negotiate the balance is revealed not only in their different attitudes toward their background and language, but also in the different ways in which they make use of traditional features of and ongoing changes in Canadian English.

It would be advantageous for teachers in the Portuguese language classroom to be aware of this complexity. Engaging with the Portuguese language is one way that students can explore their identities, not only through code-mixing of English and Portuguese, but also through the use of varieties of Portuguese learned at home (mainland Portuguese, Azorean, etc.). Although considered 'non-standard', such usage can carry important socio-symbolic meaning for students, complementing in-class practices and reinforcing connections with their heritage.

References
Armstrong, L. (2018). "With residents from all 32 World Cup countries, Toronto cheers on the world." *Toronto Star*. June 16, 2018. https://www.thestar.com/sports/worldcup/2018/06/15/toronto-cheers-on-the-world.html
Baranowski, M. (2008). The fronting of the back upgliding vowels in Charleston, South Carolina. *Language Variation and Change, 20*(3), 527-551.
Boberg, C. (2008). Regional phonetic differentiation in Standard Canadian English. *Journal of English Linguistics, 36*(2), 129-154.
Boberg, C. (2014). Ethnic divergence in Montreal English. *Canadian Journal of Linguistics, 59*(1), 55-82.
Buchignani, N., & Letkemann, P. (1994). Ethnographic research. In J. W. Berry & J. A. Laponce (Eds.), *Ethnicity and culture in Canada: The research landscape* (pp. 203-237).. Toronto: University of Toronto

Press.
Chambers, J.K. (1973). Canadian Raising. *Canadian Journal of Linguistics, 18*, 113-135.
Chambers, J.K. (2006). Canadian Raising: Retrospect and prospect. *Canadian Journal of Linguistics, 51*(2/3), 105-118.
Fridland, V. (2008). Patterns of /u/ /ʊ/ and /o/ fronting in Reno, Nevada. *American Speech, 83*(4), 432-454.
Haddican, B., Foulkes, P., Hughes, V., & Richards, H. (2013). Interaction of social and linguistic constraints on two vowel changes in Northern England. *Language Variation and Change, 25*(3), 371-403.
Hoffman, M. F. (2010). The role of social factors in the Canadian vowel shift: Evidence from Toronto. *American Speech, 85*(2), 121-40.
Hoffman, M. F., & Walker, J. A. (2010). Ethnolects and the city: Ethnolinguistic variation in Toronto English. *Language Variation and Change, 22*, 37-67.
Kettig, T., & Winter, B. (2017). Producing and perceiving the Canadian vowel shift: Evidence from a Montreal community. *Language Variation and Change, 29*, 79-100.
Le Page, R., & Tabouret-Keller, A. (1985). *Acts of identity: Creole-based approaches to language and ethnicity*. Cambridge: Cambridge University Press.
Rocha-Trindade, M. (2009). The Portuguese diaspora. In Victor Da Rosa & José Carlos Teixeira (Eds.), *The Portuguese in Canada: Diasporic challenges and adjustment* (pp. 18-41). Toronto: University of Toronto Press.
Roeder, R., & Jarmasz, L. G. (2010). The Canadian shift in Toronto. *Canadian Journal of Linguistics, 55*(3), 387-404.
Statistics Canada. (2003). *Ethnic diversity survey: Portrait of a multicultural society*. Ottawa: Ministry of Industry.
Statistics Canada. (2016). *2016 Census of Canada: Profile data for Toronto*. Ottawa: Statistics Canada.
Tagliamonte, S. (2006). "So cool, right?": Canadian English entering the 21st century. *Canadian Journal of Linguistics, 51*(2/3), 309-331.
Tagliamonte, S. A., & D'Arcy, A. (2004). "He's like, she's like": The quotative system in Canadian youth. *Journal of Sociolinguistics, 8*, 493-514.
Teixeira, C., & Murdie, R. A. (2009). On the move: The Portuguese in Toronto. In Victor Da Rosa & José Carlos Teixeira (Eds.), *The Portuguese in Canada: Diasporic challenges and adjustment* (pp. 191-207). Toronto: University of Toronto Press.

5
Portinglês Use in Toronto
Joe Correia
York University

Introduction

The Portuguese community in the Greater Toronto Area (GTA) has grown significantly since the middle of the 20th century. This increase began in the 1960 and 1970s, when many Portuguese immigrated to Canada during the Portuguese dictatorship of Antonio Oliveira Salazar in search of a better life financially and professionally (Birmingham, 2003). In Portugal at this time, Portuguese citizens lacked several rights. For instance, Portuguese women, in particular, lacked the right to vote, in addition to lacking freedom of speech. With the risk of imprisonment for citizens not abiding by the rules, many decided to move to Canada and develop a better life for themselves and their families (Higgs, 1982). With a large number of Portuguese in the same situation and attempting to restart a new life in a new country, they began to develop a community that gradually became a home away from home. The community formed an ethnic enclave in downtown Toronto, which due to the larger number of Portuguese, became known as Little Portugal. Within this ethnic enclave, community members began to feel comfortable in their surrounding, as many Portuguese shops and facilities running in the area afforded the residents the opportunity to speak the language freely while minimizing the necessity to learn or speak English.

Languages are in contact if the same person or group of people uses them alternatively within the language community (Weinreich, 1966). In the case of Portuguese Canadians, English and Portuguese are in contact, which may result in a deviation from the norms of the European Portuguese and Canadian English languages. The blend of these two languages is referred to as *Portinglês,* according to Da Silva's study from 2011. *Portinglês* will be explored in this chapter, from the perspective of English borrowing into Portuguese forms mainly through lexical interference used in the speech of 12 Portuguese Canadians from the GTA. There exists other types of *Portinglês,* such as Portuguese borrowing into English and grammatical interference from English in *Portinglês* speech. This and other terms have been used by members outside the GTA's Portuguese immigrant community, according to the speakers interviewed for this project, as a manner of interaction for those within the community. However, while Portuguese borrowing into English is a topic that requires further attention, it will not be discussed at great length in this chapter.

The aim of this chapter is to examine the role of lexical interference within *Portinglês* speech through borrowed English words, and to examine whether there are any age or gender differences in its use. Crucially, some of the terms included are English words that are pronounced and defined with characteristics from the European Portuguese linguistic system, as outlined by Mateus and D'Andrade (2001). The terms are considered *Portinglês* because they are not present in the speech of European Portuguese and because they also derive from the English language. These terms are also used by the majority of the participants and had to be considered a Portuguese dictionary term by the participant. In terms of place of birth, I do not take into account in this chapter whether a speaker is born in Canada, in the Azores, in Madeira or in the mainland part of Portugal. However, their places of birth are mentioned in their biographies. The most important requirement for participation was whether the speaker possesses a command of European Portuguese. The chapter will answer questions on gender and age difference in *Portinglês* use within the GTA, as well as other potential factors. For example, are there distinctions between male and female use of *Portinglês* within the community? Is there a difference in age when it comes to stronger use? Is the level of assimilation to English a possible factor in its usage? Is there a difference between usage in a group setting and usage in a one-on-one setting?

In order to understand how *Portinglês* works, a deeper understand of language contact is needed. One of the principal founders of research on language contact was Uriel Weinreich, who developed his interpretation on how language contact works and what it constitutes. According to Weinreich (1966), language contact is the contact of two or more languages that are used alternately by the same people. Therefore, the familiarity bilingual people have with two or more languages creates instances where the language deviates from the standard norms of the language's community. A crucial part of language contact is interference. Interference implies the rearrangement of patterns that result from the introduction of foreign elements into the more highly structured domains of language (Weinreich, 1966). Additionally, Weinreich (1966) states that differences between the phonic, grammatical, and lexical domains of languages in contact have to be achieved for interference.

Of the three types of interference, lexical interference is the most related to the study of *Portinglês* and to the language contact discussed in this paper. Weinreich (1966) describes lexical interference as follows:

Given two languages, A and B, morphemes may be transferred from A into B, or B morphemes may be used in new designative functions on the model of A morphemes with whose content they are identified. In the case of compound lexical elements, both processes may be combined. (p. 47)

In other words, the vocabulary of one language interferes with the vocabulary of another. There are different types of processes for lexical interference, and one of these is simple words. Simple words are the most common type of interference. It involves the outright transfer of the phonemic sequence and meaning from one language to another. An example of this is taken from Italian and English, where the English term *pizza pie* is borrowed into Italian and forms in the American Italian speech the term *la pizza-paia* (Weinreich, 1966). He continues that the transferred word occasionally resembles phonemically a potential or actual word in the recipient language. An example of this is from American Portuguese, where the holiday *Fourth of July* becomes *fodejulai*. In New Mexican Spanish, a word such as *truck* is borrowed from English, creating a term such as *troca* (Weinreich, 1966).

Another major type of interference involves the extension of the use of an indigenous word of the influenced language in conformity with a foreign model. An example of this is seen in the language of Yakut, where the term *tahym* means water level (Weinreich, 1966). Through Russian interference, *tahym* was extended to not only mean water level, but also all levels. Weinreich (1966) refers to this phenomenon as semantic extension, where terms such as *livraria* and *naifa*, native to Portuguese, are broadened to include their new meaning from *Portinglês*. The definition of *livraria* in Portuguese is bookstore, while *naifa* describes a type of knife. In *Portinglês*, the definitions are broadened to include the meaning of library for *livraria*, and all knives for *naifa* (Da Silva, 2011).

Weinreich (1966) also proposed other types of interference possible for multiple lexical units consisting of more than one morpheme. An example of the transfer of some elements is *home plato* in Spanish, where a word final /o/ sound is added to the word plate. It is also of note that a word like *beisemento* in *Portinglês* would fit this category.

Einar Haugen (1969) has written a great deal on bilingualism and borrowing, with some discussion on the Portuguese language in North America in 1969, specifically Portuguese settlement communities in Massachusetts. As mentioned in Haugen (1969), the Portuguese migrated there, acquired small farms, and for the most part were bounded by linguistic and religious traditions. It was noted that the younger generation of speakers were more Americanized and did not continue to use some of the cultural traits of older Portuguese immigrants. However, the older generation remained unaffected for the most part. The Portuguese borrowed many terms from English speech and applied them to their Portuguese speech, similar to the case of *Portinglês* I will be studying in this chapter. I will discuss *Portinglês* from this perspective, but will add the requirement that the words have a Portuguese linguistic trait within their usage.

Weinreich's (1966) model of interference will be used in the manner in which *Portinglês* is studied in this chapter. For the most part, simple words will have the majority of the *Portinglês* terminology, but as mentioned earlier, terms such as *checar* will fall into another category. There are also the loanwords, where the language used is reproduced and is very similar to the element it is intended to be. This will be seen in mainly proper noun terms such as *Anasteds* 'Honest Ed's' (a bargain store in Toronto, Canada), *Bates* 'Bathurst', and *Dafrim* 'Dufferin' (both street names in Toronto), where the terms do not exist in Portuguese, but exist in English and are pronounced and used as if they were Portuguese. In these *Portinglês* cases, the terms are reproduced with Portuguese linguistic traits clearly present, such as the word final fricative in *Bates* /batʃ/.

As Poplack, Sankoff, and Miller (1988) mention, "items may be borrowed from another language once and never heard again, or they may be used with great regularity" (p. 48). In fact, 75% of English words are borrowed (Poplack, Sankoff, & Miller 1988). From a Portuguese language transfer standpoint, literature has been written on the Portuguese arrival in North America and their abilities to learn English. Obviously, the Portuguese immigrants had to deal with their own versions of language contact, and this was made most apparent in Onesimo D'Almeida's (1998) story entitled "Ah! Monim dum Curisco!," which I have translated as "Money of a Man with Electricity". This is a story of a family who came to the United States from Portugal, and how the nine-year-old daughter could not understand her grandparents well. In her attempts to speak to them, she begins to use new terms, such as *monim* (in place of the English word 'money') in order to have a better relationship with them. Terms such as "*Gudívnim*" and "*Gudenaite*" were used in the book to show the language barrier and the emergence of these hybrid terms that, in this case, derive from English and are used as Portuguese speech. Linguistic changes by Portuguese families are commonplace throughout North America. In Da Silva's (2011) study *Sociolinguistic (re)constructions of diaspora Portugueseness*, two of the participants believed that the Portuguese people have been outside Portugal for too long, and have consequently adopted *Portinglês* within their community.

What is *Portinglês*?

This chapter will cover some of the *Portinglês* terms from a study done on 12 participants of speakers of *Portinglês* in the Portuguese-Canadian community. These speakers vary in age, gender, and geographical origin in

Portugal. There are nearly a hundred terms that will not be found in the Portuguese or English dictionaries. These terms are simply utilized as a mix of both languages; most of the time utilized in Portuguese speech as a popularized word that is thought to be the appropriate Portuguese form, but is instead a regional speech that would not be fully understood in the speech of native Portuguese speakers.

The goal of this study is to note the linguistic differences between Portuguese spoken in Portugal and the Portuguese (*Portinglês*) spoken in the GTA. This study also seeks to contribute to the formulation of a *Portinglês* dictionary of vocabulary terms that are specific for the community living in the GTA. Some terms do have variance and are not universally accepted by all the speakers interviewed for this project.

In order to examine the role of lexical interference within *Portinglês* speech, I have conducted 12 interviews with Portuguese-Canadian participants in mostly Portuguese to coax participants to speak *Portinglês*. I will also note any potential age and gender differences in *Portinglês* use. I have interviewed six speakers under 30 and six over 50 to provide an age gap for potential differences in usage. Six male and six female participants were interviewed to note any gender differences. This age gap was important, as the older speakers belonged to a generation that lived through the Portuguese dictatorship in some way, and the younger speakers grew up in a society not affected by this regime (Higgs, 1982). The end result would show a stronger variation in age and gender with respect to the use of *Portinglês*. A group interview was conducted that featured both younger and older speakers as well as speakers of both genders which was later analyzed to compare *Portinglês* use in one-on-one settings and group settings.

I interviewed 12 Portuguese-Canadian speakers from the GTA who not only considered themselves Portuguese-Canadians, but could also carry a conversation in both languages. The main requirement for interview was that the participants have a fluent knowledge of both the English and Portuguese languages within the GTA. Due to immigration patterns, the older speakers surveyed were born in Portugal and the majority of younger speakers were born in Canada. Place of birth was not considered to be a requirement in the testing process, as the main goal was that the speakers considered themselves Portuguese-Canadian, regardless of where they were born. As long as the speakers had lived within the GTA region for a significant portion of their lives and considered themselves Portuguese-Canadians, they were eligible.

Exclusions from the *Portinglês* study included Portuguese-Canadians who had lived outside of the GTA for the majority of their lives. This prevented outside influence from the study, and allowed for the center of the conversation with participants to revolve around their time within the community. It was also a criterion that the participants currently speak Portuguese and English on a regular basis. This was an important requirement because the speech needed to be as natural possible, and being used to speaking both is of the upmost importance for the language to come out well. In addition to this, any teachers of Portuguese were excluded from the study because Portuguese instructors make sure that their Portuguese speech is prescriptive in order to teach their students. Including any teachers would lead to a bias in their speech and would not allow for a proper analysis of the community's patterns. The 12 speakers, who are identified by pseudonyms, are as follows:

Maria, a 21-year-old female from the city of Toronto. She was born in Toronto and has lived here all her life. It is worth mentioning that both of her parents were born in Portugal and she began learning Portuguese at an early age. She also attended Portuguese school from the age of eight, and therefore was able to learn the standard language.

Brittany, a 23-year-old female also from the city of Toronto. She was born in Toronto and has lived in the city for the majority of her life. While both of her parents are Portuguese, both were born and raised in Canada and they rarely spoke the language at home. The little bit of Portuguese she grew up with she learned from her grandparents. It was because of her lack of Portuguese that she decided it was in her best interest to study Portuguese at the university level.

Sandra, a 25-year-old female from the city of Maple. She was born in Toronto and has lived in the GTA for the majority of her life. Both of her parents and all her grandparents were born in Portugal and only speak to her in Portuguese. She attended Portuguese school at a young age, and maintained the Portuguese language in her day-to-day life, whether at school or work.

Miguel, a 22-year-old male from the city of Vaughan. He was born in Toronto but moved to the north of the city at an early age. Both of his parents are Portuguese and he grew up having to speak the language at home, but he also studied Portuguese at school.

João, a 25-year-old male from the city of Toronto. He was born in Toronto and both of his parents are Portuguese, and he spoke a mixture of Portuguese and English with them at home growing up. He studied Portuguese at the elementary, high school, and university level.

Jaime, a 29-year-old male from the city of Toronto. He was born in Portugal and moved to Toronto when he was three years old. His parents spoke mainly Portuguese to him at home growing up, and he had to take ESL classes in elementary school. He considers English his first language, but says that he is fluent in Portuguese, even though he never formally studied it. He speaks Portuguese every day when he talks to his parents and grandparents. Of all the speakers, Jaime is the only one whose parents are both of Azorean descent.

Fatima, a 65-year-old female from the city of Toronto. She was born in Portugal and lived there until the age of 24. She moved to Canada and considers herself fluent in both English and Portuguese. She never officially studied English in Canada, but did study Portuguese in Portugal before she came to Canada.

Geraldina, a 70-year-old female from the city of Mississauga. She was born in Portugal and moved to Canada when she was 20. She learned English when she first moved from Portugal. However, all of her jobs have required speaking Portuguese and she has not encountered many situations where she had to have "perfect" English.

Natalie, a 75-year-old female from the city of Mississauga. She was born in Portugal and has lived in Canada since age 28. She moved to Canada because she and her husband were looking for a fresh start and a better place to live and start a family.

Manuel, a 56-year-old male from the city of Toronto. He was born in Portugal and has lived in Canada for the better part of 20 years. He moved to Canada to provide his family with better life opportunities, and moved in to the area considered to be within the Portuguese ethnic enclave.

Joseph, a 65-year-old male from the city of Toronto. He was born in Portugal and has lived in Canada since age 16. He moved to Canada in search of a better life, and learned how to speak English shortly after his arrival through experiences with his coworkers. He would use Portuguese in his day-to-day work life, but he also had to speak English, so he had exposure to both.

Vladimir, a 70-year-old male from the city of Mississauga. He was born in Portugal and has lived in Canada since he was 30. He got a job offer in Canada and moved here, and part of the requirement was knowledge of English. He has since kept exposure to both languages and continues to speak both fluently.

Seven of the 12 participants from the study were previously known to me before their participation, while the remaining were well-acquainted with other participants already selected. I conducted my interviews in Portuguese to encourage the interviewees to produce *Portinglês* words. Following the interviews, I also asked all of the participants questions relating to their uses of *Portinglês*, and I included a little bit of English dialogue in hopes of reaching the participant's vernacular, and with the intent of backing up the data in case the Portuguese speech was not retrieving adequate data to formulate this study. The average length of these conversations was approximately one hour, with some of the interviews including third parties, because of either the public setting of the interview or a well-known person of the participant that would entice a more natural speech from the interviewee. In addition to the 12 interviewees, I also include a one hour group session where six participants were recorded speaking Portuguese with each other.

All of the *Portinglês* terms analyzed were verified through the use of three Portuguese dictionaries to confirm that they are not actually Portuguese words. Three different dictionaries, including the Taylor Dictionary (1959), Oxford Dictionary (1996) and Fluminense Dictionary (2003), were all used as tests on the words. The earliest published of the three dictionaries, the Taylor Dictionary (1959), will involve the initial analysis since this dictionary is a little older. It includes terms that are strictly Portuguese without any English interference. For example, terminology such as *checar* and *beican*, included in the Oxford Dictionary (1996), is not included in the Taylor Dictionary since these are borrowed words from the English forms 'check' and 'bacon.' For this reason, the terminology was considered *Portinglês* if it is not present in the Taylor Dictionary. The other two dictionaries served as confirmation to the findings from the Taylor Dictionary. While some terms have been added that are *Portinglês*, the fact they were not included within the Taylor Dictionary (1959) suggests they are recent additions thanks to lexical interference from the English language. However, if terms were included in the two most recent dictionaries and not in the Taylor dictionary, they were not included.

Portinglês is also described as a linguistic phenomenon, which has yet to be really studied in Canada (Da Silva, 2011). In his survey, Da Silva (2011) discovered that the majority of Portuguese-Canadian speakers admit to using *Portinglês*. All of the definitions used in this paper for *Portinglês* speech were reached with the collaboration of the 12 speakers whose data were analyzed, who aided in the analysis process following their interviews. Once there was a general consensus on each term and all of the participants were satisfied with the definitions, the word was included in the list with its definition. A word was considered *Portinglês* if it contained Portuguese linguistic traits (following Mateus & D'Andrade, 2001). If a *Portinglês* term had a Portuguese linguistic trait in a position that was normally occupied by an English trait, the term was approved.

The interviews were done to entice the speakers to use the *Portinglês* terms. For example, a question asked was "what is Tropicana?." The participant would then answer sumo or *jusse*, depending on their background. The goal was to see whether the participant would use the *Portinglês* term or the Portuguese term. The interviews were done on a one-on-one basis, with one group interview between four participants during a soccer match, so as to note if more or less *Portinglês* terms were used in their speech.

Because *Portinglês* originates from Portuguese and not English speech, I provide the list of Portuguese words with how they would be sounded and spelt in Portuguese, and not English. Some are the same terms from Da Silva (2011), except spelt a bit differently to fit into Portuguese spelling and sound systems, since the speakers consider them to be European Portuguese terminology. Also, there are many proper names, which include a large number of city names, place names and people's names, which differ from Portuguese to English. An example is a city name such as London in English, which is *Londres* in Portuguese. There are place names such as Niagara Falls, called *Cataratas de Niagara* in Portuguese, which show how place names and city names can be adapted from one language to another. Words that are translated directly as loanwords from English to Portuguese are not included, such as hockey or sports team names.

Below is a list of some of the *Portinglês* terms that the participants used and believed to be terms that were part of the European Portuguese lexicon:

Table 1: *Portinglês* terms and translations

Term	Translations
Aiscrime /aɪskrim/	- A simple word (described by Weinreich 1953 as the outright transfer of a phonemic sequence from one language to another) that derives from the English word 'ice cream' /ʌɪskrim/, and is commonly found in Portuguese-spoken phrases in place of the Portuguese word for ice cream, *gelado*
Atedogue /atdɔg/	- Derives from the English word 'hot dog' /hɔtdɔg/ - Referred to in Portuguese as *cachorro quente*
Atico /atiku/	- Derives from the English word 'attic' /ætɪk/ - Referred to in Portuguese as *sótão*
Aufsaide /aufsaɪd/	- Derives from the English word 'offside' /ɔfsʌɪd/ - Referred to in Portuguese as *fora-de-jogo*
Balançar /balãnsar/	- A verb in *Portinglês* meaning 'to balance'. - Referred to in Portuguese as *equilibrar*
Bassa /basa/	- Derives from the English word 'bus' /bʌs/ - Referred to in Portuguese as *autocarro*
Beican /bekan/	- Derives from the English word 'bacon' /bekən/ - Referred to in Portuguese as *toucinho fumado*
Beisemento /besiməntu/	- Derives from the English term 'basement' /besmənt/ - Referred to in Portuguese as *cave*
Bossa /bɔsa/	- Derives from the English term 'boss' /bɔs/ - Referred to in Portuguese as either *patrão* or *patroa*, dependent on gender

Brequefesta /brɛkfɛʃta/	- Derives from the English word 'breakfast' /brɛkfəst/ - Referred to in Portuguese as *pequeno-almoço*
Checar /tʃɛkar/	- Derives from the English verb 'to check' - Referred to in Portuguese as *verificar*
Escanque /shkank/	- Derives from the English word 'skunk' /skʌnk/ - The words for skunk in Portuguese are *doninha*
Estore /ʃtɔr/	- Derives from the English word 'store' /stɔr/ - Referred to in Portuguese as *loja*
Estritcarro /ʃtritkaru/	- Derives from the English word 'streetcar' /stritkar/ - Referred to in Portuguese as *elétrico*
Farme /farmɨ/	- Derives from the English word 'farm' /farm/ - Referred to in Portuguese as *quinta*
Fixar /fiksar/	- Derives from the English verb 'to fix' /fɪks/ - Referred to in Portuguese as *arranjar*
Friza /friza/	- Derives from the English word 'freezer' /frizər/ - Referred to in Portuguese as *congeladora*
Gama /gama/	- Derives from the English word 'gum' /gʌm/ - Referred to in Portuguese as *pastilha elástica*
Garbiche /garbiʃ/	- Derives from the English word 'garbage' /garbədʒ/ - Referred to in Portuguese as *lixo*
Ginjarelle /ʒinʒarɛl/	- Derives from the English word 'ginger ale' /dʒɪnʒərel/ - Referred to in Portuguese as *cerveja de gengibre*
Jusse /ʒusɨ/	- Derives from the English word 'juice' /dʒus/ - Referred to in Portuguese as *sumo*
Livraria /livrarja/	- Derives from the English word 'library' /laɪbrɛri/ - Referred to in Portuguese as *library*
Mapa /mapa/	- Derives from the English word 'mop' /mɔp/ - Referred to in Portuguese as *esfregão*
Mole /mɔlɨ/	- Derives from the English word 'mall' /mɔl/ - Referred to in Portuguese as *centro commercial*
Naifa /naifa/	- Derives from the English word 'knife' /naɪf/ - Referred to in Portuguese as *faca*
Parcar /parkar/	- Derives from the English verb 'to park' /park/ - Referred to in Portuguese as *estacionar*
Sanwicha /sanwiʃa/	- Derives from the English word 'sandwich' /sænwɪtʃ/ - Referred to in Portuguese as *sanduíche*
Tráfico /trafiku/	- Derives from the English word 'traffic' /træfɪk/ - Referred to in Portuguese as *trânsito*
Traque /trak/	- Derives from the English word 'truck' /trʌk/

	- Referred to in Portuguese as *carroça, camioneta* or *camião*

The *Portinglês* terms included derive from the idea that the majority of Portuguese people use these words, and that someone from outside of the Portuguese-Canadian community would not understand these terms to be the accepted forms. The terms used in this study are determined by use and whether the official terminology used by these speakers is considered to be different in Portuguese speech in Portugal. Other Portuguese-speaking countries are not taken into the equation as this is strictly for members of the Portuguese-Canadian community who have a European Portuguese background. There are also other terms that were included in the study but have a higher level of debate when it comes to whether they should be included as *Portinglês* terms. These terms, which are not all agreed upon by participants, are as follows:

Table 2: Questioned *Portinglês* terms

Term	Translations
Anasteds /anaʃtɛdʒ/	- The English bargain store *Honest Ed's*, there is no Portuguese equivalent
Bates /batʃ/	- *Bates* is the pronunciation of a street name in the city of Toronto, 'Bathurst' /bæθərst/ - There is no Portuguese equivalent
Checar /tʃɛk/	- Derives from the English verb 'to check' - Referred to in Portuguese as *verificar*
Cornoflex /kɔrnfleks/	- Derives from the English cereal brand 'Corn Flakes' - Referred to in Portuguese as 'Corn Flakas''
Donata /donata/	- Derives from the English word 'donut' /donʌt/ - Referred to in Portuguese as *dawnut*
Doutor /dotor/	- Derives from the English word 'doctor' - Referred to in Portuguese as *médico* or *médica*, dependent on gender
Dupon /dupon/	- Derives from the street name in Toronto, 'Dupont' /djupɔnt/
Esparguete /ʃpargɛtɨ/	- Derives from the English word 'spaghetti' /spagɛti/ - Referred to in Portuguese as *espaguete*, but *esparguete* is also used. According to the Taylor Dictionary, *espaguete* is the only term and therefore is used in this word list

Fazer um apontamento /apontamɛntu/	- This phrase's English translation is 'make an appointment' - In Portuguese, this phrase means 'marcar uma consulta'
Frizar /frizar/	Derives from the English verb 'to freeze' /friz/ - Referred to in Portuguese as *congelar*
Ramilton /ramilton/	- Derives from the name of a Canadian city, 'Hamilton' /hæməltən/ - The name in Portuguese is the same as the name in English
Rome Dipo /romdipu/	- Derives from the name of the hardware store, 'Home Depot' /homdipo/ - The name in Portuguese is the same as the name in English
Sanamagan /sanamagan/	- Derives from the English phrase 'son of a gun' /sɔnʌvagʌn/ - Referred to in Portuguese as *filho da mãe*
Timortes /timɔrtʃ/	- Derives from the Canadian coffee shop, 'Tim Hortons' /tɪmhɔrtənz/ - The term is the same in Portuguese as it is in English

Are there distinctions between male and female use of Portinglês within the community?

Table 3: Variation of use of *Portinglês* words by gender

Gender	*Portinglês* words participants have heard and/or used before	*Portinglês* words uttered in interview
Males	190	125
Females	182	121

Overall, as shown in Table 3, the numbers for gender are very similar. Females have heard one more word than males, and the largest difference between them is the 190 words used by males in comparison to 182 by females. These numbers, based on my hypothesis, are no surprise. Gender does not play a large role in the analysis of the speech, as it depends more on the background of the participants than anything else. It is also of note that while it has been analyzed that Portuguese males attain occupations such as construction workers and females would find employment as janitors (Giles, 2002; Higgs, 1982), the greatest influence might be from whom they work with rather than what they are.

Is there a difference in age when it comes to stronger use?

Table 4: Age of participants compared to *Portinglês* term usage

Age	*Portinglês* words used	*Portinglês* words uttered in interview
Older	204	137
Younger	168	109

It is of note that the majority of the younger Portuguese speakers (only Jaime did not fit this trend) received schooling in Portuguese in Toronto. As for the older speakers, none of the speakers received schooling after the fourth class in Portugal. It is expected that the older participants would have more of a tendency to fall back on the terms that they have learned from English borrowing over the years. The younger speakers, since the majority have received school training, use the correct terms in both languages more often.

Is level of assimilation to English a possible factor in its usage?

The younger generation learned English from a young age and knows the English terminology really well, whereas the entire group of the older generation grew up in Portugal and had to learn the English terms on the fly either during work hours or through the media. The Portuguese terms the younger generation learned came from a variety of sources, and knowing that the English term is what it is may lead some of the younger generation to use the The Portuguese word over an obviously borrowed word, given their knowledge of the vocabulary system.

Is there a difference between usage in a group setting and usage in a one-on-one setting?

Some of the newer terms to the *Portinglês* vocabulary list came from this group setting, and not from the one-on-one conversations. Terms that are corporation or street names such as *Bates*, *Dafrim*, and *Timortes* originated from the dialogue between four older generation speakers and two younger generation speakers. Interestingly as well, there was a hockey game present in the background, and because of the natural aspect of the live game, the participants would forget about the recording material and continue talking about the game at hand. Terms such as *aufsaide* and *sanamagan* came from this interaction.

Suggested *Portinglês* Terms

In conversation with participants of the study following their interviews, a few new terms were suggested for usage. Natalie, Brittany, and Manuel all suggested the following terms for addition to the *Portinglês* dictionary. Those terms are provided below in Table 5:

Table 5: Suggested Additions to *Portinglês*

Name	Meaning
Agusta	Derives from Augusta Avenue, a street in Downtown Toronto. This term derives as a term generally used to replace Kensington Market. There is no Portuguese equivalent term, as the street is not known in Portugal.
Ausington	This is the street name used for Ossington Avenue in Toronto. In Portugal, this street does not exist and is therefore not used.
Baile das Velhas	General name used by the Portuguese for the building on the southeast corner of College Street and Shaw Street within the ethnic enclave of Toronto. This building is not known in Portugal and therefore not used. It received this name because it was known as the place where older women would dance.
Brica	Comes from the English term brick. In Portuguese, the correct term for brick is *tijolo*.
Clauseta	Derived from the English word closet. In Portuguese, one term used for closet is *armário*.
Estore dos Cornos	A substitute term used by the Portuguese community for the former supermarket Knob Hill Farms. This franchise never existed in Portugal during its existence, and was never used there.
Galinha do Velho	A substitute term the Portuguese community in Toronto use to call the Kentucky Fried Chicken franchise. While this franchise exists in Portugal, it is believed that the term is not used there.
Jogo da Vassoura	Alternate term used by the Portuguese community to describe the game of curling. In Portuguese, the term *curling* is used to describe the sport, however the Portuguese community has adopted this replacement form.
Paca	Derives from the English word puck. In Portuguese, the correct form for puck is *disco de borracha*.

Conclusion

Since the 1960s and 1970s when the Portuguese began to immigrate to Canada, the Luso-Canadian community within the city of Toronto has grown significantly. As time passed, the neighbourhood formed an ethnic enclave where immigrants did not need to speak English as the shops and facilities within the enclave had Portuguese speakers who could provide service in Portuguese. Due to language contact and a lack of formal education in Portugal, these speakers began to use terms they adopted from the language contact with English, and the Portuguese immigrants began to speak a mix of Portuguese and English in their terminology, creating *Portinglês*. There are many terms in *Portinglês* used by the Portuguese, which remain popular to this day, such as *traque* and *sanwicha*, and are used more often than their standard Portuguese counterpart. There are plenty of examples of these words within the community, and they spread through a variety of subjects and word forms.

The *Portinglês* study suggests that gender does not seem to be a factor in how speakers use the terms, but that age greatly influences the usage. The older generation uses *Portinglês* more than the younger one. One possible factor for this may be the kind of level of education learned by the older community back home in Portugal during the dictatorship era. There are definitely more *Portinglês* terms out there that are being used and seem to be well known to the majority of the community.

References

Almeida, O. T. (1998). *Ah! Mònim dum Corisco!* Lisboa: Salamandra.

Birmingham, D. (2003). *A concise history of Portugal.* Cambridge: Cambridge University Press.

Collins Dictionary: English-Portuguese, Português-Inglês. (2010). Glasgow: HarperCollins.

Da Silva, E. A. (2011). *Sociolinguistic (re)constructions of diaspora Portugueseness: Portuguese-Canadian youth in Toronto* (Unpublished master's thesis). University of Toronto, Toronto, Canada.

Giles, W. M. (2002). *Portuguese women in Toronto: Gender, immigration, and nationalism.* Toronto: University of Toronto Press.

Haugen, E. (1969). *The Norwegian language in America: A study in bilingual behavior.* Bloomington: Indiana University Press.

Higgs, D. (1982). *The Portuguese in Canada.* Ottawa, ON: Canadian Historical Association.

Mateus, M. H., & D'Andrade, E. (2001). *The phonology of Portuguese.* Oxford: Oxford University Press.

Weinreich, U. (1966). *Languages in contact.* The Hague, NL: Mouton.

6
A Reflection on the Challenges of Language Acquisition Outside the Portuguese Classroom

Evandro Rodrigues
University of Toronto

Introduction

Learning a new language is an opportunity to explore a distinct 'territory,' which has its own culture and values. Learners of a foreign language face this process differently and, nowadays, out-of-classroom learning has become a more common practice, mainly due to the online resources available. In this chapter, I intend to explore different scenarios based on relevant theories and my extensive experience as an instructor in foreign language education in Brazil and Canada. This chapter is a reflection on this theme with a basis on my teaching experience.

First and foremost, it is important to understand the processes of learning our mother tongue. Humans' primary natural approach with their mother tongue, which is the first encounter with a language, occurs at their very young age, at home, with their family and/or friends, playing with their siblings, cousins and friends, watching television, or listening to music, for instance.

When a child starts uttering the first sounds and syllables, their parents encourage them to say the first words correctly through repetition until they acquire accurate pronunciation. Firstly, the child learns the sounds. Then, they learn words. And, at the final stage, they learn how to create sentences while they become familiar with a considerable amount of vocabulary to express themselves and communicate with the world. Consequently, they 'officially' become native speakers before their school age – they acquire accents and speaking styles while they reach a level of cognitive development (Wadsworth, 1996). After these stages, the first and most fundamental phase in the learning of their native language has been accomplished, which leaves to the school the task of educating children on other codes of the language, such as grammar rules, writing and reading skills.

As humans grow up, they may feel confident enough to use the language in various ways, such as passing their experiences onto their children and teaching them their first words, giving a political speech to a crowd or even acting on the stage of a theatre. Adults, however, do not normally learn a foreign language through this natural process. Their identification with another language is constructed differently. They will not be born again into a family who will consider the same process to help them with the acquisition of the second language. Therefore, instead of the abnormal process of becoming a child again, some adults may seek a language course, while others may prefer less traditional learning methods.

According to the Zone of Proximal Development (ZPD) created by Lev Vygotsky (Vygotsky, 1997), learners can explore collaborative learning with the help of an instructor through social interaction, prompts and suggestions. And, with a wide variety of teaching methods, the student learns to execute a new task or understand a concept within their ability to learn at that time. Although this is the best option for most foreign language learners (L2), the journey of learning a second language in a classroom has its constraints, with the speaking time limited to a few minutes, thus leaving the learner with insufficient time for practice. Yet this is not the only reason for low achievement by many language learners. Students do not normally receive enough individualized attention by their instructors. Additionally, the instructor is probably the only native speaker in the classroom for the student to interact with, and also a reliable source that is available only for very few hours during the week.

Besides, in some scenarios, like in my own experience as a language instructor, it has often been the case that students prefer to practice with the instructor or a native speaker, and not with non-native speakers. In many cases, students tend to pick up each other's mistakes. Besides, they may not even know whether they are saying things correctly, unless the teacher is attentive enough to notice that and correct it in time before it worsens.

Despite these constraints encountered in a classroom setting, in-class education of Portuguese has a particular place and a particular value, and it is critically important to successful language learning to the point where learners can communicate effectively. Therefore, learners and instructors should be encouraged to explore valuable methods of studying and practicing Portuguese beyond the classroom setting.

Employing resources that are available beyond the classroom plays an important role in language acquisition. Language learning occurs anywhere and at any time, and not only in the classroom and during the lesson. In addition, exclusively using textbooks and establishing practices in the classroom may not necessarily engage learners in the language in a meaningful manner. Thus, it is suggested that instructors supplement the learning practices by encouraging learners to assimilate the language not only in the classroom but also outside it.

In Canada, for instance, in-class Portuguese instruction may be the only direct interaction a few adult learners have with Portuguese. After many learners leave the classroom, they return to either their English-speaking or French-speaking environment, which is where learners of Portuguese have little exposure to the Portuguese language in real settings. In the classroom, students learn the norms and values of the language. Language learning, similar to any other sort of learning, requires practice to acquire the command of the language.

On this account, it is important that instructors and learners become cognizant of the importance of the learning process when the educator is not present to collaborate. To this extent, both the instructor and the learner become mutual participants in this process while a sense of community and knowledge is created. And, fortunately, there is an abundance of resources and tools for the improvement of language learning.

Notoriously, the internet is a predominant and accessible resource available today in out-of-class language learning. With it, learners can approach a rich and meaningful use of the language. It is one of the alternatives for learners who are deprived of an authentic Portuguese environment and seek effective opportunities in their language learning.

Apart from the limitations in both in-class and out-of-class learning, there are other factors that are essential for the second language acquisition. Individual differences may affect his or her learning. According to a study conducted by Alsayed, (2003) from the Faculty of Arts and Humanities at Damascus University on the factors that contribute to success in language learning as a foreign language, there is an indication that the gender of the learner and the similarities that their native language has with the foreign language contribute to either the success or the failure in learning, and so do their attitudes, personality, interests, motivation to learn the language, cultural background, pre-existent experience with the foreign language, affective filter, and the needs for learning the language.

Learners of Portuguese

Along with these factors, in respect of learning Portuguese in Canada, there are different types of learners, whose most names I coined to associate them with special characteristics of birds – animals that can fly high to have a broader view of the intertwined language communities.

Some of these learners explore the learning of the language more than others – as proposed in the subsequent paragraphs.

1) The kinfolk budgie - whose partner's, parents', grandparents' or relatives' mother tongue is Portuguese.

For most of these learners, who have experienced Portuguese at home, even though many times, in a passive manner, their interest in the language is more related to perpetuating their families' language values and traditions, especially those learners who were not upbrought speaking Portuguese. However, they tend, in a certain way, to be more familiarized with Portuguese than those learners whose experience with the language is unprecedented. Just like budgies, which are easy to tame if acquired at a young age, the earlier the kinfolk budgie starts his or her experience with Portuguese the better s/he might be to be 'tamed' to speak the language. Consequently, most of these learners may not be considered a total beginner in the classroom or in their learning of Portuguese, but a false beginner. And, regarding out-of-class learning, these learners may not view this practice as challenging.

2) The Culture Vulture - this kind of learner has an appreciation for the art and culture of a Portuguese-speaking country or community.

These learners want to learn Portuguese so that they can have a more in-depth understanding of the culture through learning the language. Portuguese instructors in Canada often meet adult students who decided to take Portuguese lessons just because they had become friends with Portuguese or Brazilian citizens or maybe because they appreciate music styles such as *Fado*, *Samba*, *Bossa Nova*, and *Capoeira*, or because they have visited a Portuguese-speaking country and became interested in its culture.

Similar to the first example of learners, these learners are false beginners, since they might be a little familiar with some words and phrases in Portuguese. Likewise, they may not encounter great difficulty in activities beyond the classroom.

3) The Busy Hawk - learners wanting to learn the language for professional purposes.

These learners normally have a job whose duties involve dealing with Portuguese-speaking countries, such as Brazil and Portugal. In such a case, most learners seek short intensive courses or private tutoring while they try to fit the lesson into their busy working schedule. Many of these learners have a short-term goal for learning Portuguese. And, as most of them are familiarized with the internet, learning beyond the classroom on an online basis may not seem complicated to them. Real hawks normally migrate after the breeding season, so just like these birds, many of the Busy Hawks may be willing to work in Brazil or Portugal as soon as the task of acquiring some knowledge of the language is accomplished.

4) The Travelling Goose

These learners seek short intensive courses that are tailored to their specific needs, such as learning how to communicate at a dinner and order a meal in a restaurant, how to ask for directions, and how to interact with the local people. The Travelling Goose is hunger for vocabulary. The more words they know the more confident they feel.

Since a great number of these learners may not have had any previous contact with the Portuguese language, they may be considered real beginners. Consequently, out-of-class education and acquisition may be a challenging undertaking if these learners do not have a Portuguese instructor to guide them.

5) The Global Parrot

This person appreciates learning new languages. They might seek a new language for a global understanding, improvement of employment potential, or new friendships, irrespective of the aspects of the language. As they usually speak more than one language, they may be categorized as false beginners because of their ability to learn a new language. Moreover, they may find out-of-class learning a great opportunity to accelerate their knowledge of Portuguese.

Additionally, independent of these categories of learners presented above, they may also be classified as:

6) The Clever Macaw

Many of these learners are bilingual or speak more than two languages. They organize information about language, are creative, and experiment with language (Rubin, 1975). Among these learners, Portuguese instructors commonly have in their classrooms students whose mother tongue is Spanish - a language which presents many similarities with Portuguese. These students, particularly, may accidentally misinterpret Portuguese in their classroom communication, in which it is not uncommon to hear words like *pero* (but), *mañana* (tomorrow), and the false cognate *pronto* (soon), which are words that correspond to the Portuguese *mas*, *amanhã*, and *logo*, respectively. Just like real macaws, this kind of learner may also thrive on activities that challenge them.

These learners may be false beginners, since they are more inclined to have a wide perspective of the connections between the two languages. Consequently, learning beyond the classroom may be a motivating factor to them.

7) The Self-taught Owl

Although these learners rarely seek language courses, they may not know where to start and how to progress when they are not guided by an instructor. In some cases, especially for English-speaking learners, the difference between a perfect tense and an imperfect tense in Portuguese might seem confusing to them when an instructor is not present to explain the practical application of these two tenses.

It is believed that most of these learners are false beginners, and they tend to perceive out-of-class learning as a pleasurable and motivating activity.

8) The Caged Jay

Some learners experience more difficulties in their language learning, especially if they see no connection between their mother tongue and Portuguese or any other Romance language. A demonstration is the one that deals with pronunciation or word genders - why *mesa* is a feminine word and *telefone* is masculine. Usually, for these learners, seeing Portuguese or any other language as a new concept of communication might seem disturbing to them, which could create a challenging task for both the Portuguese instructor and the learner. So, the Caged Jay should be shown that there is a world of different languages to explore and not only the one s/he is 'caged in.' It should be shown to them that they can 'fly' to see that there is a broader perspective to explore.

It has been noticed that the overwhelming majority of these learners is real beginners, and they may not feel comfortable with out-of-class learning if the teacher does not properly instruct them on how to deal with the use of the language in real settings.

9) The Needy Cockatoo

As a language instructor for many years, I have met learners who have an attitude to learning which is quite the opposite of that of self-taught learners, and they mostly rely on the resources that are provided in the classroom, mainly the instructor. The sooner the teacher recognizes this category of student the more efficient and fruitful the learning will be – and, consequently, less stressful to the student. Therefore, online lessons will be better delivered to these learners if they are organized in a way that describes activities carefully and well instructively.

Apart from the sorts of learning abilities presented here, psychological variables also play a role in the success or failure in language learning. And the affective filter (Krashen, 1982) – which either facilitates or hinders language acquisition - explains these variables. The higher the affective filter, the harder the acquisition of the second language. By way of illustration, learners may not feel confident enough, or may feel anxious or shy, when asked to use the language because of the obstacles created by their high affective filter. Whereas, learners with low affective filter feel safe and empowered when using the language.

If learners could recognize which category or categories they are associated with, they would benefit much more from their Portuguese-learning so that they can anticipate the various possibilities and obstacles that will be encountered during their language learning. Obviously, discovering the right type of learner we are is not an easy task. One suggestion, however, would be to observe ourselves, our environment, current reality, strengths, weaknesses, and reactions to the variety of teaching approaches. Then, we would be able to carefully reflect on the success of our learning process.

However, it is a task that does not apply to learners only - instructors should also be aware of the individuality and the potential of every student in a classroom environment in order to provide them with efficient guidance.

Obviously, students who take Portuguese lessons will be better assisted by instructors who recognize the importance of out-of-class learning, and who are not limited to classroom activities only. Therefore, besides integrating technology into the classroom, assigning homework activities with appropriate materials and resources is one of the best practices to maintain the superior quality of the language learning process so that the learner can engage in other aspects of Portuguese which are not covered during the in-class lessons.

And in order to reach excellence in language learning quality, there is a variety of online and out-of-class activities to explore in Portuguese learning in and out of Canada that involves listening, speaking, reading, and writing skills – and even integrating two or more of these skills – so that students develop them through the combination of language and content.

For learners living in Canada, one of the many interesting experiences with Portuguese is visiting Portuguese-speaking communities where the majority comprise Portuguese Canadians. These communities present full or partial Portuguese heritage or people who migrated from Portugal and now live in Canada. And, according to Statistics Canada, Toronto has the largest number of them, followed by other large cities, such as Montreal and Vancouver, with an overwhelming population of Azorean immigrants and their Canadian-born descendants. Activities such as going to a Portuguese bakery, a coffee shop or a butchery (*talho*), attending a Portuguese or Brazilian festivity, or even attending a church service are authentic contacts with the language and a great way of practicing and interacting with native speakers of Portuguese, which will develop communicative competence out of the classroom setting and facilitate the process of learning the language.

As the learner will not be placed in a scenario set out by the teacher in the classroom, the discourse that is present in a real-life setting is caused by unpredictable and unregulated behaviour. Although this may cause learners a sense of insecurity and fear, it is the actual opportunity in which they develop their autonomy to engage in an authentic interaction and apply communicative strategies such as being encouraged to start a conversation, signaling lack of understanding, and assessing comprehension, for instance.

This meaningful interaction helps the learner to seek language fluency and it will consequently make the learner gradually eliminate both his or her insecurity and fear, and eventually feel confident.

According to a number of language scholars, being confident when speaking a language is the main goal in language learning. Without confidence, learners hesitate when they speak, and they might discourage themselves to communicate in the foreign language (Clément et al., 1994).

Another great option of speaking practice for adults in Canada is the language exchange programs and assemblies, like *Mundo Lingo* and *Babel*. In these informal encounters, learners who speak different languages interact by learning and practicing each other's languages while they make friends. These programs are a gratuitous and useful opportunity for people to socialize and reflect on the difficulties that others have when learning each other's target languages. These are opportunities for learners of Portuguese to acquire the language outside the classroom similarly to the natural approach of language learning that we are involved in at our younger age, since the speaking skill is the one mostly focused on.

Language Skills

As far as teachers and learners are concerned, listening is also a significant skill to develop in language learning (Kurita, 2012), but the other language abilities should not be ignored in this process. Reading, for instance, is a very common practice both in the language learning classroom and in a daily routine. This skill, along with writing, is the representation of literacy in any language. Students whose mother tongue is a Romance language have an advantage in learning how to read Portuguese. Latin languages such as Spanish, French, and Italian have many lexical similarities with Portuguese, especially with respect to texts with technical content. Regarding medical texts[3], for instance, even native speakers of English may not find it difficult to detect the meaning of some words, phrases or sentences in Portuguese, since a high number of the medical entries in English come from Latin, a language from which Portuguese originated.

A native speaker of English with limited knowledge of Portuguese may know the definition of the example above, although he or she may not know exactly what all the words mean. Three of those words (*típicos*, *sintomas*, and *diabetes*) are easy to translate into English, while learners who are good at languages, polyglots, or self-taught learners may understand the grammatical use and the meaning of the other words as pronouns, articles, prepositions, and verbs (*Esses, são, da*).

Although oral communication (speaking and listening) and literacy (reading and writing) are produced in different channels, both have

---

[3] *Esses são sintomas típicos da diabetes:* ... (These are typical symptoms of diabetes: ...)

important functions in the exercise of a language, so they should be fundamentally applied in language learning.

The internet is a useful source for the practice of writing and reading skills. Nowadays, learners can access web pages of the most popular media outlets from Portuguese-speaking countries as well as from many other useful and interesting websites whose contents are written in Portuguese. Social media is also a great contributor to language learning, especially when learners make Portuguese-speaking friends who write and post in Portuguese.

Equally, several accounts on social media (e.g. *Português Dicas*) dedicated to the Portuguese language supply second-language learners and first-language learners with useful suggestions about Portuguese, such as the proper use of grammar and vocabulary. Therefore, learners of Portuguese are provided with a vast number of free web pages on a variety of topics which help them develop reading habits to expand knowledge of vocabulary and structure while motivating them to read more, especially when learners can choose what they want to read. For a Google search, for instance, learners may type key words (e.g. *principais jornais brasileiros)* to find important newspaper websites.

Additionally, reading song lyrics available on numerous electronic pages (e.g. www.letras.mus.br, www.vagalume.com.br) is an entertaining activity which I believe helps language learners interact with the language, practice pronunciation and obtain a sense of confidence.

Various libraries across Canada, such as municipal and university ones, provide readers with access to a vast collection of books written in Portuguese. Toronto Public Library branches, such as the Bloor/Gladstone branch and the Reference Library, provide books of many categories, from literary novels to magazine to pulp fiction. Moreover, books may also be read online or freely downloaded from various electronic pages (e.g. http://www.bloglivroson-line.com/p/estante.html, http://www.elivros-gratis.net/, www.catracalivre.com.br).

Learners who live in large Canadian cities find newspapers and magazines, such as *Sol Português, Voice, Brasil News, Brazilian Wave, and Correio da Manhã,* which are good paper versions available in the Portuguese/Brazilian communities in Canada. Noticeably, with all these options of source for reading and writing activities, learners can explore, discuss and share them with their peers and their instructor, which will also help contribute to the revision and improvement of vocabulary and proficiency in both reading and writing.

However, learners who are not good at languages, whose affective filter is high, or who fully depend on the guidance of an instructor, may need more assistance of the instructor, as well as very clear instructions focused on making meaning of their reading and carefully assigned in-class and homework activities with individual goals so that their affective filter is lowered.

In essence, the main purpose of reading activities is to promote comprehension skills while providing an enjoyable and motivational experience. And to obtain such practice, it is expected that the learner does not struggle with difficult texts but commence their activities with texts presenting very few unknown words per page so that the reading activity motivates the learner to continue to practice reading.

Therefore, both oral and written communications should be exercised in and out of the classroom according to the objectives of the learner in order to acquire the fluency needed. Preferably, extensive writing activities should be exercised along with reading. It is the time when learners need to concentrate and reflect on what they were taught and on what they observed and acquired in the lesson period. Thus, out-of-class sources focused on reading and writing are also an excellent opportunity for language acquisition in these two skills.

Language instructors and learners should take advantage of the written form available on the internet by also exploring writing activities based on what is read, even though many students see writing as a challenge to get the instructor's approval. But it actually develops a sense of competence and autonomy, improves learners' level of both accuracy and fluency, develops skills of autonomous learning, and eventually enhances learners' confidence. And, depending on the objective of the lesson, the writing activity should be tailored to the students' needs. For instance, for a lesson on academic writing, learners should be assigned to read academic texts and observe how this type of text is structured and produced – then encouraged to create academic writing through extensive practice.

So, in today's world, it is important that instructors and learners explore the technological resources, such as online tools and apps which help learners improve their writing skills. Duolingo is a world-famous application – most commonly known as *app* - which integrates the four language skills in several languages, and the writing skill in Portuguese can be exercised from the very basic level to higher levels of the language. Likewise, instructors can apply writing activities both in class and out of class with the use of effective and motivating apps such as *Socrative*, on which students can type and share their texts anonymously, while the teacher and the whole class can read, discuss and correct them in class without exposing the learner's name, in case they make grammatical and spelling errors. Another advantage of this application is that the student can type his or her texts on it at home and post it to be reviewed in class on the following day.

As for listening practice, I believe that watching television shows, films, documentaries or online videos, as well as listening to podcasts and songs (e.g.: on Spotify), for instance, plays a significant role in improving listening skills towards language proficiency – whether the learner is exposed to them in the classroom or out of it. Music, particularly, attracts the interest of learners due to its characteristic feature of providing a sense of unstructured learning. Learners listen to music for pleasure - and the internet is one of the best resources for listening practice of the Portuguese language outside the classroom.

Therefore, when instructors facilitate learners' out-of-class listening, they consequently help them access useful materials and encourage them to explore topics that concern their interests so that learners can enjoy the materials. Moreover, in the comfort of their home, learners can better concentrate and maximize their learning during their practice time when watching a television show or a documentary, for instance, and discuss it later in class.

Similarly, numerous online videos, such as YouTube videos and Vimeo videos, provide subtitles which can help learners understand what is being said while they receive comprehensible and enjoyable listening input through new and repeated words and phrases.

Another great advantage for learners today is that they can have online access to various radio stations from Portuguese-speaking countries and podcasts in Portuguese. Obviously, practicing listening based only on the listening channel entails more careful attention from the learner, as opposed to listening to what is uttered in a movie or a video. The latter combines listening with the help of the visual channel, which may help the learner understand what she or he has heard based on face expressions and body language of speakers, for instance.

Increasingly popular streaming media, such as Netflix, Hulu and Amazon Prime are exceptional resources that allow access to an abundance of foreign language movies, including those from Portuguese-speaking countries. In summary, out-of-class resources and learning beyond the classroom should be considered towards the acquisition of Portuguese in real settings in combination with the safest environment for learners to experiment the use of the language, which is the classroom with the guidance of the instructor assisting in this language acquisition process. Considering the factors involved in the sphere out of the classroom helps influence the learning of every student, such as the affective filter as well as the type of learner they are in order to produce effective learning.

References

Alsayed, M. (2003). Factors that contribute to success in learning English as a foreign language. *Damascus University Journal, 19* (1+2).

Clément, R., Dörnyei, Z., & Noels, K. A. (1994). Motivation, self-confidence, and group cohesion in the foreign language classroom. *Language Learning, 44*(3), 417-448.

Krashen, S. D. (1982). *Principles and practice in second language acquisition.* Pergamon Press Inc.

Kurita, T. (2012). Issues in second language listening comprehension and the pedagogical implications. *Accents Asia, 5*(1), 30-44.

Rubin, J. (1975). What the "good language learner" can teach us. *TESOL Quarterly, 9,* 41-51.

Vygotsky, L. (1997). *The collected works of L. S. Vygotsky: The history of the development of higher mental functions.* New York: Plenum Press.

Wadsworth, B. J. (1996). *Piaget's theory of cognitive and affective development: Foundations of constructivism.* White Plains, NY, England: Longman Publishing.

SECTION II
DESCRIBING PRAXEOLOGICAL APPROACHES – PROGRAM DEVELOPMENTS AND PEDAGOGICAL DEVICES

7
The Role of Linguistics in the Additional Language University Classroom: The Case of the Undergraduate Portuguese Program at the University of Toronto

Anabela Rato
Suzi Lima
Natália Rinaldi
Universiy of Toronto

Introduction

The crucial role of linguistics in additional language (L2) pedagogy is unquestionable as well as the inseparable nature of the relationship between both. The development of L2 learners' metalinguistic knowledge, defined as the explicit knowledge about phonological, morphological, syntactic, lexical, and pragmatic features of the language (Alderson, Clapham, & Steel, 1997; Elder et al., 1999; Roehr & Gánem-Gutiérrez, 2009), is implicit in many language-teaching practices which entails, for example, drawing learners' attention to the various patterns and structures of language and providing them with terminology to describe them. In this chapter, we describe teaching strategies that go beyond the simplest form of metalinguistic instruction (Roehr & Gánem-Gutiérrez, 2009) and aim at promoting a deeper understanding of the Portuguese language in particular and a 'critical scientific-linguistic' thinking about language in general. We also present how research-based learning, which involves the development of cross-disciplinary research skills, is fostered in the context of an additional-language undergraduate program in a highly research-oriented university.

The skill acquisition theory (VanPatten & Williams, 2015) proposes that, after the onset of puberty, the acquisition of an additional language tends to follow different cognitive processes than first language acquisition, with learners relying more on explicit (*declarative*) knowledge in the early stages and requiring extensive practice employing explicitly learned concepts to slowly *automatize* their linguistic abilities and gain fluency. For this reason, helping learners develop explicit metalinguistic knowledge can be very useful in L2 learning, particularly for adult learners. This implies an explicit knowledge about linguistic categories and structures, about the relations between categories and how they are used, and an ability to verbalize them, and thus simultaneously the learning of terminology (i.e., the metalanguage) to talk about language itself (Ellis, 2004; Hulstijn, 2005; Roehr, 2008). On one hand, for example, explicit knowledge may simply involve identifying a Latin root shared by two or more words (such as *ambíguo, ambidestro, ambivalente*, meaning "both") and explaining how that affix causes a similarity in their meanings. On the other hand, it might involve in-depth analysis of more complex linguistic structures, such as clause formation, in which learners describe how different types of clauses are formed. The amount of metalinguistic instruction given can vary from classroom to classroom, with communicative-based classrooms relying on it to a lesser extent than more grammatically-oriented language classrooms (Kim, 2018). Nonetheless, it can be argued that adopting a teaching approach that involves some degree of metalinguistic instruction is useful in any additional language learning context (Lyster, 2007). We do not argue that any teaching approach is more adequate than another, as both implicit (communicative) and explicit (grammar-based) teaching approaches have advantages and disadvantages. Rather, we want to highlight that teaching metalinguistic knowledge, which provides learners with terminology to explain how language works, promotes a deeper understanding (i.e., awareness) and critical ('scientific-linguistic') thinking about language, thus facilitating L2 learning. It is also essential to consider that in the process of learning an L2, the learners will use their existing knowledge of other known languages, in addition to their native language, to process, compare, and acquire the new linguistic categories and structures.

In the Portuguese program, which is within the context of a research-oriented university that supports the involvement of undergraduate students in research, we encourage learners to play the dual role of student-researchers by providing them opportunities to develop cross-disciplinary research skills and analytical techniques using authentic data with the intention that this set of transferable skills and knowledge prepares students for successful (academic) careers.

The Undergraduate Portuguese Program at the University of Toronto

The University of Toronto (UofT) is a research-intensive university with over 90,000 students that supports undergraduate research and identifies *research-based learning* as one of the key elements in undergraduate education which aims to prepare students effectively for lifelong success. This has also been the *motto* of the undergraduate courses in Portuguese at the Department of Spanish and Portuguese, which promotes both the development of research skills and a 'scientific-linguist' thinking.

The three programs in Portuguese - specialist, major and minor - offer a wide range of courses that range from Lusophone literature and culture to Portuguese linguistics and language. The profile of the student population of the program varies between heritage speakers of Portuguese who were exposed to Portuguese at home – which is *per se* an heterogeneous group due to the type and amount of language exposure they have received – and L2 learners who started studying Portuguese in the formal classroom context at UofT and did not have consistent exposure to Portuguese prior to taking the courses. Both groups of native English-speaking learners have heterogeneous language backgrounds, including the knowledge of other second language(s) such as French, Spanish, among others. Therefore, we adopted the term Portuguese as an additional language (PAL).

The courses are generally divided into language courses, in which students have to follow a proficiency sequence to complete the program, from beginner to advanced Portuguese, and content courses, which include the linguistic courses. These courses focus on the discussion of issues, questions, and debates pertaining to linguistics so as to develop pertinent research questions and methods for answering them in a small class setting with a maximum enrollment of 25 students. The courses are developed to cultivate not only metalinguistic knowledge and critical "scientific-linguistic" thinking but also to promote the learning of research methods, academic writing and oral presentation skills, which are required of successful undergraduate students. The linguistic courses consist of 12 two-hour class meetings which include lecture, discussion, small-group in-class activities, and group research projects that are carried outside of class hours but scaffolded over the semester. The language courses consist of a weekly two-hour lecture and a one-hour tutorial, which combine a wide range of in-class activities either individually or in pairs or groups. The language courses are designed to develop and practice the fundamental language skills of listening, speaking, reading, and writing with an emphasis on communication.

Developing a "Scientific-Linguist Thinking"

In this chapter, we support the idea that undergraduate students have already had enough experience with language so that they have the potential to reflect about languages in a more conscious and scientific way. We also introduce the concept of what we call *scientific-linguist thinking*, why we consider its relevance in language courses and how it can be developed at different linguistic domains: phonology, morphology, syntax, semantics, and discourse. All examples shared are real in-class situations – more specifically, activities and projects – that, as instructors, we developed throughout the advanced courses of the undergraduate program in Portuguese at UofT.

The concept of what we call *scientific-linguist thinking* could be defined as a scientific way of reflecting or thinking about a language. In this sense, any language would be seen as a combination of a system and its (non-chaotic) variation. In other words, we should consider that not only languages can be systemically described but also their variation. The advantage of assuming that undergraduate students should develop, in their language and linguistics courses, a scientific-linguist thinking is multifaceted:

- Improvement of their ability to reason and to scientifically reflect about language, since they already have an established linguistic system and experience;
- Improvement of their language dominance, fluency and capacity of creating;
- Demystification of the idea of languages as "isolated worlds";
- Demystification of the idea of learning an additional language by purely memorization.

These benefits lead students to become more conscious speakers – not only in their first language but also in other languages they might know. As a very important piece of the puzzle, instructors should frequently expose their students to classes that work on the development of this scientific-linguist thinking.

In the next section of the chapter we describe the role of linguistics in five upper-level (i.e., third-year) courses taught in the Portuguese undergraduate program at UofT: i) Advanced Portuguese I & II; ii) Introduction to Portuguese Linguistics; iii) Brazilian Indigenous Languages and the Research Excursion Program; (iv) Portuguese Language in the World; and (v) Portuguese Language and Society. The section describes the structure and objectives of the courses that introduce students to research in linguistics and provides examples of research-based assignments and projects designed to promote, on one hand, a metalinguistic knowledge of Portuguese and, on the other hand, a set of research skills transferable to other disciplines.

Case Studies

Case study 1: Advanced Portuguese I & II

The main goal of this course is to provide the tools for intermediate Portuguese students to advance their use of Portuguese in different domains (spoken, written, comprehension). As discussed in the introduction, the profile of the Portuguese students at UofT varies between heritage speakers and Portuguese as an additional language (PAL) learners, whose first language is mostly English. Given the different types of linguistic background of the students, an important topic to be discussed is dialectal variation. Concepts from linguistics were used in this course to show the students that the variation observed across different dialects is not chaotic and that one can identify regularities and elaborate hypotheses to explain them.

In general, these in-class activities and projects we developed with the students consisted of tasks in which students were supposed to find patterns and variation in Portuguese. The examples we provide here show how the development of a scientific-linguist thinking can be applied in five different linguistic domains: phonology, morphology, syntax, semantics and discourse.

Advanced Portuguese I
Phonology

The purpose of this activity was to find a rule for the variation presented by the prefix *-in* and its variant *-im*. In this activity, students were required to list as many words in Portuguese as possible that can have the prefixes *-in* or *-im* attached. Then, they were asked to compare such words with their translation in English: i) *-in* (inacreditável 'incredible'; incapaz 'incapable'; indecente 'indecent'; intacto 'intact'); ii) *-im* (impossível 'impossible'; impaciente 'impatient; exception: imbatível 'unbeatable') etc. In this activity, which was guided all the time by an instructor, students were not asked to simply memorize the variation *-in/-im*, but to reflect about the language as a system with a reasoning behind it. At the end of the task, students would be able to:

i. conclude that *-in* is the most common prefix and the rule to be generally applied;
ii. conclude *-in* changes its form to *-im* before *p* or *b*;
iii. learn that /p/ and /b/ have common features: they are labial consonants;

iv. learn that /n/ and /m/ have distinctive features: they are non-labial and labial, respectively;
v. learn the *linguistic* motivation for this variation – assimilation;
vi. compare the same motivation with English - and see if it applies or not.

Morphology

The main goal of this activity was to improve students' vocabulary in Portuguese. They were asked to highlight all words ending in *-dade* in two texts – which they had already worked with in class. For example, words, such as *criatividade* 'creativity', *produtividade* 'productivity', *compatibilidade* 'compatibility', *capacidade* 'capacity' etc., were listed by students. After that, they had to translate them into English and to conclude that the suffix *-idade* in Portuguese is equivalent to *-ity* in English. The exercise after consisted of the creation of new words in Portuguese by applying the rule. This type of exercise can also be extended to other suffixes and prefixes, such as *-ation, -ism, under-* etc., and to explanations regarding exceptions etc.

Syntax

This activity aimed to expand their vocabulary in terms of intensifiers in Portuguese (*muito, bastante, super* etc.) and to show that there is variation due to extralinguistic factors, not only in Portuguese but also in English. The instructor asked students to identify words used to boost meanings or to intensify ideas in two types of material (a written personal experience and a filmed interview with a politician). For instance, words such as *super* ("foi um dia super legal"), suffix *-ão* ("ela é um mulherão"), *muito* ("trata-se de uma situação muito complicada"), suffix *-íssimo* ("são pessoas educadíssimas"). At the end of this exercise, students could:
i. conclude that there are different ways – other than *muito* – to intensify ideas in Portuguese;
ii. conclude that there is variation in terms of style (formal vs informal);
iii. conclude that there is variation in terms of grammatical gender (male vs female);
iv. conclude that languages change, and new forms enter the system;
v. reflect about their own language by comparing whether or not the conclusions drawn for Portuguese could be applied to English.

Semantics

The goal of this activity was to work with the different meaning that a modal verb can express and to show that this ambiguity is not restricted to Portuguese. Students were required to identify 3 modal verbs (*poder* 'might', *dever* 'must' and *ter que* 'have to') in a list of sentences randomly extracted from Brazilian websites and social media. Then, the instructor asked the meaning of these verbs in the context where they were applied. For example, *dever* expresses possibility in "Amanhã <u>deve</u> chover", but it conveys internal obligation/desire in "Nós <u>devemos</u> acabar com a violência neste país" etc. This exercise not only provided students with knowledge of their own language but also instigated their curiosity to discuss the situations where they would use *might* or *must, must* or *have to,* for example, in Portuguese and in English. Given that they had already been introduced to the fact that variation in language might be related to extralinguistic factors, such as age, sex, social class etc., they also mentioned this possibility as a way to explain why speakers use different modal verbs depending on the context.

Discourse

This activity consisted of a small project where students had to interview a native speaker of Portuguese. The aim of such an exercise was to analyze discursive markers and to decide if they were empty or full in terms of expressing meaning. In a sentence such as "<u>Então</u>... <u>Bom</u>, eu num tava lá, <u>né</u>? Então, o que eu posso dizer é que ouvi que ele tava <u>tipo</u>, meio que fugindo da situação porque ele ficou nervoso, acho eu...", the words *então, bom, né,* and *tipo* are used in a speech act to convey no specific meaning. They are mainly used to determine whose turn to speak it is, to ask for a confirmation etc. By the end of this project, students were aware of their own discursive markers in both languages (Portuguese and English). They were also able to point out that some of them might reflect a variation due to age (younger vs older people) or to gender (male vs female). Additionality, some learners mentioned the fact that speakers contract words when they are speaking (reduction of verb *estar*, for instance), that they use slang and alter their pronunciation. Although the idea of this project, i.e. to create a general corpus collected and composed by the students, could not be accomplished, the outcome of it was completely positive, as the level of student's thinking, discussing and reflecting was high.

In sum, in this course, we attempted to show how undergraduate students can be more linguistically productive in language courses if their instructor adopts the idea of what we call *scientific-linguist thinking*. At the university level, they should comprehend that languages can be scientifically seen, analyzed and learned as a combination of a system and its (non-chaotic) variation. Activities at any level of grammar should also have as a goal the development of this scientific-linguist thinking so that students can become more conscious and critical speakers in any language. The exercises presented here are examples of tools that provide: i) the improvement of students' ability to scientifically reflect; ii) the improvement of their language dominance and knowledge; iii) the demystification of the idea of languages as "isolated worlds", as they can make comparison and find similarities; and iv) the demystification of the idea of purely memorization.

Advanced Portuguese II

In class, group exercises were used to explore the more general characterizing features of Brazilian and European Portuguese. For example, in one of the exercises proposed, the students were exposed to two Brazilian Portuguese dialects: the dialect spoken in São Paulo and Rio de Janeiro. In groups, the students had to hear speakers of one of the cities and describe the variation in the pronunciation of the phonemes /r/ and /s/ in different positions within the words and in different phonemic environments (between vowels, between a vowel and a consonant, etc.). We can identify two advantages of this exercise:

a. *Encourage students to be independent thinkers*: the students developed research abilities, as they had to identify variation in the data, elaborate a hypothesis and then explore the predictions of their hypothesis by putting it to test when pronouncing other words with similar properties;

b. *Expand the range of comprehension of Portuguese (within and between dialects)*: by showing the differences across different dialects and between spoken and written language. We considered critical to show the students that spoken and written languages are not equivalent and vary (Marcuschi, 1997).

Other than exercises, the students were also exposed to the results of academic studies on the topic. One strategy to facilitate the presentation of the academic studies for Portuguese-learning students was to present media coverage on those projects, which included the discussion of technical jargon, for non-specialists. These in-class discussions included an overview of different factors that might impact language variation such as age, gender, geographic location, register (level of formality). In sum, even though most of our students had no background in Linguistics, they were able to follow the discussion and to find it meaningful as they actively thought about the phenomena by means of exercises.

In the same course, another activity developed by the students in groups was a research paper. Four topics were explored by the groups:

Topic 1: Regência verbal

Task: in class, we saw that there is dialectal variation as well as variation in oral and written Portuguese with respect to *regência verbal* (Bagno, 2013, pp. 206-207): *essa criança não a obedece* 'this child does not obey' *(European Portuguese, Brazilian Portuguese)* vs. *essa criança não obedece (Brazilian Portuguese)*. The students were encouraged to find more examples of the same phenomenon in written and oral texts.

Topic 2: Pronunciation

Task: the students had to choose two dialects (for example, two dialects spoken in Brazil, or two dialects spoken in Portugal or one dialect from Brazil and one dialect from Portugal) and discuss the variation in pronunciation of certain graphemes. For example, the grapheme <s> might be associated with a variety of different phonemes in Portuguese.

Table 1. Possible pronunciations of the grapheme <s> in dialects of EP and BP.

Grapheme	Phoneme	Phones	Examples
<s>	/z/	[z]	abusa
	/s/	[s]	sapato
	/ʃ/	[ʃ]	Casca

(partially based on Caetano e Barroso 2016, Table 3)

Topic 3: Pronominal objects in Brazilian Portuguese

Task: a well-described feature of Brazilian Portuguese is the variation in the use of pronominal objects (clitic and non-clitic forms). The students were encouraged to find more examples of the same phenomenon in written and oral texts in the linguistic environments that favored the use of the clitic form in Brazilian Portuguese.

(1) a. Não te chamei (BP/EP)
        not ACC.2SG called
    b. Não chamei você (BP)
        not called-1SG you
    "I didn't call you."

(2) a. O João não lhe perguntou (BP/EP)
        the João not DAT.3SG called
    b. O João não perguntou a ela (BP)
        the João not called PREP her
    "João didn't call her."

(Luís & Kaiser, 2016, p. 225, based on Galves, Moraes, & Ribeiro, 2005)

Topic 4: Pronominal placement in spoken BP

Task: in class, we saw that the most common position where clitic pronouns in Brazilian Portuguese occur is preverbal. The students had to find more examples on the topics provided, from oral and written texts (magazines, newspapers, websites):

(3) a. Me chamo Maria. (BP)
ACC.1SG call Maria
b. Chamo-me Maria. (EP; BP (rare))
call-ACC.1SG Maria
"My name's Maria."
(Luís & Kaiser, 2016, p. 223, based on Galves, Moraes, & Ribeiro, 2005)

Alongside with the discussion about language variation and the difference between descriptive and prescriptive grammar, we have also problematized in class the difference between variation and error. Error in Linguistics is what is not possible in any dialect of a language, not what is not in agreement with a prescriptive grammar. This discussion is important in L2 classes as it encourages students to think about linguistic prejudice and their consequences not only in the language they are studying, but also in their first language, as language variation is observed in all languages.

Finally, in this course the students were exposed to the situation of multilingualism in Brazil. The same could be done using a different country of reference. This is also important as a strategy to show that countries are multilingual spaces; in the specific case of Brazil, not only because of the multiplicity of Brazilian Portuguese dialects, but also because of the presence of other languages. More specially, in the course we discussed the existence of Brazilian indigenous languages: nowadays, approximately 170 languages (Massini-Cagliari, 2004). We have also discussed the lexical influence of Brazilian indigenous languages on Brazilian Portuguese (based on Dietrich & Noll, 2010).

In synthesis, in discussing dialectal variation (Brazilian and European Portuguese as well as internally to each dialect) we aimed for the improvement of the students' Portuguese oral and written abilities. We have also promoted student research, which is an important step in encouraging students to become independent thinkers.

Case study 2: Introduction to Portuguese Linguistics

This course was an introduction to Portuguese linguistics studies based on the contrast between dialects of Brazilian Portuguese and European Portuguese. The learning objectives of this course were the following: (i) be able to identify linguistic properties that characterize Brazilian and European Portuguese; (ii) know the technical terms of the different areas of knowledge (phonology, morphology, syntax, semantics); and (iii) become familiar with methods of research in the field of linguistics and employ them in their activities as students and researchers of Portuguese.

The main material used in this course was *The Handbook of Portuguese Linguistics* (Wetzels, Costa, & Menuzzi, 2016). In this book, all chapters presented a comparison between Brazilian and European Portuguese. The students in the course had to prepare weekly summaries of the chapters they read. Other than the weekly summaries, the students took part on what we labeled as fieldwork activities: the students developed a short questionnaire on the theme of their final project and surveyed L1 speakers of Brazilian and European Portuguese who visited the class. Different types of tasks were included in the questionnaires, including production tasks (e.g., where the consultant has to describe a picture, an event or complete a sentence, provided a context), grammaticality tasks (e.g., where the participants heard certain sentences and evaluated whether they were grammatical or not) and comprehension tasks (e.g., where the participants had to evaluate whether a particular sentence was possible or not in a particular context or when presented with two sentences, the participant had to choose which option was more adequate given a particular context). In this course the students had to develop a research project on an aspect of a Portuguese dialect.

In class, the students had the opportunity to reflect on their own use of Portuguese and how that contrasted with other speakers/dialects. Before discussing theoretical terminology, some classes started with an exercise intended to explore the students' intuitions about Portuguese. An example of this type of exercise is presented below. A phenomenon studied in the linguistics literature is the possible collective and distributive interpretations of the sentence "Three architects designed four buildings" which can be interpreted as three architects designed four buildings each (a total of 12 buildings were built) or three architects worked together in the design of four buildings; these correspond to the distributive and collective interpretations of these sentences, respectively. Following Ussery's studies in English (1998), we explored in Portuguese, in a class activity, whether the verb used in a sentence influenced the likelihood of a collective or distributive interpretation of the sentences. In this occasion, the students answered a forced choice task; their answer to the question determined whether they were favoring a collective or distributive interpretation of the sentences (example 3). After the exercise, we discussed their answers and explored some hypothesis to explain the pattern observed in class.

(4) Três mulheres comeram seis pedaços de chocolate [Distributive]
       Three women ate six pieces of chocolate.

       Quantos chocolates foram comidos? ( ) 6   ( ) 12
       How many chocolates were eaten?

Quatro pessoas elegeram dois deputados.
Four people elected two deputies.

Quantos deputados foram eleitos? () 2   () 8
[Collective]
How many deputies were elected?

Três homens carregaram dois mesas.
Three men carried two tables

Quantas mesas foram carregadas? () 2   () 6
[Ambiguous]
How many tables were carried out?

Overall, these exercises put the students – advanced Portuguese speakers – in the central role of their learning process and encourage them to build hypothesis and to explore them in their dialects and dialects of their classmates.

Case study 3: Brazilian indigenous languages and the Research Excursion Program

This course was an overview of linguistic diversity in Brazil, centered on Brazilian indigenous languages and peoples. Students from different backgrounds – not necessarily Portuguese speakers – were introduced to current practices in the maintenance and revitalization of Brazilian indigenous languages and current strategies for empowering indigenous peoples (such as training indigenous filmmakers and music production). We have also studied aspects of the grammar of Brazilian languages through the analysis of small data sets, and we discussed the influence of Brazilian indigenous languages on Brazilian Portuguese.

In this course, the students interviewed professionals who are directly involved in the work with Brazilian Indigenous communities, such as 1) specialists of language documentation; 2) filmmakers; 3) prominent members of non-governmental organizations. The students have also prepared from scratch (or improved) a Wikipedia article about an indigenous language spoken in Brazil. Each pair of students was responsible for a different language. By building the Wikipedia article, the students were also contributing to the dissemination of information about Brazilian indigenous languages as well as developing skills in the presentation and summarization of linguistic data and analysis.

We evaluated that the existence of such a course in a Portuguese program was critical as it introduced the students to linguistic as well as socio-cultural aspects of Brazil. This course has led to a related initiative, the course "Brazilian Indigenous Languages: documentation, language maintenance and revitalization", offered by the Research Excursion Program, at the University of Toronto. The Research Excursion Program is a UofT program where a small group of third-year students contribute to a faculty-led research project in an off-campus setting. Two groups of students have travelled to Brazil and learned about the research developed on Brazilian languages and had a brief experience with data elicitation. These experiences were documented in the blog of the course (https://uoftbrazil.blog). These included not only observations on the research work such as the following:

'Today was the first day of real work with speakers of Baniwa, Neenghatu, Guarani Ñandeva, and Marubo' (T. Gelvez); 'We often remarked at how much data we were getting from a single day. Fieldwork is a challenge – it's difficult to prioritize and ask the right questions – but also immensely rewarding'; 'It is especially interesting to work with Patxohã since it is a reconstructed language, and very little linguistics research has been done on it' (V. Elango & N. Londoño) but also descriptions of the cultural and social experiences "From *bobó* to *tapioca* and *aguaçu* to *graviola* everybody enjoyed a decadent lunch and bonded over linguistics' (N. Londoño); 'The exhibition on Indigenous cultures in Rio and Brazil (Museu de Arte do Rio) interwove a variety of indigenous art and artifacts with the history of Rio de Janeiro. It was an enlightening experience to see the historical and cultural context of the work we were doing, in a hands-on way'. (C. Janik-Jones)

While one of the core goals of Portuguese programs is to give the students the opportunity to improve their language skills and to learn about the literature and other forms of cultural manifestations in Portuguese-speaking countries, we believe that experiential learning opportunities – such as the REP program – as well as courses that integrate a research component – as the ones described in the case studies presented in this section – are critical in the education of undergraduate students. We also would like to emphasize that linguistics can be a useful tool in the process of encouraging the students to be independent thinkers and to take a more active role in the process of learning Portuguese, by building hypothesis and identifying patterns across dialects.

Case study 4. Portuguese Language in the World

This course aims to provide an overview of the varieties of Portuguese spoken in the world and to discuss the structural similarities and differences between them. The course also comprises a concise historical background to world Portuguese, reviews contact language situations in immigration and border communities, and introduces linguistic concepts for the understanding of dialectal variation in contemporary Portuguese.

This course is divided into two parts: in the first six weeks, students are introduced to linguistic concepts, confronted with myths about the Portuguese language (Bagno, 2007) which include a discussion of the unity and diversity in contemporary Portuguese in terms of phonetics, morphosyntax and lexicon, and an overview of the Portuguese language both in time and space. One of the main aims of this course is that students may come to appreciate and be able to recognize the linguistic differences and similarities between the varieties of Portuguese and link those to the previous (or acquired) knowledge about the Portuguese-speaking countries, cultures and literature.

In the early weeks of the course, students are asked to build a peer-reviewed glossary with key terms for the course for which they have to construct their own definition and example of terms such as accent, (macro) dialect, speech community, among many others, as exemplified next.

ACCENT is the term used to describe the pronunciation features that identify the speech of a group of people for a certain language or dialect (Gupta, 2017). Usually, these groups of people are determined by geographic location, socio-economic status, or level of education. An accent is different from a dialect in that it does not include grammatical or lexical variation, but only differences in pronunciation.

Example: The palatalization of /t/ and /d/ before a front high vowel ([i]) is a pronunciation feature of Brazilian Portuguese (<tia> [tʃi]a, <dia> [dʒi]a) which does not occur in European Portuguese ([ti]a, [di]a).

To explore the cross-dialectal variation among the Portuguese varieties, students were given a set of exercises which consists of analysing authentic speech samples (audio and video) and written excerpts and identify how certain linguistic structures behave. For example, by following a list of linguistic structures, students would annotate excerpts of literary texts in European Portuguese (PE), Brazilian Portuguese (PB), Angolan Portuguese (AP) and Mozambican Portuguese (MP), by identifying the structure and then describing how it behaves:

For example: (1) direct object clitics (*lhe, lhes* or *o/a/os/as* ('ninguém lhe/o culpa'; 'eu lhe/o imitava'); (2) progressive verb tenses (gerund: 'os meninos foram correndo'; gerundial infinitive: 'os meninos foram a correr'); (3) presence or absence of article before possessive determiner ('(o) meu avô'); (4) the use of the verb *ter/haver* (e.g., 'Na saída da escola, tinha/havia um vendedor'); (5) prepositions (e.g., 'chegaram na/à sala: em/a'). The aim of this type of exercise is to make the learner aware of the variation within the same language across varieties. After training in identifying linguistic structures that vary across the Portuguese varieties, students are asked to analyse them on the media. In the following assignment - Portuguese language varieties on the media – learners are asked to give a 2-3-minute in-class oral presentation about a linguistic aspect of a Portuguese variety (e.g., European, Brazilian, Angolan, Mozambican, Cape Verdean Portuguese) and identify and explain a linguistic aspect pertaining to that Portuguese variety, by selecting an authentic written or oral text from print, broadcast or online media to analyse. In this task, (i) L2 learners analyse Portuguese language varieties, (ii) identify linguistic variation in authentic texts, and (iii) describe how linguistic structures vary within a Portuguese variety.

Another context in which Portuguese shows variation is in language contact situations such as those in the borders (e.g., Brazil and Uruguay, Portugal and Spain) or in diaspora contexts such as in Canada, where there is a large Portuguese-speaking community mostly from Portugal and Brazil but also from other Portuguese-speaking countries. Due to this fact, students can easily be exposed to/experience hearing Portuguese spoken in Toronto and many of them have familial and friendship relationships with Portuguese speakers, from either the first or second generations. In this activity - Portuguese in contact with English in the Great Toronto Area - learners are asked to interview a bilingual Portuguese-English speaker in Portuguese (15-20 minutes) and summarize their main findings in a short report. The objectives of this task are the following: (i) to learn about the linguistic features of Portuguese in contact with English; (ii) to identify linguistic phenomena in Portuguese that derives from language contact; and (iii) to acquire skills in qualitative data analysis.

The two-page report should include the main findings including demographic information about the participant, method (i.e., information about the interview), and analysis of a linguistic feature which shows English contact-induced variation in the speech of the participant. This activity is scaffolded into five phases: (i) preparation of the interview, which should include 12-15 questions about themes such as work, school, neighbourhood, childhood, dreams, family traditions, among other themes; (ii) interview; (iii) selection of the linguistic feature and examples; (iv) transcription of the selected examples from the interview; (v) report.

In the second half of the course, students are asked to prepare a poster presentation, which is a frequent medium of communication in academic settings, and further explore the analysis of an authentic speech sample of a Portuguese variety, by expanding the assignment 'Portuguese language varieties on the media.' The main goals of this project are to further the learners' knowledge about the linguistic structures of Portuguese and its linguistic varieties; to obtain practical experience in the preparation of a study, and to acquire skills in qualitative data analysis. This project is also divided into two phases: (i) the written research proposal which involves the formulation of the research question(s) and hypothesis(es), review of previous literature on the topic selected, and outline of the method; and (ii) poster presentation, which comprises the aspects presented in the proposal, by addressing feedback provided by the instructor and peers, as well as presenting the qualitative results of the analysis. Besides the specific course aims in terms of the integration of pedagogy and research, this course has three goals: to train students in aspects of research, to cultivate information literacy, and to provide opportunities for academic writing and oral presentation.

Case study 5. Portuguese Language and Society

The main aim of this course is to examine variation in contemporary Portuguese language and explore the extent to which social factors such as gender, age, social class, and ethnicity affect the use of Portuguese and determine its characteristics, by analyzing authentic spoken and written texts. It is also a goal of the course that students learn to appreciate the linguistic diversity of the Portuguese language and one's own sociolinguistic situation, that is, the diversity of languages and dialects that are part of their lives.

The course is therefore designed to give students the opportunity to apply their previous metalinguistic knowledge to the analysis of language usage so as to understand how language varies and is used by social subgroups. A sample of assignments has been selected to show how we aim to achieve the aforementioned goals.

In the first assignment - language variation in the Portuguese-speaking media – learners are asked to identify the type of linguistic variation (diatopic, diachronic, diastratic, diaphasic, etc.) that can be observed in different samples of authentic language from the media so that they can practice analyzing Portuguese language in use and describing how linguistic features vary with social factors. To present the results of their analysis, students prepare a brief oral presentation in which they identify one linguistic structure which carries marked social meaning, for example in evoking particular ethnic, age, class, or gender identities and explain its meaning.

This course involves also the development of activities that promote reflection about language use and variation. The next example is an in-class exercise which aims to reflect sexism in the language system and to what extent Portuguese is an (inherently) sexist language by looking at symmetry and asymmetry in the lexicon (e.g., the use of the generic masculine pronoun), marked and unmarked terms, and semantic derogation using examples from authentic speech (music, news, adverts, and institutional texts, among others). Social constructionism, dominance and difference theories are among some of the explanations for gender differences that are discussed (Wareing, 2004).

In the following exercise, students are asked to rewrite the sentences with a more gender-neutral language and different suggestions are discussed in class.

a) *A palavra de <u>um homem</u> é o reflexo do seu caráter.*

b) *<u>Os encarregados de educação</u> devem comparecer na escola na próxima segunda-feira.*

c) *<u>Os portugueses</u> avançaram muito na pesquisa.*

d) *No final da aula, <u>o professor</u> deve pedir <u>ao delegado de turma</u> que identifique <u>os alunos</u> que vão à visita de estudo.*

To identify the diversity of languages and dialects that are part of the students' life, through observation, students are asked to describe the multilingual profile of their neighbourhood, based on the following questions:

1. What languages are present in the 'linguistic landscape' of your neighbourhood?

1.1 How many languages do you hear spoken in the course of a single day, and how often do you hear them?

1.2. Is there multilingual signage in street names or on signposts?

1.3. What languages do you see on shop windows and on packaging of merchandise? Or on posters and billboards?

1.4. What languages are used in the media, for example in the local press or on the radio?

2. Do you think your residential area could be described as a speech community? What characteristics indicate that? (Adapted from Bell, 2014).

This assignment promotes not only training of the "scientific-linguist" thinking about language system(s) but also the reflection about how the multilingual context of Toronto is built through language(s). In another research activity - *the Portuguese linguistic landscape in Toronto* – students are encouraged to reflect specifically on the sociolinguistic situation of the Portuguese language in Toronto and, consequently, on their own. The students are asked to build a portfolio with photographs of a street or a block in Toronto with all the signage (official/public or commercial signs, graffiti) in Portuguese, and a one-page reflection with their interpretation of the 'semiotic landscape' of Portuguese in Toronto, by answering questions such as: What do the signs and their language use tell you about the sociolinguistic situation of Portuguese in Toronto?, How do the signs construct the public space?, What would the space be like without any or some signs?. They are also encouraged to talk to the producers of some signs (such as shop owners) about what they have done with their signs and why and/or talk to passers-by about their understanding of or reaction to the signs and to relate the producer's and the audience's perceptions with each other (Adapted from Bell, 2014). The students' main findings of this research project were published in the Brazilian newspaper *Jornal de Toronto* (March 28, 2018, p. 4), "A língua portuguesa na paisagem linguística de Toronto', which included the following:

> (…) Currently, the presence of Portuguese is not limited to the area called Little Portugal, extending to other areas of the city such as Weston-Pellam Park (…) in commercial establishments, financial institutions, offices and cultural and sports associations. (…) Public signs are visible, for example, on Dundas Street West, identifying "Azores Street". (…) We can also find, scattered through the streets of the West side of Toronto, graffiti with words or phrases written in our language. And we can see in many establishments the national flags of the Portuguese-speaking countries, images of symbols and cultural icons and toponyms that appeal to an identity with the Portuguese-speaking cultures. [our translation]

Some of the students' observations while conducting this study were also included such as (i) "Ter visto a Bandeira de Portugal e a palavra 'Lisboa' me fez sentir como se estivesse em casa" (Seeing the Portuguese flag and the word 'Lisboa" made me feel as if I was at home); (ii) "Little Portugal parece um pedacinho de Portugal ou do Brasil" (Little Portugal seems like a little piece of Portugal or Brazil); (iii) "Não é possível caminharmos por estes espaços urbanos sem reparar na língua portuguesa" (It is not possible to walk through these spaces without noticing the Portuguese language).

To further the study of language variation, integrate community-engaged learning in the course, and contribute to a larger corpus of speech data entitled "Heritage Language Variation and Change" (Principal Investigator: Naomi Nagy, University of Toronto, http://projects.chass.utoronto.ca/ngn/HLVC/0_0_home.php), the course research project -Portuguese heritage language variation in Toronto – was carried out over the semester.

The research project aimed at studying Portuguese heritage language variation in Toronto by identifying linguistic features that show English contact-induced variation. This is also a strategy to trigger learners' knowledge of English and Portuguese and promote awareness of the structural linguistic differences (and similarities) between both languages. This project also trains students in research methods used in sociolinguistics, namely conducting a sociolinguistic interview and transcribing speech using an appropriate software (ELAN, v. 5.0), and in quantitative data analysis. This project was scaffolded over the semester as follows: (i) preparing the interview in class; (ii) conducting a one-hour sociolinguistic interview with an English-Portuguese bilingual in pairs; (iii) transcribing half of the interview and peer-revision of the transcription of the other half done by their pair; and (iv) an oral presentation of the demographic information about the participant, description of the method and procedures (including challenges and/or limitations), and analysis of a linguistic structure which shows contact-induced variation in the speech of the participant.

Conclusion

In this chapter, we discussed the role of linguistics in the undergraduate Portuguese program at the University of Toronto by describing the learning objectives and research assignments of five upper-level linguistic research-based courses. We also discussed an approach to the study of Portuguese as an additional language which entails developing not only a deeper and explicit understanding – metalinguistic knowledge - of Portuguese, and a "scientific-linguistic" thinking about language, but also the learning of transferable research skills and analytical techniques that can be applied to the study of other disciplines. Moreover, several examples of assignments were provided that show how concepts of theoretical linguistics and research skills can be applied to the learning of Portuguese as an additional language. We also argued that following a language teaching pedagogy that implies some degree of metalinguistic instruction is helpful in adult L2 learning and provided examples of how to foster a deeper and critical reflection about language. Examples of research-based learning were also presented to illustrate how to encourage students to pose relevant research questions and apply adequate methods for answering them in their role as student-researchers, being the ultimate aim their training and preparation for a successful career. In sum, we presented a range of pedagogical methods and activities that integrate the instruction of form (phonological, morphosyntactic, lexical, semantic) and use (social context) to promote students' development of metalinguistic knowledge throughout their Portuguese language-learning process and learning of cross-disciplinary research skills.

References

Alderson, J. C., Clapham, C., & Steel, D. (1997). Metalinguistic knowledge, language aptitude and language proficiency. *Language Teaching Research, 1*, 93–121.

Bagno, M. (2002). *Preconceito linguístico: o que é, como se faz*. São Paulo: Loyola.

Bagno, M. (2013). *Gramática de bolso do português brasileiro*. São Paulo: Parábola Editorial.

Bell, A. (2014). *The guidebook to sociolinguistics*. Malden, Oxford, & West Sussex: Wiley Blackwell.

Caetano, A., & Barroso, H. (2016). Desvios na representação grafemática por aprendentes de Português L2 em Timor-Leste: o caso das fricativas. *Revista Diacrítica, 30*(1), 5-30.

Dietrich, W., & Noll, V. (2010). O papel do tupi na formação do português brasileiro. *O português e o tupi no Brasil. São Paulo: Contexto*, 81-103.

ELAN (Version 5.0) [Computer software]. (2018, January 6). Nijmegen: Max Planck Institute for Psycholinguistics. Retrieved from https://tla.mpi.nl/tools/tla-tools/elan/

Elder, C., Warren, J., Hajek, J., Manwaring, D., & Davies, A. (1999). Metalinguistic knowledge: How important is it in studying a language at university? *Australian Review of Applied Linguistics, 22*, 81–95.

Ellis, R. (2004). The definition and measurement of L2 explicit knowledge. *Language Learning, 54*, 227–75.

Galves, C., M. Moraes, & Ribeiro, I. (2005). Syntax and morphology in the placement of clitics in European and Brazilian Portuguese. *Journal of Portuguese Linguistics, 4*, 143-177.

Hulstijn, J. H. (2005). Theoretical and empirical issues in the study of implicit and explicit second-language learning: Introduction. *Studies in Second Language Acquisition, 27*, 129–40.

Kim, S. H. (2018). Metalinguistic Knowlegdeknowlegde. In J. I. Liontas (Ed.), *The TESOL encyclopedia of English language teaching* (pp. 1-6). Wiley-Blackwell.

Luís, A. R., & Kaiser, G. A. (2016). Clitic pronouns: phonology, morphology, and syntax. *The Handbook of Portuguese Linguistics*, 210.

Lyster, R. (2007). *Language and teaching languages through content: A counterbalanced approach*. Amsterdam: John Benjamins.

Marcuschi, L. A. (1997). Oralidade e escrita. *Signótica, 9*(1), 119-146.

Oliveira, G. M. (2002). Brasileiro fala português: Monolingüismo e preconceito lingüístico. In F. L. da Silva & H. M. de Melo Moura (Eds.), *O direito à fala – a questão do preconceito lingüístico*, (2nd ed.), revised edition (pp. 83–92). Florianopolis: Insular.

Rato, A. (2018, March). A língua portuguesa na paisagem linguística de Toronto. In *Jornal de Toronto*, p. 4. https://jornaldetoronto.ca/2018/03/28/a-lingua-portuguesa-na-paisagem-linguistica-de-toronto/

Roehr, K. (2008). Linguistic and metalinguistic categories in second language learning. *Cognitive Linguistics, 19*, 67–106.

Roehr, K., & Ganem-Gutierrez, G. A. (2009). The status of metalinguistic knowledge in instructed adult L2 learning. *Language Awareness, 18*(2), 165–81.

Ussery, C. (1998). *Processing plural DPs: Collective, cumulative, and distributive interpretations*. Amherst: University of Massachusetts.
Wareing, S. (2004). Language and gender. In L. Thomas et al. (Eds.). *Language, society and power* (2nd Ed.) (pp. 75-92). London & New York: Routledge.
Wetzels, L., Menuzzi, S., & Costa, J. (Eds.). (2016). *The handbook of Portuguese linguistics*. Wiley Blackwell.

8
A Personal Writing Device, with Heritage Language Speakers, at the University of Toronto

Luciana Graça

Camões, Instituto da Cooperação e da Língua, I. P.

University of Toronto

Introduction

In the last two decades, the difficulties shown by students in writing in general, and in academic writing at the university level in particular, have been taking on an obvious and growing place in research carried out in multiple countries. However, this research has been mainly conducted in the field of Portuguese as a first language (from now on, L1) (Pereira, Aleixo, Cardoso, & Graça, 2010; Bork, Bazerman, Correa, & Cristóvão, 2014; Barbeiro, Pereira, & Carvalho, 2015; Dolz-Mestre, 2016; Pereira, Graça, Marques, & Cardoso, 2016; Pereira, 2019), and also in that of Portuguese as a second language (PL2) or foreign language (PFL) (Aguilar, 2010; Siopa & Pereira, 2017; Tavares, 2008;). However, and despite the various efforts already undertaken, there are still very few studies that are particularly interested in the development of writing skills among students for whom Portuguese is the heritage language (henceforth, PHL) (Cardoso, 2016; Gontijo, 2010a, 2010b; Graça, in press; Silva, 2008, 2010; Souza, & Lira, 2017) commonly conceived as a minority language acquired in the context of migration, and generally within the family, although in permanent (inter)relationship with the language(s) of the respective host country (Flores, 2013; Melo-Pfeifer, 2018). Since this acquisition is mainly made at the level of oral proficiency already developed by students, it is even more essential not only to better understand the difficulties that may be specific to this audience, but also to design, test and assess possible new ways of teaching, capable of filling the main gaps highlighted by students in this specific area of language.

In the Canadian context, although Portuguese has already been gradually present in the programmes of university institutions, as well as a progressive interest on the part of teachers and researchers in this particular field of study of PHL has been noticed (Ferreira & Rolim, 2010; Marujo, 2016; Ribeiro, 2016, 2019), the truth is that not all Portuguese language programmes at university level already offer specific Portuguese language courses for heritage speakers. When this happens, students enroll in other language courses, according to the linguistic proficiency they reveal, which is a specific challenge for the teachers, who create curricula with different opportunities to differentiate teaching, explore the students' own prior knowledge, and stimulate mutual help between them (Cardoso, 2016). In the case of the University of Toronto, the Portuguese Program comprises a subject specifically aimed at such heritage students: *PRT219: Academic Portuguese*, created in the academic year 2015/2016, and offered to meet the specific needs of students who have had an exposure to spoken Portuguese, in an informal context, without an exposure to the so-called written Portuguese. Moreover, although this Programme includes, in the teaching-learning process, the various communicative competences, we will highlight here only the writing device created. This device is broadly characterized by the fact that it seeks to stimulate in students, and through certain verbal productions in writing, not only a greater immersion in the process of writing itself but also a reflection on their own identity as a writer (and speaker) in Portuguese, in their host society, in case they immigrated at a young age with their families, or simply in the society of their own, where they make their lives. This is possible because this device was conceptually based on a theoretical system founded on two important groups of principles. On one hand, the following aspects contributed to our "exploratory practice" (Ellis, 2010): i) genre pedagogy, with textual genres being conceived of as an organizing axis of teaching practices, as they are perceived as didactic tools capable of unblocking the textual production itself, by students, by exploring the knowledge they already have regarding the transversal dimensions to all genres; and ii) the set of revisions involved in the writing process itself, since it is not so linear. On the other hand, the approach of the so-called *meaningful literary instruction*, developed by Hanauer (2011), which proposes a more humanized L2 or FL curriculum, incorporating revealing writing activities, personally and socially speaking, and addressing experiences and emotions experienced by the students themselves, also contributed to it. It will be this *meaningful literary instruction* - in close accordance with the theoretical principles advocated and followed by the "Grupo ProTextos", of which we are also part and which we will also explain later - that will be used, in our case, in the writing component itself presented to these students, who are learners of Portuguese as an heritage language; an experience like this has also been carried out by Loureiro-Rodríguez (2013), but in the context of a class for speakers of Spanish also as an HL.

Thus, the organization of this text will include the following parts: in the first part, with the theoretical contextualization, we will present and explain our main options; in the second part, we will describe the exploratory study carried out by us, both teacher and researcher; then, in the third part, we will present the analysis of the written textual productions of three students. The final part is kept for the conclusion, in which we will try, *grosso modo*, not only to make a synthesis of the main results obtained but also to make certain considerations on the subject under study.

Theoretical Contextualization

Traditionally, investigative approaches perceive the acquisition of HL as an incomplete acquisition in relation to that of the native speaker, which means that an attempt is being made to compare the productions of heritage learners with those of native - and (perhaps) mostly monolingual – speakers. Moreover, native speakers are considered to be more legitimate and therefore more competent at the level of various language skills, such as in the areas of lexicon, grammatical domain, and even the writing ability itself (Flores, 2013; Melo-Pfeifer, 2018; Polinksly, 2007). However, this trend "does not account for the systematic interactions between the languages of the students' repertoires and their ability to use both codes in expressing their double (or triple) linguistic and cultural affiliation" (Melo-Pfeifer, 2018, p. 1168). After all, heritage speakers do not learn languages in isolation; it is therefore increasingly important to put more emphasis on everything that students are already capable of doing, than to focus on the supposed deviations (Melo-Pfeifer, 2018).

In the last decade, in some publications in the field of HL, there have been proposals for approaches that contradict the traditional method, with an emphasis on comparison with the "mythical native speaker". Traditionally, the focus was on the acquisition of the so-called prestige varieties, the development of linguistic registers associated with a more formal writing, and the teaching of vocabulary and grammar itself. In this new perspective, the varieties of heritage speakers are brought into the classroom as a starting point for students to build knowledge from what they already know; only after students master their own varieties should the standard varieties also be brought as one (other) way to promote their own language development. That was the case in the study conducted by Loureiro-Rodríguez where standard Spanish is seen as another register to add to students' linguistic repertoire rather than a replacement for their home variety (2013); thus, the same principle applies to any other language.

These new understandings naturally require new ways of teaching. On one hand, by considering a sociolinguistic component, in order to help students "reflect on why and how all those varieties have attained the sociopolitical/linguistic status that they have over the years" (Correa, 2011, p. 317; cited in Loureiro-Rodriguez, 2013, p. 45). On the other hand, through the consideration of the learner in all its complexity and *uniqueness*; in fact, authors are often unanimous in recognizing the heterogeneity of students, at the level of their linguistic profile as learners, and as HL speakers. Therefore, there is a need to *humanize* the language class (Hanauer, 2011), exploring the existing affective bond itself (Melo-Pfeifer & Schmidt, 2012).

In a (even) more direct transposition to the teaching of written production, the creation of writing activities that raise the student's awareness not only about the relationship between language and identity, but also between attitudes towards the language and its use (Bartolomé & Macedo, 1999; Leeman, 2005; Loureiro-Rodriguez, 2013), begins to be defended. To this end, it is necessary to abandon the *decontextualisation* and *dehumanisation* that have characterized language teaching, as mentioned by Hanauer (2011). In this context, the teacher should pay attention not only to cognitive abilities but also to the experiences that students have already lived, as well as to the emotions that they have already experienced and still experience. Says Hanauer (2011): "Learning a language is a human endeavor which interacts with a wide range of human capacities. It is an emotional and embodied experience in addition to being a cognitive process" (p. 108). In this context, the challenge will be to create and update, *in loco*, the teaching of language, in general, and of written production, in particular, as a significant, contextualized and personal activity for the learner, which is perceived as a living, historically situated human being, at the center of the language learning process (Hanauer, 2011). In other words, in addition to writing being a complex individual process, in which multiple dimensions are involved, the learning activities proposed to students should also be perceived by them as being not only relevant, and with a controlled cognitive load, but also sufficiently motivating, for a greater involvement and commitment to the task.

Based on this understanding of the language learner, Hanauer (2011) develops a set of four principles that guide the teaching of writing production to students, specifically of L2 or FL, although they can be adapted to the approaches that have emerged for the teaching of HL:

"1. AUTOBIOGRAPHICAL WRITING: Employs writing that utilizes memory, imagination and personal experience to explore and understand the self.

2. EMOTIONAL WRITING: Promotes a student writing process that activates and elicits emotional responses from the writer and the reader and endorses the expression of personal feelings.

3. PERSONAL INSIGHT: Integrates a reflective process that leads to a deepened appreciation and understanding of personal experience (and, ultimately, greater understanding of the human condition).

4. AUTHENTIC PUBLIC ACCESS: Situates writing within a social process of presenting personally held beliefs, understandings and feelings to others in the language learning classroom and beyond the classroom to people and communities who are of significance to the writer."

Traditionally, HL university courses have tended to focus on developing already advanced literacy skills in order to provide students with wider written production repertoires (Reznicek-Parrado, 2014). In this way, it is conceivable to offer the possibility of developing writing, anchoring this learning in the oral proficiency already developed by students, which we have already mentioned. However, if there is already some work done at the level, for instance, of the differentiation between the informal oral registers that students already know and the more formal (written) academic genres, there is still a long way to go to analyze, for example, the role that personal narrative - in the first person, or autobiographical narrative - can play as a functional component of such courses (Pavlenko, 2007). According to Pavlenko (2007, p. 165), three types of autobiographical narratives are commonly analyzed, in the study of sociolinguistics of bilingualism and SLA: i) "diaries and journals, written either spontaneously or in response to teachers' and researchers' request"; ii) "linguistic biographies and autobiographies, that is life histories that focus on the languages of the speaker and discuss how and why these languages were acquired, used, or abandoned"; iii) "published linguistic autobiographies, to avoid influencing speakers' responses through elicitation procedures." The advantages of using these autobiographical narratives are diverse and evident:

> [A]utobiographic narratives offer three major contributions [:] [f]irst of all, they offer insights into people's private worlds, inaccessible to experimental methodologies, and thus provide the insider's view of the processes of language learning, attrition, and use. Secondly, they highlight new connections between various learning processes and phenomena, and, in doing so, point to new directions for future research. Thirdly, autobiographic narratives constitute a valuable information source for historic and diachronic sociolinguistic research in contexts where other sources are scarce. (Pavlenko, 2007, pp. 164-165)

As we can see, according to the theoretical assumptions presented, the research works that have been carried out, namely in the areas of L2 and FL, and whose principles can be brought to the teaching of HL itself, in general, and of written production, in particular, have contributed to considering that it is important to place the student him or herself at the center - or at the heart - of teaching (Cardoso, Lopes, Pereira, & Ferreira, 2019; Dodman, Cardoso, & Tavares, in press). In addition, all the work already developed in the field of Portuguese as a L1 (Cardoso, 2009; Graça, 2010; Pereira, Aleixo, Cardoso, & Graça, 2010; Graça, Pereira, & Dolz, 2014; Graça, & Pereira, 2015) was also very important. Still in this regard, we would also like to refer, once again, to the aforementioned "Grupo ProTextos", in what concerns its model of teaching writing, in particular, in order to highlight the three main dimensions that guide the process of (teaching) this competence, and which will be important to combine, in any language program: i) the social dimension - the multiple uses of language trigger different textual genres that enable communication, when choosing and adapting these ones, that we perceive in line with the socio-discursive interactionist (SDI) approach and the School of Geneva (Coutinho, & Miranda, 2009; Schneuwly *et al.*, 2004); ii) the procedural dimension - the procedural models of written production, focusing on the mental processes of elaboration and organization of the information, have significantly contributed to change the typical paradigm of school composition (Camps, 2008); and, finally, iii) the personal dimension - the so-called relationship that each writer maintains with writing itself; a relationship that "each student feeds, from an early age", and that is "dynamic, and continuously reconfigured in the various contexts in which the student writes and that largely influences his or her writing investments" (Cardoso, 2016, p. 449). In fact, only in this way can we obtain a teaching context that is not only properly *contextualized* - and in which the emphasis is (more) placed on what the student already knows, including at the level of the writing process itself in general, and not on what it does not yet master, in terms of the specific systems of writing in HL (Martinez, 2005; Melo-Pfeifer, 2016) - but also, and especially, *humanized*. After all, "the language learner's memory, experiences, feelings, beliefs, history and social environment are the [real] context of language use" (Hanauer, 2011, p. 109). Therefore, in addition to the concept of "humanized" that we bring here, we would like to present here another one: "personalized." This personalized teaching, which could only arise from a precisely *humanized* teaching, would refer to a teaching which, due to the strategies used, is characterized by being, simultaneously, personal and individualized, after considering the individuality of each student.

Stories with People Inside: The *Personal Writing* Device

Context

The exploratory study here described was carried out at the University of Toronto. Toronto has an estimated population of around 2.8 million, making it the fourth most populous city in North America and the most populous city in Canada, with multiculturalism all too evident, as shown by the fact that there are more than 150 languages and cultures active throughout the city (Ribeiro, 2016). Among the most widely spoken languages in the Greater Toronto Area, the Portuguese language occupies the ninth place, clearly demonstrating the importance of this language in this context (Statistics Canada, 2012), even though its presence is also significant in the country. Obviously, the long history of Portuguese emigration to Canada - which officially and legally began in 1953, with the signing of several bilateral agreements between the governments of the two countries - contributed to it (Ribeiro, 2019).

The Course of *PRT219: Academic Portuguese*

The course of *PRT219: Academic Portuguese* is one of the language courses offered in the Department of Spanish and Portuguese. In addition to these courses, the Portuguese Program also offers courses in linguistics, literature and Lusophone culture. This course aims to meet the needs of all students who have already had an exposure to spoken Portuguese, in an informal context - living in a Portuguese-speaking country or with a Portuguese-speaking family - but with little or no exposure to written Portuguese. The ability to speak and understand Portuguese - which can vary from a basic level to a relatively high level of proficiency - and the limited or non-existent formal education in HL are, therefore, prerequisites to enter this course.

Since we were aware not only of the specificities of PHL, by comparison with those of L2 or FL, but also of the potentialities of the approach of the *meaningful literary instruction* - developed, as we have seen, by Hanauer (2011), and used in the writing component itself presented to the students -, we have created the syllabus of the course (also) incorporating, precisely, the writing of texts that stimulate both a more solid immersion in the process of writing *per se,* and a reflection on one's own identity as a writer (and speaker) in Portuguese, within the Non-Lusophone country where they live.. This does not mean, of course, the erosion of a work at the level of the various communicative competences, in a learning process that is always equally regulated by the assessment, permanently dynamic and providing indications for the pedagogical-didactic performance itself, as defined by several authors, summarized by Alavi and Taghizadeh (2014), and also recommended and implemented by other colleagues, also working in the context of the HL (Cardoso, 2016).

The Writing Device

Although this contribution focuses exclusively on one of the assessment components of this course, we consider it appropriate to present, in general, all the elements according to which students are assessed in the course *PRT219: Academic Portuguese*, in the academic year 2017/2018, with a total of 24 classes per semester, with two lessons per week, for a total of three hours. A more detailed description of the "personal texts" will be presented immediately after the following table.

Table 1.
Evaluation in PRT219: Academic Portuguese

Domain	Assignment	First term	Second term	Weight
Preparedness and effort	*Class attendance and participation*	5%	5%	10%
Summative assessment	*Grammar tests* (3+3)	4%	4%	24%
	Final exam	------	30%	30%
Interpersonal communication	*Personal texts* (2+2)	2%	2%	8%
	Academic texts (3+3)	2,5%	2,5%	15%
	Cultural project 1	6,5%	------	6,5%
	Cultural project 2	------	6,5%	6,5%
Cultural commitment	*Cultural events* (extra credit)			Up to 5%
			TOTAL	100 %

In relation to the production of written texts - which, as we have already seen, is divided into two large groups -, the teacher tries to make it meaningful for students, regardless of its nature. On the one hand, there are the academic texts and, on the other, the personal texts. The six academic texts proposed to students cover different genres that are characteristic of the academic sphere, such as the following three: letter of application for an exchange programme abroad; letter of complaint; and opinion article. On the other hand, the "personal texts" - autobiographical narratives -, in a total of four, led the students, in turn, to address not only personal aspects but also cultural and social topics relevant to and according to their own linguistic experience. More specifically, each student had to address each of the following topics in each of their personal texts: i) "Who am I?"; ii) "When do you use Portuguese and English languages in your life?"; iii) "Will I teach the Portuguese language to my children, in the future?"; iv) "What role could the writing of these personal reflections have played in you?". All texts were written individually by the students, outside the classroom, and sent, in word format, to the teacher, who would evaluate them. As all of these genres were always explicitly worked in the classroom, and since the teacher was always available to provide the necessary clarifications and support during the writing process itself, it was decided that this writing device would not include the sending of an initial draft prior to the sending of the (final) text itself.

The Students

In the academic year 2017/2018, 11 students enrolled in PRT219; in line with the definition of heritage speakers, they all grew up in a house where Portuguese was spoken and in a context where the Portuguese language was a minority language. This contribution will only focus on the personal texts written by three of these students, who elaborated these texts in detail, covering a larger number of requested topics: António, Mário and Paulo - pseudonyms chosen by us.

Stories With People Inside

António: *"Being bilingual is an unforgettable treasure that I'm proud to have"*

Born in Toronto to Portuguese parents, António started living with his grandparents and his maternal aunt when his mother died, just at the first months of his life. He only went back to live with his father, and his stepmother - whom he had started to call "mother," a treatment that we will also keep here - years later. It was while living with his grandparents that he started to speak Portuguese, because, as he indicates, "we lived with my great-grandmother and, if I would like to talk to her, it had to be in Portuguese, because she didn't understand English". Although he was born in a country where English is one of the two official languages, he also recognizes that, in the family environment in which he grew up, most of his relatives always spoke to him in Portuguese. Entering the Canadian school was the decisive moment to start learning, and using, the English language. António believes that the contact between the two languages, Portuguese and English, gave him, right from the start, several comic situations. He remembered three episodes:

    i. on his first visit to mainland Portugal, when he heard his mother, on the telephone, telling a relative that she would like to go to a "marisqueira", António, who loved "carne" (meat dishes), immediately interrupted her to ask her to go to a "carneira", by analogy with the word "marisqueira", derived from "marisco" ("seafood"), which designates an establishment where seafood is sold, all this immediately causing the parents' laughter;

ii. on his first visit to the Azores, despite the cousins' insistence that he should speak English with them, António did not give up on his desire to practice Portuguese and, therefore, agreed that the cousins could speak to him in English, while he would keep using Portuguese, to respond - and, as António reflects, "apparently, the majority of tourists who visit relatives do not know the language, and those who know the language do not want to speak it, because they do not enjoy it" ;

iii. still on a visit to mainland Portugal, António mentions that, in a café he went to, one of the employees said he didn't speak Portuguese and, therefore, António had to make the request in English; António "[found] shocking that, in Portugal, there were employees who didn't want to learn the language of the country where they work", despite being a markedly tourist area. The way he reflects on the value of memories, in the construction of knowledge, is also quite interesting: "[Although] there are certain encounters where conversations are badly spoken, this is how one learns and makes the memories".

The transmission of Portuguese to his children, in the future, is seen by António as an absolute certainty. After all, and in his words, Portuguese "is [his] mother tongue" - and this, we remember, even though he was born in Canada. He still adds: "being bilingual is an unforgettable treasure that I'm proud to have" and, thus, he also would like to transmit it to his eventual descendants. In fact, and as he also stresses, "it is essential to learn the mother tongue in order to appreciate our roots and our cultural traditions". The advantages of learning Portuguese are not only multiple but also of a different nature. António highlights four main reasons for early learning of the Portuguese language:

Understanding a Romance language such as Portuguese helps children learn other similar and Romance languages, such as Spanish, French and Italian. There are always great opportunities to comment on issues that non-Portuguese speakers do not understand. [...] In addition, our language has untranslatable expressions for other languages. [...] Finally, I would like to teach my children Portuguese to help them connect to a family identity and to feel part of a community of Portuguese.

Moreover, if "being Portuguese is [even] an huge characteristic of who [António is]", the strong involvement he has with the Portuguese community, in Toronto, in particular, is in fact another important and defining characteristic:

Through the folk ranch, to which I belong, I have met some of my best friends. Dancing at the folk ranch has given me more pride in showing my culture and also makes me have another respect for my ancestors, and this in a way that I can't explain well; all I know is that it's wonderful.

The relevance of the elaboration of these personal narratives is quite significant for António, for instance, in terms of the possibility he had to go back in time and better understand some decisions of his family members, such as, for example, the learning of the Portuguese language itself, from such an early age:

> In one of the texts, I reflected on my childhood - on having learned Portuguese before I started to learn English; on having gone to Portuguese school every Saturday, from the age of 4 to the 12th year; on having had to communicate in Portuguese with my relatives who lived in Portugal, because they did not know English, etc. And writing about it helped me to better understand my parents' decision to force me to learn about my roots, even though I complained so much at the time. This decision, taken by my parents, gave me another dimension, and an invaluable appreciation of the Portuguese language and culture.

Mário: "For me, Portuguese is very important, it is part of my roots, and it is my mother tongue, a sentimental connection mainly with my grandparents and with Brazil"

Mário, whose parents are Brazilian, was born in Brazil, where he lived until he was five. At five, he moved to Canada. He lived in Spain for five and a half years, in France for six months, and in Brazil for another year and a half, before returning to Canada at the age of 16 to complete his secondary education and enter university. His knowledge of languages is vast: "Portuguese, English, Spanish, French and, currently, Italian."

He spoke exclusively Portuguese until the age of five, while living in Brazil. The first contact with English has already been made in Canada, and in a school context. At home, with his parents, he continued to speak only Portuguese. Learning English was easy, because he arrived as a child in Toronto, as he explains. And the truth is that, despite the country in which they might be living, Mário's parents always continued to speak exclusively to him, and to the other two children, in Portuguese. And, according to his words, his parents didn't just transmit him the language; they also managed to create a truly umbilical relationship with his roots:

> Portuguese and English are part of my life today and I feel very comfortable speaking these two languages. For me, Portuguese is very important, it is part of my roots, and it is my mother tongue, a sentimental connection mainly with my grandparents and with Brazil. English is the most widely spoken language in business circles today and I've learned to like it. Finally, I am very proud to have these two languages in my life history.

The transmission of Portuguese language to his children is unequivocal for Mário. There are two main reasons for this:
> In addition to being a widely spoken language today, [...] it is also, from a personal point of view, my mother tongue, full of sentimental and cultural values. In my family, speaking languages has always been important, and because it is a Romance language, it has made it very easy for me to learn Spanish, French and Italian, which is an enormous advantage today. For these reasons, I believe that my children should learn Portuguese.

In Mario's opinion, the role of the family in making such transmission possible is unquestionably essential. In this regard, Mario recalls a very revealing family episode:
> I remember that when I came to Canada at the age of 5, my teachers told my parents to speak to us only in English, but my parents disagreed and continued to speak to my brothers and to myself in Portuguese. They did so, because they believed that English would be easily learned because we were in contact with teachers and friends for most of the day. And they were right! The same thing happened when we lived in Spain: Portuguese was only used at home, Spanish was used at school and with friends, and English was kept as a language school. Three languages were spoken without any problems. What a cultural heritage I had, because my parents had this vision of life! Of course, this is much easier, if both parents speak Portuguese and agree.

And Mario's reflection continues with a new topic: is it possible to grow and learn several languages, without damaging each other? The answer is indisputable. Yes, it is.
> I know the case of my neighbors, who are Portuguese who arrived in Canada only 6 years ago. Currently, the only 9-year-old son doesn't speak Portuguese and barely understands the language, because his parents wanted to adapt their son to English as soon as possible. It's a shame, because the boy could speak both languages fluently. Nowadays, when his grandparents come to visit him, because they don't speak English, they can barely communicate, making cultural ties and, worse, family ties, difficult. [...] I have the same opinion as my parents: the more languages we know, the better! I am an example that one can have an education with several languages and none of them harm the other.

The writing of personal narratives was also an indubitable added value for Mario, at various levels: "improvement of the written part, better understanding of grammar, use of verbs, accentuation, and increased my vocabulary". And the increase in confidence, as he expresses himself in this language, is also underlined: "I feel more confident to write and express myself in this language." However, the positive aspects of these writing activities go beyond the boundaries of the language:

In addition, this course gave me the opportunity to work with Luso-Canadian and Brazilian colleagues, who made me better understand the characteristics of this language both in Brazil and in Portugal, in addition to the Lusophone cultural traditions, which are part of the general culture that I highly value.

Paulo: "The Portuguese language allowed me to create and maintain a close connection to my roots and to a cultural identity"

As soon as Paulo was born in Toronto, he was immediately taken by his parents to what he considers to be "his homeland, the land of seeds and bananas, the island of Madeira." His exposure to Portuguese language since he was a child was due not only to his daily contact with his parents, but also to his trips to Madeira. These trips are part of what Paulo considers to be "the few lucid memories" of his childhood. His parents and all of his family have always spoken to Paulo in Portuguese. However, Paulo has also always watched television shows in English. Therefore, in his opinion, his first language was neither Portuguese nor English, but a "mixture" of both languages.

When he entered school, the use of English language began to dominate his daily life, when he was away from home. Even so, and sometimes, Paulo still used a few words in Portuguese, when he spoke to colleagues who only knew English. The visits to Portugal helped Paulo to keep Portuguese language alive in his life, because it was in Portuguese that he communicated with his family there, which also helped him to "create friendships with his cousins and to understand the stories of past generations." The level of proficiency in the language is directly proportional to the increase in the number of trips to Portugal, also in Paulo's words: "My conversations became more fluid and the shyness that I used to have to speak in Portuguese disappeared." Paulo also highlighted the fact that his mastery of the Portuguese language allowed him to enter the world of the arts.

> Besides the context of oral communication, being bilingual allowed me to appreciate other means of expression in the Portuguese language, such as literature, music, and cinema. Reading *Blindness*, written by Saramago, created in me an huge interest about this writer and the Portuguese literature in general.

Because he was born and raised in Canada, Paulo assures us that it was the Portuguese language that allowed him to create and maintain a "close connection" to his roots and to a "cultural identity." And, by recognizing the importance of this, Paulo would like to make the same decision taken by his parents. Paulo's thinking makes explicit a very interesting question, to which he also answers:

But what is a Portuguese cultural identity for, in a country that has its own culture? After all, learning a language is no easy task, due to the large number of hours spent learning the tiny details of grammar. However, the learning of Portuguese to my future children would be useful not only for them to know their origins, but also for them to be aware that there is more world, beyond the place where they grew up, and this world can also be discovered, by them, through various linguistic tools, as is the case of language.

The benefits arising from the writing of personal narratives, highlighted by Paulo, are also diverse. Here are just a few: a self-discovery not only of his personality but also of his life goals - for example, he volunteered at a Portuguese school, went on an exchange program at a Portuguese university and is currently in another Portuguese university, taking an advanced Portuguese course, and preparing his application to a Portuguese university:

In addition to the fact that these texts were an excellent way for me to practice writing in Portuguese throughout the semester, they also helped me to discover my personality and my goals, thanks to the personal aspect of the texts. In other words, the writing of these personal texts made me reflect on my path, not only in relation to the Portuguese language, but also on my identity as a Portuguese-Canadian and my ambitions. In fact, these reflections also helped me to achieve my desire to actively participate in the Portuguese community in Toronto - for example, I volunteered at the school where I had already been a Portuguese language student as a child.

Before I improved my writing in Portuguese to the level it is today, I often made the mistake of writing as follows: first, I wrote in English and only then I translated what I had written into English.

It is undeniable that the frequent writing of texts has helped me to develop a mentality that forms thoughts, as well as phrases, in the Portuguese language. Of course there will always be some influence of English on my writing in Portuguese; after all, most of my training, specifically in writing, was in English. However, with more practice and more experience in all forms of communication in Portuguese, I foresee that my dependence on English will be less and less. Finally, this improvement in my writing in Portuguese language has also helped my social life. Now that what I want to say to my Portuguese family and friends is built immediately on one sentence, I feel much less anxiety, I take much less time to answer and I am no longer so afraid of making mistakes in what I am saying.

Thus, the student started to communicate in more contexts, and in more registers, not only expanding, in a very significant way, all his contacts with the language, but also enriching his own relationship with the Portuguese language.

Conclusion

Working with HL writing must be a dialogical process between multiple dimensions, because writing is a complex operation, which is operated through the confluence of several components (Dolz-Mestre & Gagnon, 2018; Pereira, 2019). Without wanting to hide the relevance that the syllabi of the HL courses continue to include the acquisition/improvement of the standard variety and of more formal writing registers, the truth is that it is also important to provide students with contextualized activities, in personal and social terms, in order to contribute to a more effective involvement and development of students in the language. In fact, in our opinion, the analysis presented here revealed more potentialities associated with the inclusion of personal writing activities, such as the writing of personal narratives, whose advantages go beyond the academic sphere itself, as it has already been demonstrated in other research developed in the field of Portuguese teaching. Students were more aware of their own relationship with the Portuguese language in general (Dodman, Cardoso, Tavares, in press), and with the writing in particular (Cardoso, 2016; Melo-Pfeifer, & Simões, 2017; Cardoso, Lopes, Pereira, & Ferreira, 2019; Graça, in press). There were students who explained the considerable evolution they felt in mastering the language, in all its aspects. Some students started to think in Portuguese, before also writing in it. There were students who were thus strengthened in their confidence to use Portuguese in a greater number of contexts. There were students (re)discovering themselves in their own language and Lusophone culture. Students have seen themselves as a more obvious part of a culture that ties them with others, even though they come from - or their relatives come from - different countries. Some students finally had the courage to nurture new aspirations, including in their family members' own countries of origin. And why did all this happen? Because, in addition to being able to think, speak and write in Portuguese, the language we speak also allows us to dream. It is therefore important that we, as teachers of heritage speakers, should always be able to combine the necessary efforts and strategies to ensure that our students' *flights* are then commensurate with their real aspirations. And, to do so, using the repertoire of languages already known, and/or mastered, by the students, seems to be a useful option that can be used by the teacher. After all, languages do not establish any competition among themselves; rather, they can support each other to help the student to go further (Melo-Pfeifer & Schmidt, 2012).

In this context, in addition to the teaching of PHL as a language-culture, we consider the need to integrate, in this relationship, a third vertex, that of the person himself. The teaching of PHL as a language-person-culture would thus include, in addition to a culturally contextualized use of the language, the student's own consideration in all its uniqueness, as a unique person, and that, therefore, would also bring all his individuality to the classroom, at various levels. And so it would become, without any doubt, much richer each of our classes (Souza, & Lira, 2017), because we would really have a *personalized* - and *humanized* – teaching, to which we previously referred. After all, and especially based on our own experiences in teaching, is it not the feeling of belonging to a language and culture that is intrinsic and truly characteristic of an HL speaker?

References

Aguilar, L. (2010). Método de comunic-ação para o ensino e aprendizagem do português língua estrangeira. *In* José Pedro Ferreira & Manuela Marujo (eds.), *Ensinar português nas universidades da América do Norte* (pp. 133-142). Toronto: Department of Spanish & Portuguese/Instituto Camões.

Alavi, S. M., & Taghizadeh, M. (2014). Dynamic assessment of writing: the impact of implicit/explicit mediations on L2 learners' internalization of writing skills and strategies. *Educational Assessment, 19*(1), 1-16.

Barbeiro, L., Pereira, L. Á., & Carvalho, J. (2015). Writing at Portuguese universities: students' perceptions and practices. *Journal of Academic Writing, 5*(1), 74–85.

Bartolomé, L., & Macedo, D. (1999). (Mis)educating Mexican Americans through language. *In* T. Huebner & K. Davis (Eds.), *Sociopolitical perspectives on language policy and planning in the USA* (pp. 223-241). Philadelphia: John Benjamins.

Bork, A. V. B., Bazerman, C., Correa, F. P. P., & Cristóvão, V. L. L. (2014). Mapeamento das iniciativas de escrita em língua materna na educação superior: resultados preliminares. *Prolíngua, 9*, 2-14.

Camps, A. (2008). Escribir e aprender a escribir. *Aula de Innovación Educativa*, 175, 10-14.

Cardoso, I. (2009). *A relação com a escrita extra-escolar e escolar. Um estudo no Ensino Básico.* Aveiro: Universidade de Aveiro.

Cardoso, I. (2016). Experiências didáticas com a escrita em PLNM: questionando vias de promoção de (des)envolvimento. *In* Maria Luisa Ortiz Alvarez & Luís Gonçalves (Org.), *O Mundo do Português e o Português no mundo afora: especificidades, implicações e ações* (pp. 427-471). São Paulo: Pontes.

Cardoso, I., Lopes, C. G., Pereira, L. Á., & Ferreira, J. (2019). A relação com a escrita ao longo da escolaridade básica: imagens fixadas ou flexíveis? Contributos do grupo ProTextos. *APP, Palavras - Revista em linha, 2*, 35-54.

Coutinho, M. A., & Miranda, F. (2009). To describe genres: problems and strategies. *In* C. Bazerman, A. Bonini, & D. Figueiredo (Eds.), *Genre in a changing world* (pp. 35–55). Colorado and Indiana: Parlor Press and WAC Clearinghouse.

Dodman, M. J., Cardoso, I., & Tavares, V. (in press). Communicating and understanding the other through experiential education: Portuguese language and culture in Toronto. *In* M. Jeon, M. Figueredo, F. Carra-Salsberg (Eds.). *Globally Informed Design and Praxis in Languages, Literatures and Linguistics Curricula*. University of Toronto Press.

Dolz-Mestre, J. (2016). As atividades e os exercícios de língua: uma reflexão sobre a engenharia didática. *DELTA: Documentação de Estudos em Lingüística Teórica e Aplicada, 32*(1), 237-260.

Dolz-Mestre, J., & Gagnon, R. (eds.) (2018). *Former à enseigner la production écrite. Acquisition et transmission des savoirs*. Villeneuve d'Asq, Presses Universitaires du Septentrion.

Ellis, R. (2010). Recherche sur l'enseignement et la pédagogie des langues. *Le Français dans le monde: recherches et applications*, 48, 46–65.

Ferreira, J. P., & Rolim, R. (2010). O ensino de português no Canadá: algumas observações sobre dinâmicas universitárias. *In* José Pedro Ferreira & Manuela Marujo (eds.), *Ensinar português nas universidades da América do Norte* (pp. 101-113). Toronto: Department of Spanish & Portuguese/Instituto Camões.

Flores, C. (2013). Português Língua Não Materna. Discutindo conceitos de uma perspetiva linguística. *In* R. Bizarro, M. Moreira, & C. Flores (orgs.), *Português língua não materna: investigação e ensino* (pp.35-46). Lisboa: Lidel.

Gontijo, V. (2010a). Motivation and attitudes in Portuguese classes. *In* José Pedro Ferreira & Manuela Marujo (eds.), *Ensinar Português nas Universidades da América do Norte/Teaching Portuguese in North American Universities* (pp. 59-67). Toronto: Department of Spanish and Portuguese/Instituto Camões.

Gontijo, V. (2010b). *The Role of Heritage, Attitudes and Motivation among Learners of Portuguese*. M. A. thesis. North Dartmouth, MA: University of Massachusetts Dartmouth.

Graça, L., & Pereira, L. Á. (2015). O papel transformador das ferramentas didáticas nas práticas de ensino e no objeto ensinado: o caso da escrita do artigo de opinião. *Contrapontos, 15*(1), 17-32.

Graça, L. (2010). *O papel das ferramentas didácticas nas práticas docentes de escrita*. Tese de doutoramento europeu. Aveiro: Universidade de Aveiro.

Graça, L. (in press). A escrita significativa, em português: Um dispositivo de escrita pessoal para uma personalização do ensino, com falantes de língua de herança. *In* K. Silva & C. Martins (Org.), *Geopolítica do Português: História, políticas e ensino*. São Paulo - Campinas: Mercado de Letras.

Graça, L., Pereira, L. Á., & Dolz, J. (2014). Resistências e obstáculos na formação contínua de professores: um estudo de caso sobre o ensino da escrita em diferentes disciplinas. *Estudos Linguísticos/ Linguistics Studies*, pp. 261-282.

Hanauer, D. (2011). Meaningful literacy: writing poetry in the language classroom. *Language Teaching, 45*(1), 105-115.

King, K. A., & Ennser-Kananen, J. (2013). Heritage languages and language policy. In C. A. Chapelle (ed.), *Encyclopaedia of applied linguistics*. URL: https://onlinelibrary.wiley.com/doi/pdf/10.1002/9781405198431.wbeal0500

Leeman, J. (2005). Engaging critical pedagogy: Spanish for native speakers. *Foreign Language Annals, 38*(1), 35- 44.

Loureiro-Rodríguez, V. (2013). Meaningful writing in the heritage language class: a case study of heritage learners of Spanish in Canada. *L2 Journal, 5*, 43-58.

Martínez, G. A. (2005). Genres and genre chains: post-process perspectives on heritage language writing in a South Texas setting. *Southwest Journal of Linguistics, 24* (1 & 2), 79-90.

Marujo, M. (2016). O ensino do português no Canadá – A província do Ontário. *In* A. A. C. Luís, C. S. G. X. Luís, & P. Osório, P. (Orgs.) *A língua portuguesa no mundo* (pp. 287-301). Lisboa: Edições Colibri / Universidade da Beira Interior.

Melo-Pfeifer, S. (2016). *Didática do português língua de herança*. Lisboa: Lidel.

Melo-Pfeifer, S. (2018). Português como língua de herança: Que português? Que língua? Que herança?. *Domínios da Linguagem, 12*(2), 1161-1179.

Melo-Pfeifer, S., & Schmidt, A. (2012). Linking "Heritage Language" education and plurilingual repertoires development: Evidences from drawings of Portuguese pupils in Germany. *L1-Educational Studies in Language and Literature, 12*, 1-30.

Melo-Pfeifer, S., & Simões, A. R. (Eds.). (2017). *Plurilinguismo vivido, plurilinguismo desenhado: estudos sobre a relação dos sujeitos com as línguas*. Instituto Politécnico de Santarém / Escola Superior de Educação.

Pavlenko, A. (2007) Autobiographic narratives as data in applied linguistics. *Applied Linguistics, 28* (2), 163-188.

Pereira, L. Á. (2019). A Produção de Textos na Escola – um Percurso para uma Didática (da Literacia) da Escrita. *In* I. P. Martins (org.), *Percursos de Investigação em Educação no CIDTFF: um itinerário pelas Lições de Agregação* (pp. 795-839). Aveiro: UA Editora.

Pereira, L. Á., Aleixo, C., Cardoso, I., & Graça, L. (2010). The teaching and learning of writing in Portugal: The case of a research group. *In* C. Bazerman, R. Krut, K. Lunsford, S. McLeod, S. Null, P. M. Rogers & A. Stansell (eds.), *Traditions of Writing Research* (pp. 58-70). UK, Oxford: Routledge.

Pereira, L. Á., Graça, L., Marques, V. R., Cardoso, I. (2016). Country Report: Portugal. *In* Otto Kruse, Madalina Chitez, Brittany Rodriguez, Montserrat Castelló, *Exploring European Writing Cultures: Country Reports on Genres, Writing Practices and Languages Used in European Higher Education* (pp.163-178). Zurich University of Applied Sciences: Working Papers in Applied Linguistics, 10.

Polinsky, M. (2007). Heritage language narratives. *In* D. Brinton, O. Kagan, S. Barckus (Eds.), *Heritage Language Education: a new field emerging* (pp. 149-164). New York: Routledge.

Reznicek-Parrado, L. M. (2014). The personal essay and academic writing proficiency in spanish heritage language development. *Arizona Working Papers in Second Language Acquisition and Teaching, 21*, 71-83.

Ribeiro, A. P. T. (2016). O ensino do português no Canadá: especificidades, mudanças e expectativas. *In* Maria Luisa Ortiz Alvarez & Luís Gonçalves (org.), *O Mundo do Português e o Português no mundo afora: especificidades, implicações e ações* (pp. 331-351). São Paulo: Pontes.

Ribeiro, A. P. T. C. (2019). *O ensino-aprendizagem do português no Canadá: um contributo para a sua promoção*. Lisboa: Universidade Aberta.

Schneuwly, B. *et al.* (2004). *Gêneros orais e escritos na escola*. Campinas Editora.

Silva, G. (2008). Heritage language learning and the Portuguese subjunctive. *Portuguese Language Journal*, 3, Fall. URL: http://www.ensinoportugues.org/wp-content/uploads/2011/05/HLSubjunctivePLJSilva.pdf

Silva, G. V. (2010). Maintaining (?) Portuguese in Southeastern Massachusetts. *In* José Pedro Ferreira & Manuela Marujo (eds.), *Ensinar português nas universidades da América do Norte* (pp. 69-81). Toronto: Department of Spanish & Portuguese/Instituto Camões.

Siopa, C., & Pereira, L. Á. (2017). Escrever português como segunda língua: Perceções e experiências de aprendizagem de estudantes universitários. *Indagatio Didactica*, 9 (4), 351–366.

Souza, A., & Lira, C. (Orgs.) (2017). *O POLH na Europa – Português como língua de herança*. Londres: JN Paquet Books.

Statistics Canada (2017). *Canadian diversity and multilingualism in Canadian homes*. Ottawa: Industry Canada. URL: http://www12.statcan.gc.ca/census-recensement/2016/as-sa/98-200-x/2016010/98-200-x2016010-eng.cfm

Tavares, A. (2008). *Ensino-aprendizagem do Português como Língua Estrangeira*. Lisboa: Lidel.

Van Deusen-Scholl, N. (2003). Toward a definition of heritage language: sociopolitical and pedagogical considerations, *Journal of Language, Identity & Education*, 2 (3), 211-230.

9
Teaching Portuguese Language and Lusophone Literatures at York University: Innovating Curriculum and Enhancing the Student Experience

Inês Cardoso
University of Aveiro, CIDTFF[1] & Polytechnic of Leiria

Maria João Dodman
York University

Creation, Evolution and Program Trends

Although course offerings in Portuguese at YU existed since the 1980s, it was only in the fall of 2008 that an official program in Portuguese Studies was established. As one of Canada's largest post-secondary institutions, YU is one of only two universities that offer such a degree[2]. The creation of the program served to establish a more formal relationship with the Camões Institute[3], but also as a way to affirm the university's commitment to global diversity[4], multiculturalism and, in particular, the recognition of Portuguese language (PL) and cultures within local and global communities[5]. In addition to pursuing a Bachelor of Arts (BA) or an

---

[1] Research Centre on Didactics and Technology in the Education of Trainers: http://www.ua.pt/cidtff/entrada.
[2] The other institution is the University of Toronto, whose offerings in Portuguese date back to 1947.
[3] *Camões, Instituto da Cooperação e da Língua* – Camões, I. P. – is a cultural and educational branch of the Portuguese Ministry of Foreign Affairs: https://www.instituto-camoes.pt/.
[4] In addition to Toronto having one of the largest Portuguese-speaking communities, YU is also host to students from over 180 countries, and thus one of the most visible and varied multicultural institutions.
[5] According to a Statistics Canada's National Household Survey 2016, the Portuguese

Honours Minor, students may also enhance their degree by pursuing a Certificate of Language Proficiency in Portuguese. Over the past decade, the program has changed and evolved. For instance, it now offers more student-oriented platforms and, in the fall of 2013, an Experiential Education (EE) course – the first of its kind in foreign language at YU – was created that, while honouring the program's relationship and commitment to the community, also provided students with immersive, hands-on professional and personal opportunities. Another important change was the program title – from "Portuguese Studies" to "Portuguese & Luso-Brazilian Studies"[6] (PORL) – in 2014. This change boasted a decisive commitment to all Portuguese-speaking countries, their rich and varied cultures and regional expressions, and aimed to more adequately reflect the program's curriculum that addresses, for instance, colonial, post- and neo-colonialist trends of vast territories and immigrant communities. In addition to our language courses that highlight and value variation and regionalism, our courses on culture, film and literature provide insights on nation-building, emerging ideologies, historical and cultural revolutions, while addressing the richness of the several national and marginal Lusophone literatures[7].

In addition to the pioneering EE discipline, the program ties to the communities have increased significantly. As the majority of Portuguese immigrants in Canada immigrate from the Azores, the discipline "The Culture and Literature of the Azores", the only of its kind in Canada, acknowledges the region's unique identity and its literary and cultural

---

represent almost 1,5% of the Canadian population, esteemed to be about 482 610. The peak of Portuguese immigration occurred between 1966 and 1974, yet, over the last couple of decades there has been a growth of other Portuguese-speaking communities in the Greater Toronto Area (GTA), namely Brazilians and Angolans - 36830 the former, and 2955, the latter.

[6] Upon careful consideration of many proposals, the program decided that the terms Portuguese, Luso- or Lusophone and Brazilian must be included in the new name. The reasons for this choice are explained as follows: i) Portuguese: expresses the program's appreciation of the unifying language of the Portuguese-speaking countries in their shared historical and foundational linguistic backgrounds. It supports our commitment to our international Portuguese Partner (Camões, I. P.), to our communities (the large Portuguese community in Canada and especially in the GTA), and to our Portuguese-speaking heritage students; ii) Luso-: meaning related to Portuguese, included in Lusophone, names the program's commitment to interdisciplinary and internationalization which includes course offerings representative of the entire Portuguese-speaking world beyond Portugal; iii) Brazilian: specifies the program's strategic development towards strengthening our ties with the growing Brazilian communities in the GTA; our commitment to Brazilian studies through course offerings and research in the area; our participation in the Centre for Research on Latin America and the Caribbean (CERLAC) and in the Brazil Studies Seminars.

[7] For more information on our courses: http://portuguese.dlll.laps.yorku.ca/courses/.

productions. By exploring themes such as poverty, isolation and insularity, this discipline also aims to develop students' enhanced empathy and understanding of the Azores and its migration saga. York's specific context as the post-secondary Canadian institution with the largest numbers of researchers of the Lusophone world (survey by J. A. Ferreira & Rolim, 2010), boosts our research profiles[8] and consequently enriches the overall student experience. Hence, students have access to scholars and courses from varied backgrounds and disciplines as well as student associations, co- and extra-curricular opportunities. Students are in fact encouraged to explore courses in other disciplines and the program officially recognises a number of multidisciplinary credits[9]. Beyond courses, the program's outreach and EE opportunities (on and off campus) promote the enhancement of the student experience in a variety of ways: from language and cultural immersion to formal sponsored and co-sponsored opportunities, such as, among others, film festivals, career panels, community placements, and volunteering[10].

We have been navigating then in narrows of local demand, opportunities, and constraints. Portuguese is a world language, and there is a large and unique contingent of speakers locally; yet Portuguese, as a world language, is not *primus inter pares*, and it is a complicated colonial history giving rise to its status, and particularly, in the context we operate, to the heterogeneity of students whose families are from Portuguese-speaking countries, former Portuguese colonies. We will further characterize our student population later. Other sections will focus on pedagogical options and theoretical foundations while also remaking our relationship with the local communities which use PL, striking what we find a difficult but successful balance in attending to the various publics and demands.

Student Demographics - Characterization, Motivations and Relationship with the Language

As a post-secondary institution, YU is well known for its multiculturalism, and a choice university for students who are either the first in their families

---

[8] York is home to, among others, the Canadian Center for Azorean Research and Studies http://ccars.apps01.yorku.ca), the Lusophone Studies Association (http://lsa.apps01.yorku.ca), and the Portuguese-Canadian History Project (https://pchp-phlc.ca).
[9] See http://portuguese.dlll.laps.yorku.ca/courses/additional-courses.
[10] Any York student with an adequate level of proficiency can volunteer to assist in the language classes. These opportunities, in addition to the linguistic and cultural enrichment, are acknowledged via York's co-curricular record:
http://portuguese.dlll.laps.yorku.ca/students/volunteer-opportunities/.

to attend university and/or first generation Canadians[11]. In this contribution, we will bring to light specific data about our students in PORL, collected through mandatory online placement tests. These tests are designed to assess students' language proficiency and their relationship with the language, and they also provide insights into students' cultural backgrounds. The idea of a "relationship with…" is adapted from previous notions focusing on learners' complex relationships with knowledge, language and school systems (Charlot, 1997) and with writing (Barré-De Miniac, 2000; Cardoso, 2009). Pedagogically and theoretically, we adopt this notion of "relationship" since it places the emphasis on the "Subject/Individual" and considers personal and unique ways, whether conscious or unconscious, that s/he brings, alongside experiences, knowledge, ideas, and concepts. We are then acknowledging, in this personal relationship with the language, the individual's agency and attitudes oscillating between enthusiastic and diverse use of the language to a personal detachment from it. These relationships encompass practices of use (type, contexts, and frequency); affective aspects (opinions, images or representations about the PL, motivations to learn); and cognitive dimensions, namely conceptions about its learning, the way subjects express themselves in relation to the language, and learning strategies. However, this positioning or relationship is not static in time – hence it is of interest to collect this data for the development and application of a pedagogical approach that leads to a renewed expression and reshaping of this relationship, as didactics research demonstrates, in particular regarding certain images about languages (Melo-Pfeifer & Simões, 2017; Pfeifer & Schmidt, 2012). This is the main reason why we will include students' voices in this paper, which might be relevant to our knowledge of their relationship with PL: to acknowledge its contribution, from the diagnosis and throughout the academic year (through means we will describe when talking about the classroom dynamics), to the design of pedagogical tools and projects.

We will consider the placement tests' data between 2014 and 2017; although there were 246 entries, 15 were incomplete, thus our data is composed of 231 questionnaires. One hundred and thirty-four students identified themselves as being from a Portuguese-speaking (Lusophone) home background, while 97 were of other origins/languages' backgrounds. Under "Student information," participants were asked to provide personal data, ethnicity, and formal or informal knowledge of languages used daily and/or others. Students were also required to provide linguistic and sociocultural perceptions, and self-assessments of all the languages that they

---

[11] http://vpap.info.yorku.ca/files/2014/04/SMA-York-Final-Appendix-Long-Version-of-SMA-April-14-2014.pdf.

have learnt or mastered/have been somewhat exposed (formally or informally), indicating which categories best described their knowledge of those languages, in regards to listening, speaking, reading, and writing separately: Excellent, Very good, Good, Fairly, Barely.

Although a large number of our students tends to be from Lusophone backgrounds[12], other students from a diversity of backgrounds also pursue studies in Portuguese. The data we are considering, as stated before, is retrieved from the language placement test: the majority of students who fill it out will in fact enroll in the language classes. However, the sample we are considering in this chapter presents us with 58% of self-identified Lusophone students and 42% from other backgrounds. Nonetheless, the typical trend when we consider our language classes enrolment is 70% of heritage learners (Ferreira, Graça, & Cardoso, 2020; Melo-Pfeifer, 2018) and 30% of other students from different language and ethnic origins. Most, from both groups, desire to learn, both locally and abroad, a second or third language for personal and/or professional reasons. Almost all students hold positive and even memorable connections with the language and its speakers, particularly through cultural expressions such as dance and music. The need to improve upon and polish more formal language skills ranks high among heritage learners, who, according to Bastos and Melo-Pfeifer (2017), are those whose language was acquired within the family and the community of origin relocated to a new place where a different language is majorly spoken. In this case, Portuguese as a heritage language is a language with a high flexible degree of "strangeness" for the students, from a language heard or heard about but not spoken to a language spoken in many contexts, depending highly on the practices of family communication and transmission. This group of heritage learners/speakers shows vulnerabilities common of those who learn and speak the language sporadically and in familiar or informal settings (Valdes, 2014). They tend to view their language heritage as "broken" or "incomplete" and desire to fulfill a more holistic relation to their language and family. It is therefore vital to encourage the already positive relationship to the language and culture of their ancestors via affective and identity ties (Cardoso, 2016).

Our corpus includes all answers to the question "Write down honestly the first three «things»/words that come to mind about the PL", a sum of 656 words (Figure 1), among which 153 were written in Portuguese. Interesting enough is that the heritage learners, expected to master the language more comfortably in the case they can be placed among those

---

[12] Most identify as Luso-Canadians, while other students from Brazilian and Angolan backgrounds also enroll into our program.

more familiarized with the language[13] – Lusophone students – only wrote 55 Portuguese words.

Figure 1: Cloud of the 656 words

Figure 1 reveals the compilation of the 656 words collected as the result of the students' spontaneity to describe the language. While the vastest Portuguese-speaking territory, Brazil, appears, students also wrote of its Latin and romance roots, and its positive linkage to family. Following a content analysis, we have placed occurrences in the categories presented here in a decreasing fashion, followed by their number (table 1):

Table 1: Results from content analysis: categories and occurrences

Categories	Number of occurrences (total)	Lusophone Students	Non-Lusophone students
Positive values	134	89	45
Lusophone cultures	106	65	41
Origin/language families/interlingual comparisons	58	24	34
Lusophone countries	54	8	46
Sociolinguistic skills – dialects, accents, and intra-linguistic variety	52	27	25
Family relationships	47	45	2

---

[13] Although, following Dabène, M. Bastos and S. Melo-Pfeifer also note the continuum "known-unknown" where the heritage learners navigate throughout their lives in terms of being very familiar-not familiar at all with the language (Bastos & Melo-Pfeifer, 2017).

Sociolinguistic skills - linguistic markers of social relations, rules of politeness	42	25	17
Gastronomy	31	20	11
Geographical and climatic references	30	17	13
Learning and performance	26	19	7
Communication settings – examples in Portuguese	20	11	9
Lusophone people - characteristics, attitudes	12	8	4
PL in the world language ranking	13	8	5
Linguistic biography	10	7	3
Learning goals	10	5	5
Friendship/love relationships	8	3	5
Lusophone personalities	3	1	2

In general, the vast majority qualified Portuguese as beautiful (33), interesting (21), romantic (13), fun (10), familiar, exotic. In other instances, comfort, elegance, liveliness, musicality and wealth - mainly historical -, are also present. PL provokes fascination and attraction, it is even considered sexy, described as a simple and natural language, necessary, popular, powerful, important, sympathetic, intelligent, inspiring, and connected with happiness. From the references to Lusophone cultures to the individual's heritage, we found football, *saudade*, a range of musical expressions and the growing popularity of *samba* and *fado*, and an interest in history. Also relevant are language diversity and knowledge, and occasional allusions to colonialism, Camões, religion, dictatorship, tradition, festivals, Diaspora, soap operas, and folklore groups. In the latter references, there seems to be an acute awareness of Portuguese-speaking countries and territories, as well as diversity.

When comparing the results between Lusophone (134 students with Portuguese-speaking backgrounds) and non-Lusophone (97 students with other linguistic backgrounds), we noticed, as we anticipated, the strong presence of family and, naturally, a greater exposure to the PL among

Lusophone students. These students revealed greater awareness of speech modalities, speed, and varieties as well as sociolinguistic knowledge. Non-Lusophone students tended to express more global references, such as the Portuguese-speaking world with varied references to its cultures as main motivators to learn the language. Language comparison is more prominent in this group and awareness of language and accent variants is almost as high as in the other group, suggesting that there is a well-known awareness of such variations. We could infer that this awareness of variation and diversity could be driven by two main influences: the large "Lusophone concentration" visible in Toronto and the GTA, and the other, a cognizance of certain tensions between traditional Portuguese and/or Lusophone "organizations" and the individual's agency, between uniformity and variability, and between exclusion and inclusion (Da Silva, 2015, 2012).

Summing up, Lusophone students show a greater focus on specific and local realities connected to the Lusophone world, and the Portuguese-speaking communities. No identity dilemmas were perceived, although there is a subtle reference to certain "stereotypes" pervasively associated with the Portuguese-speaking "ethnoclass" (Garcez, 2018), in particular those regarding unskilled migrants, and academic underachievement. Based on their responses mainly regarding what we called "positive values" (table 1), one may infer these students, however, do not seem to feel negatively impacted by Portuguese-speaking negative labels. On the contrary, they seem proud and wish to excel in their proficiency. Moreover, Lusophone students emphasize learning a great deal (they are responsible for 19 out of 26 replies falling under this category – table 1), seeking to become legitimate language users and mastering what they deemed to be "proper Portuguese". Their references to learning are indeed more abundant than those of non-Lusophones, who, considering they are learning Portuguese as a foreign language for the first time, would be expected to know less Portuguese[14] and, therefore, to focus more on their learning goals in these responses. Many, even if they incorporate the so-called "ethnoclass", come across resilient and eager to perhaps change traditionally class-associated stereotypes. On the other hand, non-Lusophone students hold wider perspectives. They signal mobility and global professionally-driven advantages of Portuguese, and the interlinguistic connections they may develop, while revealing an allure of

---

[14] Again, considering the fluid notion of heritage learner explained above, we should acknowledge that some heritage learners might know as much or less Portuguese as a non-Lusophone learner, although the majority of heritage learners are more exposed to the language in family contexts, which surpass the exposure that non-heritage students generally have access to (Valdes, 2014).

Portuguese-speaking cultures. Concerns regarding language profitability are then predominant among non-Lusophone students, although it is interesting to note that, in a different context, Montreal, speeches of profit and promotion have been arising despite the decrease in enrolment of heritage language (see Scetti, this volume).

These results mirror Garcez's (2018) recent ethnographic study conducted with children of Brazilian migrant families in Toronto. The diversity of socioeconomic profiles visible in the neighbourhoods the families live in and the professions of the parents correspond to contrasting language ideologies. In fact, much like our Lusophone group, Garcez found participants from lower-class families assigned mainly local values to the Portuguese language and demonstrate a sense of pride in keeping the language. Children of middle/upper-class families are more preoccupied with career success and global markets, a trend more in line with our non-Lusophone group. In general, though, the value attributed to the language was common among all families (see also Garcez, Dias, & Bess, this volume). These divisions and complementary visions of the values assigned to Portuguese substantiate, in our perspective, the vast complexity of the ethnolinguistic market of Portuguese in Canada, or in the GTA more particularly. As we stand for a pluricentric language perspective (Clyne, 2012; Melo-Pfeifer, 2018), we must consider not only all the variation of the language, but also its associated and diverse representations. The PL classroom serves as an extension of the real world, and it should welcome all socio-linguistic backgrounds and promote democratic dialogue regarding the diversity, and often negative stereotypes of Portuguese speakers. Engaging students in such dialogues can lead to more positive images and a more informed and engaged relationship with the language and its many cultural expressions especially for those students with limited conceptions of the language and its users. This dialogue, however, involves learners, instructors, and the community at large in a call for action and global citizenship. Moreover, we strive to empower subjects via the language and its cultural benefits in local and international contexts.

Beyond the Traditional Language and Literature Classroom

Student-focused Learning Platforms: Scaffolding the Learning Process

Our learning approach includes continuous interactive, evaluative, and reflective methods. As our emphasis is a communicative one, we encourage students to communicate not only with one another but also within a variety of registers and genres while assessing and referring to his/hers evaluative process (Cardoso, 2016). Learning is also not confined to the classroom. We view it as an autonomous and empowering process upon which students can excel, for instance, via several online platforms, such as My Portuguese Lab (Jouët-Pastré et al., 2013), Escola Virtual[15], Moodle, Facebook group[16], Twitter[17], Skype, WhatsApp, and Messenger. The instructor's guidance focuses on the student as an individual, and it is a relationship nurtured by the insights regarding the students' sociolinguistic and cultural repertoires and their intimate relationship with the language and its cultures. This information was collected firstly through the online placement test, which we exemplified in the previous section, and later via several assignments that provide additional data and inform our teaching and research throughout the year(s).

In the language courses, there is progressive scaffolding from a more oral approach at the beginners' level (53% weight in evaluation out of the entire course load) to 50% weight both to oral (listening and speaking) and written skills (reading, writing) in intermediate, and a more written production focus at the advanced level, with a 55% weight. Evaluation is also more focused in class at the beginners level, while as students' progress through the courses, they also acquire a more creative and autonomous relationship with the language; as such, the evaluation must reflect this nuance. The curriculum then includes varied activities both in and out of class designed to develop student confidence and autonomy. From the student-led flipped classroom and oral and written interaction with native speakers[18] to free and creative writing and students' projects and portfolios, there is always a structured invitation for meaningful engagement with a myriad of situational contexts and genres. Despite the aforementioned structure, students hold free agency to determine their goals and tasks according to their individual commitment to the course load (Dodman, Cardoso, & Tavares, forthcoming).

In the culture and literature courses there is an emphasis on reading and research skills at the introductory culture course, while the advanced courses focus on writing and the development of essay writing and argumentative skills. While there is substantial academic assistance for students on campus, we find that, due to many reasons, students generally do not make use of such services. Thus, our approach in the introductory course is to create meaningful and valuable experiential learning opportunities. The readings in POR2600 – Luso-Brazilian Cultures and

---

[15] http://www.escolavirtual.pt/.
[16] https://www.facebook.com/groups/544944348971440/.
[17] https://twitter.com/YorkUPorL.
[18] Considering the substantial Lusophone community in Toronto, and the partnerships prepared so that students may interact with native speakers of Portuguese, they will be provided with plenty of opportunities to do so.

Cinemas, our introductory course – aim to mirror the panoramic diversity of such cultures, but also to capture a wide variety of students' interests. Thus, the readings tend to be inter and transdisciplinary allowing for a multitude of approaches. While students engage with seminal pieces, they are also exposed to modern and complex interpretations. This is the case, for instance, surrounding the usage of Portuguese worldwide and the term Lusophone in relationship to a troubled colonial past and the exclusion of diverse non-Lusophone ethnicities, histories and cultural manifestations within the so-called Lusophone official sphere. The complexities and possibilities are then discussed through the lenses of art and fiction. Students read how colonized nations take ownership of the language of the colonizers by honouring local ethnicities and by adopting and adapting oral and local traditions in literary texts. They also delve deeper in well-known topics. For instance, most students are quite familiar with *capoeira*. Yet, very few understand the history and the racial/class implications of its practice. In the 2017-18 iteration of the course, students read an article that spoke of *capoeira*'s elitist and government appropriation and thus transforming it into political currency while rejecting and excluding Black consciousness. Students also met *capoeiristas* and participated in a workshop. The *capoeiristas*' treatment of the practice focused on education about Brazil's troubled slave past and the value of *capoeira* as the keeper of stories of slavery, resilience and community strength. The curriculum for this discipline includes a major research project organized around students' interests. The initial project is then enhanced via the development of research skills, library visits, and a research fair where students celebrate their efforts and showcase their findings through a poster presentation. The evaluation, much like in the language courses, promotes autonomy while offering continuous feedback for improvement and proper research skills that can be applied across disciplines and personal pursuits.

Enhancing Students' Relationship with Reading and Writing

Writing is another privileged curricular and research area (Cardoso, Pereira, Lopes, & Lopes, 2018)[19]. Moreover, internal demands for academic literacy training in higher education as well as external demands from the local communities for collaboration toward an improved outlook for the educational and social prospects of social groups somehow identified as connected to Luso-Brazilian studies are great reasons for the focus on reading and writing that we will cover in this section. In this realm,

---

[19] In fact, Inês Cardoso, the Camões lecturer at York (from October, 2013 to June, 2019), in partnership with the Camões Coordinatorship of PL teaching in Canada, participated and led teacher-training initiatives that revealed both the teachers' difficulties with teaching proper writing skills as well as students' poor written scores.

we consider three dimensions of writing that, through our research, also inform our pedagogic and didactic approaches: i) the cognitive demands of (re)writing and revision processes, ii) the social nature of writing, and iii) the personal approach to writing. Our research has revealed that there must be a multifunctional and procedural perspective underlying the learning and teaching process of writing (Cardoso, 2009). For example, cognitive writing research exposes a high complexity of the writing processes, the difficulties that writers endure – in our case, issues related to L2, heritage and foreign language writing. However, it also provides guidance for the implementation of instructional methods to tackle such difficulties: procedural scaffolding, self-regulation and revision strategies, oral corrective feedback, collaboration and interaction.

Additionally, 'writing' for social purposes – and within multiple cultural and societal textual genres – informs us of our students' needs so we can best offer tools for effective communication (both orally and written), according to the students' flexibility and goal setting. We also anchor our writing teaching approach in the framework of socio-discursive interactionism as developed by Bronckart (1997) and influenced by Vygotsky (2005). Our interests reside mainly in the following pedagogical aspects: how we learn and how we foster development through learning, considering the importance and centrality of logocentrism and social-linguistic context within language practice as an instrument of human development itself. Therefore, our mission in L2 is to widen the learners' horizons with useful and diverse language activities. Hence, we must provide a variety of models aimed at transforming language imitators into authentic language users. Hence, the central position we attribute to any textual genres is always strictly connected to the language activities in which they thrive. Initially, when students are exposed to diverse textual genres, they tend to imitate them. However, in due time, they will acquire autonomy to be authors on their own terms. If they already engage in a variety of contexts and modalities (i.e. opinion articles, emails, short stories, etc.) in their L1, they can apply certain global macro-characteristics to their texts in their L2. Thus, we must present and orient the teaching of genres in a transversal manner, accepting their individual cultural backgrounds and building on to use language as a marker of symbolic knowledge about the world. This idea is fundamental to the understanding of the rules that structure and organize a textual genre in their transversal role in languages (Bronckart, 2008; Guasch, 2000). Some multilingual contexts have benefited from this "integrated plurilingual language planning" (Bikandi & Valls, 2008; Hyland, 2007) by teaching/learning the same textual genre in different languages. Whereas the individual's management of the writing process in the L1 may also be transposed to the writing process in the L2, we can therefore assume that those individuals who demonstrate high literacy skills in L1 will transpose such skills into L2, consciously or not. Following this same logic, the opposite is equally plausible (Chenoweth & Hayes, 2001).

Guided by these findings, one of our didactic approaches focused on textual genres in communicative contexts is grounded in what we call a teaching (or didactic) sequence (Dolz et al., 2004; Pereira & Cardoso, 2013)[20]:

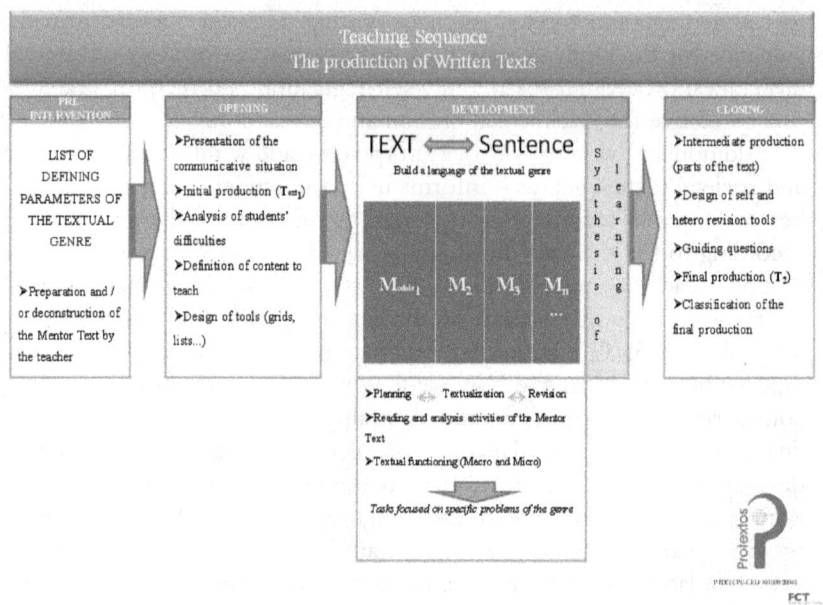

Figure 2: Teaching Sequence (translated from Pereira & Cardoso, 2013, p. 52)

A teaching sequence acknowledges the role of mentor texts in the target language and the clear identification of the communicative situation. Reading is addressed to support writing in learning more about the organization of the text and specific linguistic features – in this case, in the L2. Checking, revising, and assessing tools play a major role in order to determine the following writing steps. This didactic tool has proven quite effective in aiding students to master a specific text genre, in particular more formal registers such as letters of complaint. Students understand the main characteristics of the textual genre, and linguistic resources available to them. In-class assessment criteria include genre-based activities,

---

[20] See more of our research group «"ProTextos" - Teaching and Learning of Writing» at http://protextos.web.ua.pt/.

considerations of the textual infrastructure level, and the elements found on a letter of complaint; for instance; the enunciation, and general issues of morphology, syntax and lexicon[21].

Last, but not least, we consider the personal nature of writing as a practice and as a measure of individual expression also in the L2, a conclusion supported by six years of students' textual guidance, collection and analysis. Indeed, personal writing in the L2 is not only possible, but also quite fruitful (Cardoso, 2016). The connectivity between the cognitive, social, and personal dimensions of writing can lead to a positive reshaping of the students' relationship with writing, and thus can encourage them to invest in their written production while improving their language skills. For instance, discovering that writing can be a useful and/or a meaningful experience in a certain communicative context may foster a positive personal connection to writing. As such, this personal connection may encourage and engage students in the writing processes, by leading them to invest in improving their texts—for instance, developing language skills. We evoke here our guiding principles of the writing process (cognitive dimension) whether it takes place within a creative and personal writing in the L2 or embedded in a social context. Ultimately, both creative and "social" writings may "live" beyond the classroom and "spill over" into real communication with readers.

In class, when students are prompted to create a written output, the other skills – reading, listening, speaking – will certainly provide a basis for planning their texts – that means providing content to enrich students' knowledge/vocabulary about any content-based topics and activities. Such activities allow students to be cognizant of their writing tasks and textual purposes. On the other hand, the reading can be writing-oriented, following the type of activities conducted within a teaching sequence: reading to learn how to organize/write a similar text of the same textual genre.

Outside the classroom, another main component of the "writing program" occurs through the computer-mediated corrective feedback of free writing assignments. In these cases, students write on their subjects of interest in complete autonomy according to their level and capabilities. Corrective and personalized feedback by the instructor follows. While the role of corrective feedback has been an issue of controversy (Hyland, 2010; Van Beuningen, 2010), we have found it useful in our case. Based on

---

[21] We will not analyse the letters of complaint here, but the results were previously presented in Cardoso (2017). Experiências didáticas em PLNM: discutindo vias de promoção de (des)envolvimento na escrita. WEBINÁRIOS. AOTP 2017 – American Organization of Teachers of Portuguese, with the support of *FLAD – Fundação Luso-Americana para o Desenvolvimento*, September 6.

available experiential evidence, offering learners the opportunities to notice the gaps in their developing L2 systems, and engaging them in metalinguistic reflection, shows that written corrective feedback has been conducive to foster proficiency (Cardoso, 2016). We believe this to be linked to the free nature of the task as well. In fact, it seems that despite a common "negative attitude" towards academic writing, some students do in fact enjoy writing as a cathartic activity, considering the subjects they choose to explore in their free writing assignments, and the fact they use them to talk about the importance of writing these texts, although these are not typical tasks of academic foreign language writing in higher education. More analysis of these free texts needs to be done to deepen our knowledge about the role of free writing in foreign and heritage language learning. This fact has influenced and informed our research and our teaching experiences in an attempt to foster an epistemic affinity with the mechanism of L2 writing (self-regulatory strategies to improve linguistic skills), anchored in a more personal and holistic writing outside of the structured classroom. While correctness and fluency are important, we aim at strengthening a more comfortable relationship with the PL, aligned with our previous research that largely explores the students' relationship with writing also in their L1 (Cardoso & Pereira, 2015). Many of these free writings result in publications in newspapers and magazines in Lusophone communities.

Hence, having the same writing freedoms in L2 as in L1 has been beneficial for students. Assuming that there is a positive relationship with writing in the L1, we must transpose it to the learning of the L2. Affection, a factor that scores high in students' attitudes regarding writing, must then also be present and harnessed for progress. At times, students should be permitted to write of private matters should they wish. In addition to ensuring confidentiality, we encourage students to keep writing freely with no anxiety or stress, along with timely and gentle corrective approaches to ensure that past errors are not repeated. The feedback is varied according to the different assignments, but always meant to be comprehensive and corrective in general or specific, direct or indirect ways[22], and always aligned to the learner's level (Cardoso, 2016). Written feedback is important because it allows students to return to it often and revise texts accordingly.

Anonymous excerpts can also provide material to be revisited and corrected in class, in particular when there are reoccurring collective errors. By promoting the needed detachment from their own texts, writers can

---

[22] For instance, the instructor can offer general commentary about the text combined with specific corrections at the sentence level by providing solutions and explanations available or offer clues designed to promote self-correction.

better detect the errors of others. Collaboration also guides students' creative projects. Such is the premise behind the short stories booklets[23], destined for underprivileged children in Lusophone countries. Students collaborate in all aspects of the process, from research to writing and revising through online platforms[24]. To date, this project has been one of the most meaningful for two main reasons. On the one hand, students learn and create culturally-appropriate narratives. And, on the other hand, they can assess their progress and growth throughout while realizing the potential and the global reach of the language.

The relationship between the cognitive, social and personal dimensions of writing – and by extension reading – has proven fruitful in the advanced literature courses as well. When students approach literary texts, they must acquire reading practices that are twofold: understand the cognitive benefits of reading and its impact on the subject, and the ability to draw connections based on the historical, social and cultural impact of such readings, always anchored by contextual references. The challenges surrounding the teaching of literature are very significant and were addressed in an earlier chapter (Dodman, 2010). Yet, it might be useful to summarize some of the systemic and prevailing issues. Students continue to exhibit difficulties in terms of reading comprehension, analytical skills, and writing. Although the reasons can be several, we do know that very few students declare a love for reading or even read on a regular basis. In addition, according to the National Survey of Student Engagement (NSSE) of 2017 almost half of first-year students surveyed work off-campus, and the number rises to a staggering 60.5% in 4th year[25]. Therefore, time or lack thereof is a considerable factor. Teaching foreign literature in our case is also challenging in terms of the availability of materials and proper modern editions. The situation is even more precarious in the small availability of translated works[26]. Ultimately, the teaching of literature, even seminal pieces, must be presented in ways that address and reflect universal values. For instance, students learn and apply readings of Camões and Gil Vicente through guided discussions and written reflections of gender, class, religious, and racial distinctions. On another occasion, such as in the making of Brazilian identity, students confront certain realities that serve

---

[23] Booklets were sent to East Timor in 2018, and Guinea Bissau in 2019: see "Books of Short Stories for Portuguese-Speaking Countries" at
http://portuguese.dlll.laps.yorku.ca/creative-corner/students/.
[24] https://storybird.com/; https://www.storyjumper.com/.
[25] It is also highly problematic that 11% of 1st year and 18.7% of 4th year students work full-time. For the NSSE see http://oipa.info.yorku.ca/nsse-reports/.
[26] According to Hephzibah Anderson in a world where English dominates, only about 2 to 3% of works written in other languages are translated into English:
http://www.bbc.com/culture/story/20140909-why-so-few-books-in-translation.

the ideologies of the generation of the 1930s or the creativity of Brazilian modernists. In this case and others, literature is neither mere entertainment nor escapism, but rather a dangerous weapon for change through its power to reflect and also deconstruct ideologies (Deats & Lenker, 1999). As for reading, we never encourage reading for the mere sake of reading. Engaging with a literary text can only occur when students become aware of the specific contexts mirrored in fiction. Therefore, ample situational information must be conveyed in order to develop the necessary tools and sensitivity to approach and understand any text. In addition, and as Enscoe & Russell (1969) evidence, a deeper understanding of the elements of fiction contributes to an overall improvement not only in the quality of the experience with fiction, but also in the reading act itself, making the reading a more pleasurable and successful activity. Once students understand the intricacy of such elements as well as the sequence and structure of fiction, they are better suited to engage imaginatively. It is also crucial for students to understand the cognitive benefits of reading fiction; Blakey Vermeule (2010) explains that, among other benefits, fiction, contrary to other mediums, offers depth and doubt, complexity and shadow, and most importantly perhaps, the capacity to make us think. Lastly, it is the emerging field of narrative empathy that in the past few years has guided us in both our selection of readings and our pedagogical approach to the teaching of fiction. As this topic has been discussed elsewhere[27], we will not expand here. Suffice to say that empathic responses hold deeper meanings and range that goes beyond the classroom towards universal human values.

It Takes a Village: the Role of the Portuguese-Speaking Communities

Although Portuguese and Luso-Brazilian Studies created a pioneering experiential education course only in 2013[28], experiential opportunities are a major foundation of the program and such opportunities abound in all our courses. In addition to the ones already mentioned, PORL has, for instance, organized events that showcase the intra-linguistic variety of the language, promoted meetings with Portuguese-speaking professionals, held open-houses, participated in several cultural initiatives: film screenings and festivals, literary circles, art exhibits. In addition, each academic year, there are regular events on campus aimed at providing easy access to meaningful experiential education that reflect the curriculum and current topics of interest in the Portuguese-speaking world. The

---

[27] See chapter by Dodman, Cardoso, & Tavares – references.
[28] More information of the EE course "Language in Context: Portuguese in the GTA" can be found in the chapter by Dodman, Cardoso & Tavares.

"Lusophone Coffee Hour" is only one example of such regular events. On occasion, the program offers independent studies at the advanced levels in order to promote intensive research and build mutually beneficial interactions between the students, PORL and the communities at large. Topics such as education, the teaching of Portuguese in multilingual environments and children's literature have presented both dynamic and stimulating opportunities for engagement with language and the Portuguese-speaking communities locally and abroad.

The support and engagement with our community partners[29] has far surpassed our expectations. In addition to welcoming our students in professional settings, our partners offer students a plethora of diverse placements, real-life language and cultural interaction. It is also the community that financially support our program awards[30]. Faculty members in the program have affective ties in the community and have organized, co-organized, and participated in a number of initiatives deemed mutually important. In addition to guest lectures, presentations, language and formative workshops, literary events, teacher training, school visits, among other community engagements, faculty members in the program were at the forefront of Faculty-wide initiatives. For instance, professors in the Portuguese & Luso-Brazilian Studies program launched the very first Faculty community conversation series in 2016. This first community conversation focused on the academic struggles of Portuguese Canadians and it was made possible due to the continued collaborative relationship with Working Women Community Centre, one of our partners that, through important activism and mentoring programs, has provided educational, personal and community support to Portuguese and Spanish-speaking youth affected by academic underperformance. Following this important conversation, the program's addressed the community's need by establishing another pioneering initiative: a youth Summer program (ages 14-18)[31] that sought to attract, although not only,

---

[29] Camões Coordinatorship of PL teaching in Canada; newspapers/magazines *Milénio Stadium/ MDC Media Group* and *Etc. & Tal magazine*; FPTV; SATA – Azores Airlines; Working Women Community Centre; Rodrigues Law LLP, and Portuguese Canadian History Project.

[30] For all information on program awards:
http://portuguese.dlll.laps.yorku.ca/students/program-awards/. Two grants are financed by business enterprises, and the other one by a non-profit community association.

[31] Both editions of this weeklong program – "The Lusophone World: Local and Global Communities" in 2017 and "The Lusophone World; Musical and Artistic Expressions" in 2018 – were free to all participants and included all meals and transportation costs. This was possible due to the goodwill of our campus partners and collaborators, and financial support from the Faculty, and from one of our community partners and philanthropist Manuel da Costa. For additional information: http://portuguese.dlll.laps.yorku.ca/youth-summer-program/.

at-risk youth from marginalized communities. As agents of change, our desire was not only to promote the role of a foreign language degree in an increasingly competitive global market, but also to showcase the university as a democratic communal space in the pursuance of academic matters, but in particular, to promote the unique, varied and complete Lusophone based curriculum and research at York.

In addition to our local communities, the global reach of the program is visible in our established relationship with the Camões Institute and the government of the Azores. Both of these institutions have supported the program in a myriad of ways, from financial to archival and cultural resources. We wish to highlight in particular the involvement of both institutions in the program's major international conference (fall of 2018)[32], as well as major literary events and exhibitions on campus[33].

Concluding Remarks
We have outlined the creation and the evolution of a foreign and heritage language program within the specific context of a large Canadian multicultural institution, surrounded by noteworthy Portuguese-speaking communities, in order to contribute to a reflection about such situated complexities that may be enlightening for others in different yet comparable situations. In fact, the importance of the Portuguese-speaking communities (on and off-campus) in the support of academic and experiential education opportunities cannot be overstated. Students are exposed to a variety of cultural and linguistic variations as well as interdisciplinarity, flexibility, community participation, volunteering, and placements. Our teaching philosophy reflects our holistic approach to impact not only the intellectual and academic growth of students, but also their personal and humanistic interests. Summing up, this descriptive contribution of our path was intended to evidence how we have been responding to the various potentially divergent demands, striving to conciliate and create linkages between the students' diverse own motivations, higher education goals, and Lusophone communities and partners' expectations on our program.

Learning foreign languages and cultures enhances one's place in the world by becoming more sensitive and empathic, more engaged and more willing to contribute to the well-being of others. While addressing the personal and social context of our students, we seek to provide them with

---

[32] http://portuguese.dlll.laps.yorku.ca/conference-2018/.
[33] The sponsorship of visits of Portuguese writers David Machado and Afonso Cruz, among others; or several exhibitions, such as "Economic Potential of the PL", "The History and Evolution of Portuguese Cinema", and "Pessoa unveiled", only to name a few.

the tools necessary to engage with the rest of the world, to question their own ideas and their relationship with knowledge, to see language, culture and literature as a space for growth, critical thinking, free agency and, most of all, intellectual and personal fulfillment.

References

Barré-De Miniac, C. (2000). Le rapport à l'écriture: aspects théoriques et didactiques. In *Savoirs mieux*. Presses Universitaires du Septentrion.

Bastos, M., & Melo-Pfeifer, S. (2017). O Português em Moçambique e na Alemanha: da diversidade de estatutos à diversidade de abordagens didáticas. In A. C. Monteiro, C. Siopa, J. A. Marques, & M. Bastos (Eds.), *Ensino da Língua Portuguesa em Contextos Multilingues e Multiculturais*. Porto Editora.

Bikandi, U. R., & Valls, A. T. (2008). El tratamiento integrado de las lenguas. *Textos de Didáctica de La Lengua y La Literatura, 47*, 7–9.

Bronckart, J.-P. (1997). Activité langagière, textes et discours. Pour un interactionisme socio-discursif. In *Sciences des discours*. Delachaux et Niestlé.

Bronckart, J.-P. (2008). La actividad verbal, las lenguas y la lengua - reflexiones teóricas e didácticas. In A. Camps & M. Millian (Eds.), *Miradas y Voces. Investigación sobre la educación lingüística y literaria en entornos plurilingües* (pp. 27–44). Grao.

Cardoso, I. (2009). *A relação com a escrita extra-escolar e escolar. Um estudo no ensino básico. Tese de doutoramento*. Universidade de Aveiro.

Cardoso, I. (2016). Experiências didáticas com a escrita em PLNM: questionando vias de promoção de (des)envolvimento. In M. L. O. Alvarez & L. Gonçalves (Eds.), *O Mundo do Português e o Português no mundo afora: especificidades, implicações e ações*. Pontes.

Cardoso, I., & Pereira, L. Á. (2015). Le rapport à l'écriture extrascolaire et scolaire: une étude menée auprès d'adolescents. *Revue Canadienne de Linguistique Appliquée/ Canadian Journal of Applied Linguistics, 18*(2), 28–44.

Cardoso, I., Pereira, L. Á., Lopes, C. da G., & Lopes, R. P. A. P. (2018). Os jovens e a escrita: práticas escolares e extraescolares em Portugal. *Educação Em Revista, 34*, 1–35. https://doi.org/http://dx.doi.org/10.1590/0102-4698180899

Charlot, B. (1997). *Du rapport au savoir. Eléments pour une théorie*. In *Poche éducation 1*. Anthropos.

Chenoweth, N. A., & Hayes, J. R. (2001). Fluency in writing. Generating text in L1 and L2. *Written Communication, 18*(1), 80–98.

Clyne, M. (Ed.). (2012). *Pluricentric languages: Differing norms in different nations*.

Da Silva, E. (2015). Sociolinguistic tensions in the portuguese/lusophone community of Toronto, Canada. In L. P. M. Flores (Ed.), *Global Portuguese: Linguistic Ideologies in Late Modernity* (pp. 124–143).

Da Silva, E. (2012). Sociolinguistic (re)constructions of diaspora Portugueseness: Portuguese-Canadian youth in Toronto. *Dissertation Abstracts International Section A: Humanities and Social Sciences.*

Deats, S. M., & Lenker, L. T. (Eds.). (1999). *Aging and identity: a humanities perspective.* Praeger.

Dodman, M. J. (2010). O Ensino da literatura portuguesa na York University: do século XVI ao século XXI. Conteúdos, métodos e estratégias. In J. P. Ferreira & M. Marujo (Eds.), *Ensinar Português nas Universidades da América do Norte. Teaching Portuguese in North American Universities* (pp. 129–132). Department of Spanish and Portuguese - University of Toronto. Instituto Camões.

Dodman, M. J., Cardoso, I., & Tavares, V. (forthcoming). Communicating and Understanding the Other through Experiential Education: Portuguese Language and Culture in Toronto. In M. Jeon, M. Figueredo & F. Carra-Salsberg (Ed.). *Globally Informed Design and Praxis in Languages, Literatures and Linguistics Curricula.* University of Toronto Press.

Dolz, J., Noverraz, M., Schneuwly, B., Rojo, R., & Cordeiro, G. (2004). Sequências didáticas para o oral e a escrita: apresentação de um procedimento. In B. Schneuwly & J. Dolz (Eds.), *Gêneros orais e escritos na escola* (pp. 81–108). Mercado de Letras.

Enscoe, G. E., & Russell, R. W. (1969). *The disciplined imagination: an approach to the reading of fiction.* Addison-Wesley Publ. Co.

Ferreira, J. A., & Rolim, R. (2010). O ensino de Português no Canadá: algumas observações sobre dinâmicas universitárias. In J. P. Ferreira & Manuela Marujo (Eds.), *Ensinar Português nas Universidades da América do Norte. Teaching Portuguese in North American Universities* (pp. 101–113). Department of Spanish and Portuguese - University of Toronto. Instituto Camões.

Ferreira, T. S., Graça, L. & Cardoso, I. (2020). Formação de professores de Português Língua de Herança: possibilidades do recurso a atividades "na pele dos aprendentes". In M. L. Gonçalves & S. Melo-Pfeifer (Coord.). *Português língua de herança e formação de professores.* Lidel (978-989-752-517-9).

Garcez, P. de M. (2018). Quem é estudante falante de português em famílias de origem brasileira em Toronto, Canadá? Questões de classe. *Linguagem Em (Dis)Curso, 18*(3), 729–749.

Guasch, O. (2000). La expresión escrita. In U. R. Bikandi (Ed.), *Didáctica de la segunda lengua en educación infantil y primaria* (pp. 273–300). Síntesis.

Hyland, F. (2010). Future directions in feedback on second language. *International Journal of English Studies, 10*(2), 173–182.

Hyland, K. (2007). Genre pedagogy: language, literacy and L2 writing instruction. *Journal of Second Language Writing, 16*(3), 148–164. https://doi.org/10.1016/j.jslw.2007.07.005

Jouët-Pastré, C. de, Klobucka, A., Sobral, P. I., Moreira, M. L. de B., & Hutchinson, A. (2013). *Ponto de Encontro: Portuguese as a World Language* (2nd ed.). Pearson.

Melo-Pfeifer, S. (2018). Português como língua de herança: Que português? Que língua? Que herança? *Domínios de Lingu@gem*. https://doi.org/10.14393/dl34-v12n2a2018-18

Melo-Pfeifer, S, & Simões, A. R. (Eds.). (2017). *Plurilinguismo vivido, plurilinguismo desenhado: estudos sobre a relação dos sujeitos com as línguas*. Instituto Politécnico de Santarém / Escola Superior de Educação.

Melo-Pfeifer, S., & Schmidt, A. (2012). Linking "heritage language" education and plurilingual repertoires development: evidences from drawings of Portuguese pupils in Germany. *L1 Educational Studies in Language and Literature, 12*(special issue), 1–30. https://doi.org/10.17239/L1ESLL-2012.02.11

Pereira, L. Á., & Cardoso, I. (2013). A Sequência de ensino como dispositivo didático para a aprendizagem da escrita num contexto de formação de professores. In L. Á. Pereira & I. Cardoso (Eds.), *Reflexão sobre a escrita. O ensino de diferentes géneros de textos* (pp. 33–65). UA Editora.

Valdes, G. (2014). Heritage language students: profiles and possibilities. In N. L. . Willey, J. Peyton, D. Christian, S. Moore (Ed.), *Handbook of Heritage, Community, and Native American Languages in the United States* (pp. 27–35). http://www.linguas.net/LinkClick.aspx?fileticket=pvMGYpDt200=&tabid=695&mid=1356&language=en-US

Van Beuningen, C. (2010). Corrective feedback in L2 writing: theoretical perspectives, empirical insights, and future directions. *International Journal of English Studies, 10*(2), 1-27,184. https://doi.org/10.6018/ijes/10/2/119171

Vermeule, B. (2010). *Why do we care about fictional characters*. The John Hopkins UP.

Vygotsky, L. S. (2005). Pensamento e linguagem. In *Psicologia e pedagogia* (3ª). Martins Fontes.

10
Challenging Cultural Stereotypes in the Pluricentric Portuguese as a Foreign Language Classroom

Vander Tavares
York University

Introduction

According to Statistics Canada (2017), Portuguese is the first language of at least 237,000 people in the country. The diverse community of Portuguese language speakers has continued to grow over the years, especially as a result of immigration, which began in as early as the 1950s. The steady growth of the Portuguese-speaking community has had direct implications for the teaching and learning of Portuguese in Canada: in addition to being currently sought as a foreign language, Portuguese has also become a heritage language to students born to Portuguese-speaking parents, in parallel contact with English, French, and many other languages spoken in Canada in the public or private dimensions. The European and Brazilian varieties of Portuguese are the most prominent within the immigrant community, although the two varieties co-exist in a linguistically synergetic environment as the number of Portuguese speakers from other backgrounds continues to rise in Canada (Statistics Canada, 2017).

This chapter offers a contribution to two areas of research within applied linguistics. First, while a number of educational institutions across Canada provide Portuguese language courses today, research exploring the teaching and learning of Portuguese as a foreign language from and within the Canadian context remains underexplored, though it is of great importance in view of the linguistic and demographic trends highlighted above. Second, culture has been a traditional component of foreign language teaching. Yet, considering the complexity of both the term and the task, culture teaching as a topic has attracted ongoing discussion and much debate by instructors/researchers. However, mainstream applied linguistics continues to focus on considerations of culture teaching primarily from a perspective of English as a second or foreign language. By exploring the cultural stereotypes of students of Portuguese as a foreign language in an advanced-level undergraduate course, this chapter seeks to strengthen and diversify research on culture teaching.

Stereotypes and Language Teaching

Almost a century ago, in the field of psychology, stereotyping was introduced conceptually as a necessary cognitive feature in humans (Langenhove & Harre, 1994). Lippmann (1922) held that direct exposure to new experiences by humans was remarkably limited because of the complexity, dynamicity, and extent of the real world, to which humans only have minimal access during their life time. Accordingly, stereotyping would then function as a mechanism to compensate for the knowledge gaps that would otherwise be acquired naturalistically. Despite the view of stereotyping as a biologically intrinsic and automatic coping strategy, Lippmann maintained that it was, nonetheless, "a very partial and inadequate way of representing the world" (p. 72).

Stereotypes are still often seen as overgeneralisations of the *other* (Hughes & Baldwin, 2002), which may be assigned uncritically to individuals of another national and/or cultural group. However, stereotyping is not always the product of a lack of direct personal experience with individuals from different groups. In fact, Peng (2010) suggests that stereotypes "may not be reduced even if direct observation of the target culture proves them to be wrong" (p. 246) (see also Kramsch, 1993), likely because of the level of complexity in individual factors, such as sociocultural and psychological experiences in life, that come into play in our interaction with the world. In the foreign language classroom, where structured input to target language and culture are received primarily *within* the classroom context, the instructor is then tasked with creatively identifying and developing continuous opportunities in which students' stereotypes can be discussed and challenged.

Instructors and researchers generally agree that stereotypes are difficult to change or reduce. For instance, although Chinese and Japanese societies are discussed consistently as collectivist societies, Matsumoto (2002) and Peng (2003) argue that their research exploring cultural attitudes of younger Japanese and Chinese, respectively, toward the self and society as a whole do not support the stereotypical image of these societies as "being collective-oriented and seeking life-long ties" (Peng, 2010, p. 246). Therefore, stereotypes are difficult to change because they "solidify" over time within our broader framework of cultural reference (Itakura, 2004; Lyons & Kashima, 2003), and also because the acquisition and development of stereotypical images are informed by exposure to multiple channels of information related to the target group, such as literature, advertising, and tourism.

Peng (2010) defines stereotypes as "images, understandings or knowledge of culturally different others which are caused by inaccurate cultural knowledge or incomplete information" (p. 246). In this chapter, stereotypes are regarded as both overgeneralisations and underdeveloped representations which do not accurately portray the other. Central to this chapter is also the understanding that stereotypes resulting from erroneous information can interfere with effective intercultural communication and relationships (Ting-Toomey & Chung, 2005).

In the pluricentric Portuguese classroom, students can draw on their own personal intercultural experience to explore and challenge stereotypes. As high as 70% of students in the Portuguese language and Luso-Brazilian studies program at York University come from immigrant families from Portugal, Brazil, Angola, and other Portuguese-speaking countries or territories (Dodman, Cardoso, & Tavares, in press). Often, these students are first-generation Lusophone-Canadians who grow up in the multicultural and multilingual context not only of their immediate homes, but also of distinctively diverse Toronto and Canada (Statistics Canada, 2017). Based on this context of experience, these students bring to the Portuguese language classroom unique introspective cultural perspectives, which become resources for the instructor.

This cultural identity-related introspective resource can be accessed through structured classroom activities like the one presented later in this chapter. The pedagogical process which students experience requires that they first look into the target culture—the one they also occupy, partially or fully, depending on their individual sociocultural and linguistic involvement with it—but from an outsider's Anglophone Canadian viewpoint, and then simultaneously position themselves also as recipients of these stereotypical representations. In other words, the activity affords the students the opportunity to view themselves as the other, but also respond to this assigned stereotype from this *other* position—a type of proficiency of the multicultural self.

Byram and Esarte-Sarries (1991) view language students as ethnographers of the target culture. In this sense, rather than only receiving culture-related input in the classroom, traditionally through fact-like figures, students should also be instructed to develop analytical skills that can help them assess and reflect on cultural material. In addition to assessing input related to the target culture that originates from indirect sources, students should assess discoveries which result from their own exploratory experiences, both individually and in collaboration, which may at times be contradictory to previously consolidated knowledge (Itakura, 2004). This student-led ethnographic work can involve interviews with individuals from the target culture and contrastive reflections that help students view the target culture in less dichotomous or ethnocentric ways (Cardoso & Dodman, this volume; Ho, 2009; Kramsch, 1993).

In discussing cultural images in the foreign language classroom, it is essential to reinforce the notion that cultures are not static. Although a number of activities can highlight the dynamic and interactive nature of culture, the first-generation students of a Lusophone background bring first-hand experience of intercultural contact into the classroom from having grown up within a shared cultural space in Canada. Cultural images can change as cultures interact, and the students in this pluricentric Portuguese language course are the very representation of this cultural phenomenon, sharing subject positions and identities which not only meet at the cultural boundary, but also permeate into each other's bi-cultural space, modifying each other as a result of this dialectical and transformative contact (Pavlenko, 2006).

Plurilingualism and Cultural Images
Although plurilingualism refers to linguistic and cultural knowledge in more than one language, this knowledge is normally seen as a single competence. Beacco (2007) explains that plurilingual competence is comprised of varying degrees of linguistic proficiency in several languages. Thus, being plurilingual is not the same as having achieved a high level of proficiency in all languages one knows, but rather "the ability to use more than one linguistic variety to [different] degrees... for different purposes" (p. 36). A linguistic variety may be used for a particular communicative activity, such as writing a text message or an academic essay, and as direct exposure to the context in which these activities are embedded increases or decreases over time, so does the degree of proficiency in that particular linguistic variety, since contextual use and language proficiency are understood to be related.

Plurilingual and pluricultural competencies are closely intertwined, and may often be theorised by some as a singular competence. A strong argument has proposed that acknowledging and acting upon—and within—plurilingual competences, both at the individual and societal levels in which linguistic and cultural knowledges are integrated, may support better intercultural participation with and understanding of one another in linguistically and culturally diverse societies, especially those currently characterised by active immigration (Flores, 2013; Knowles, 2016). Plurilingual competence is then understood to lead to a communicative context in which cultural differences might have less weight in influencing intercultural relations.

The plurilingual Portuguese classroom is envisioned as a communicative environment where plurilingual inter-comprehension among students may be fostered. The Portuguese language courses at York University bring students together whose objective is to learn or improve their target variety of the Portuguese language, most typically the European and Brazilian ones. Since these varieties naturally come into contact in the classroom, the learning experience affords students an instructor-mediated opportunity to develop not only an awareness of the differences and similarities among the linguistic varieties, but also an understanding that within these differences, effective communication can still be possible as students acquire and build upon their knowledge specific of language (variety) in context (Araújo e Sá & Melo, 2007).

In a similar vein, as the varieties of Portuguese interact, opportunities for the development of intercultural knowledge emerge. Through interactive and reflective activities in which cultural material—imagery, text, video, and students' lived experiences, for example—is shared, students can learn about the culture of the other in conjunction with its particular linguistic variety. These learning opportunities are expected to expand the plurilingual-pluricultural repertoire of students by integrating knowledge of language and culture into one dynamic competence (Coste, Moore, & Zarate, 2009). In this chapter, students' plurilingual-pluricultural repertoire is expanded through an activity in which cultural images in the form of stereotypes are foregrounded.

Images of the Other: Portuguese and Brazilian People

Stereotypes by Portuguese people toward Brazilians and vice-versa have existed for a long time given the extensive historical ties between the two countries. Stereotypes toward one another have been the product of not only early intercultural contact between the two countries, especially through mass immigration, but also a number of channels that disseminate cultural information, such as literature, tourism, and popular media, which altogether continue to propagate old and new images of Brazilians and Portuguese as two distinct, homogenous cultural groups. These stereotypes evoke images of one another that are as diverse as the kinds of channels through which these images are circulated in the two countries and internationally.

The role literature has played in disseminating stereotypes of Portuguese people—men, in particular—cannot be underestimated. In the romance novel *O Cortiço* (1890) by Brazilian writer Aluísio Azevedo, which tells the story of different ethnic groups working and living together in a Rio de Janeiro's tenement, one of the central characters is an "exploitative and parasitic" immigrant Portuguese man named João (Rowland, 2001). In the novel, João is obsessed with enriching himself, and achieves this by cheating the legal system and exploiting others, but mainly a run-away slave who helps him with the arduous business work. João not only forges the slave's manumission document, but also readily leaves her when the opportunity to marry the wealthy neighbour's daughter presents itself—a move he makes to ascend socially.

Rowland (2001) has argued that the cultural image of the Portuguese as wily and opportunistic still persists today, despite more than a century since the last mass immigration of Portuguese people into Brazil occurred. In most cases, the Portuguese were depicted in two dominant stereotypes: the wealthy Portuguese immigrant, whose business management was successful due to exploitation and cheating, whom Brazilians were hostile toward because a Portuguese commerce person would supposedly only hire other Portuguese to work in their stores; and the unintelligent Portuguese person who would subject themselves to inferior work for a quick salary, work which local Brazilians would refuse to undertake (Castro, 2013; Rowland, 2001). Of course, in presenting intercultural relations between these two groups, Brazilians were also stereotypically portrayed as having a clever and lazy attitude in relation to work.

Between the Portuguese and Brazilians, one gender has become the major target of stereotypes for each cultural group: the Portuguese man, and the Brazilian woman. Alves and Junior (2019) discuss the prevailing ways in which the Brazilian woman is portrayed in Hollywood productions, including animated cartoons, such as the Simpsons: beautiful, sensual, tanned, and provocative. A research study at the University of Coimbra found that the image of the Brazilian woman in Portugal can often be one of a prostitute, while the Brazilian man's image is one of an unreliable and untrustworthy individual (Oliveira, Cabecinhas, & Ferin, 2011; Vitorio, 2007). The study suggests the tourism and media industries may have contributed to the proliferation of these images over a period of several years.

The stereotype of the typical Portuguese man by Brazilians has also been depicted through a specific physiognomy and physique. Pais (2016) explains this stereotype originated in the nineteenth and twentieth centuries as Portuguese immigrants arrived in Brazil: "on the welcome cards [of restaurants] there was a caricature that represents the Portuguese man prototype: big-bellied and bouffant moustaches; the big belly signaling the passion for food and drink; the moustache corresponding to a physical trace of more difficult explanation" (p. 10) [translated from Portuguese]. Research which has sought to explore common cultural images held by the two national groups toward one another has been growing, but still demonstrates that these stereotypes are not easily reduced (Machado, 2018).

The Activity

This activity[37] required students to listen to a conversation centred on cultural stereotypes. Each individual speech in the conversation was numbered so that students could follow the sequence of events in a series of numbered cartoons in which the story was visually presented. To

---

[37] Ferreira, T. S., Soares, S. C., Melo-Pfeifer, S., & Favero, M. (2015). Lado a lado - Nível A1. Ensino Português no estrangeiro. Porto, Portugal: Porto Editora.

complete the activity, students had to log into the online learning platform, access the activity, listen to the conversation (often with headphones), and answer questions aloud, which were recorded into the learning platform system with the use of microphones. The conversation used in the activity has been transcribed, translated, and provided below. In it, a group of strangers from Portugal, Brazil, and France come together after being assigned the same table at Patricia's wedding reception.

1. **Priest:** I declare you husband and wife.

2. **Simone:** Congratulations! Congratulations to both of you!
3. **Patricia:** Thank you, auntie!

4. **Simone:** What is our table? Oh, here it is. The table of the camellias. How interesting! Each table has the name of a different flower!
5. **Gabriel:** Yeah, how original...
6. **Silvana:** It doesn't matter. It's romantic!

7. **Simone:** Good afternoon! Looks like we'll be spending the afternoon together!
8. **Gabriel:** What fun to spend the afternoon with strangers! This keeps getting better…

9. **Simone:** My name is Simone, this is my husband Caio, and these are our children: Gabriel, Ana Marta and Silvana. We live in Aveiro. I'm the bride's aunt!

10. **Ana:** Nice to meet you! I'm Ana, Gontran is my husband and Jojo is our daughter. We are French. We are in Portugal for this wedding ceremony, because Gustave is my nephew. He's my sister's son.
11. **Gabriel:** And on top of that they're French…

12. **Joanna:** What did you say?!
13. **Gabriel:** Who, me? Nothing... I said I really like French crepes.
14. **Joanna:** Ah, I thought I had heard something else.

15. **Simone:** Oh, yes? Are you French? But you speak such good Portuguese!
16. **Ana:** My parents are Portuguese, but they have been living in France for 40 years now. My sister and I were born in France. But my parents always speak to me in Portuguese, and I try to do the same with Jojo, but it's not always easy.

17. **Gabriel:** Jojo? What a name...
18. **Joanna:** Jojo is for friends. For you, it's Joanna.

19. **Joanna:** I think this napkin is mine. At least in France the napkin is placed on the left side.
20. **Gabriel:** The French and their obsession with etiquette and manners...

21. **Gabriel:** Well, here in Portugal the napkins belong to whoever grabs them first.
22. **Joanna:** It seems true that the Portuguese are rude with no manners.
23. **Gabriel:** Don't you know it's bad to let out the secrets?!
24. **Simone:** Gabriel, hey! Why these manners? Do not mind him, Joanna! Gabriel is in a bad mood. He did not want to come to the wedding.
25. **Silvana:** Yeah, he turned 12 last month, but he thinks he turned 18!

26. **Joanna:** Look, she's Brazilian!? You must be nicer than your brother.

27. **Gabriel:** Oh, this game is awesome! I'm always playing this on my phone!
28. **Joanna:** So, why don't you play it now? If you are so bored...

29. **Silvana:** That's because the smart guy here forgot to charge the battery of his cell phone.
30. **Joanna:** If you want, we can play it together.
31. **Gabriel:** Really?! Cool!

A few hours later...
32. **Gabriel:** That's a good one! I know another one, listen: a French, an English and a Portuguese get on an airplane...

33. **Patricia:** We have a souvenir for you! So, are you guys having fun?
34. **Simone:** Everything is great!

35. **Gabriel:** It's the best wedding ever! If you get married again, invite me and I will come!
36. **Simone:** What, Gabriel?!

A number of exercises followed the conversation presented. The first exercise tested students' listening comprehension skills in Portuguese. In this exercise, students were required to match items in the first column with items in the second based on what they had heard in the conversation so that they could identify which character held a stereotype toward a given character. The second exercise tested students' analytical skills in relation to the content. In this exercise, students were given three choices and asked to identify which one was the factor influencing the characters' opinions of one another prior to getting to know them. The choices were (a) physical aspect, (b) nationality, and (c) language. The correct answer was nationality. The third exercise required students to identify the cultural ideas emergent in the conversation with respect to: French people (value placed on etiquette and good manners), the Portuguese (rude and impolite behaviour), and Brazilian people (friendly attitude).

The fourth exercise is the focus of this chapter. This exercise shifted the emphasis from testing students' comprehension skills to exploring their individual relationships with cultural stereotypes about the other as well as the self. In part one, students were asked whether they had previously heard those stereotypes associated with French, Portuguese, and Brazilian people. Additionally, students were asked whether they also held these cultural images. In part two, students were asked to share ideas they held (1) toward their own cultural group—which varied according to the students' individual cultural, national, and linguistic backgrounds, though largely Lusophone (Portuguese, Brazilian, and Angolan), but with some students being citizens of more than just one country—but also (2) toward Canadians, since students' personal experiences were situated in the Canadian sociocultural environment. In part three, students were asked first to reflect on whether they believed others had a preconceived opinion of them, and second to identify the possible factors sustaining these preconceived opinions.

Fourteen students completed the activity. The recordings of their oral responses to questions in all three parts were transcribed, translated, and analysed. The process of analysis involved reading and categorising each response under important themes (Creswell, 2013) within the broader topic of cultural stereotypes, such as nationality, dress code, race, among others. In this sense, the analysis focused directly on what students said (content), rather than how they said it (form). As for understanding the process of language and culture learning, this study adopted a constructivist approach, wherein students engage in experiences that foster and centre on individual agency, creativity, social collaboration, and that position students as co-constructors of knowledge (Rüschoff, 1999). Abrams (2002) has proposed that exploring cultural stereotypes through a constructivist approach is appropriate because it leads students to "access their existing cultural frameworks and actively analyze supporting or contradictory evidence to refine their hypotheses" about the target culture (p. 144).

Part I: Relating to Stereotypes

In general, the majority of students, all of whom have been assigned pseudonyms, reported hearing these specific stereotypes before. Within this group of students, those of a Portuguese background either challenged or rejected the stereotypes associated with their nationality and culture presented in the activity. To challenge or reject the negative stereotypes, students drew typically on their positive, immediate family experiences. However, in the case of Clara (1) and Jane (2), their responses suggest that cultural association can still play a significant role in how students see other members in their own multigenerational and multicultural families. In other words, despite being family, the students still viewed their family members primarily through the lenses of cultural stereotypes.

    1. I have my own opinion of French people because my mom is French. (Jane)

    2. I have heard these stereotypes about French people before, that they have a certain etiquette. I've never heard these stereotypes about the Portuguese, that they are brute and rude. I don't think that is true because my family is Portuguese, and they're friendly and kind people. (Clara)

    3. I've heard all these stereotypes about all three groups, but I don't agree with all these ideas. I don't think it's true that Portuguese people lack politeness. In general, they are friendly and helpful. (Camila)

Yet, Clara's response (4) demonstrates that her stereotypical view of her French family members changed after a two-month visit with them. This experience may be considered a kind of ethnographic involvement in which the student had her views changed through first-hand live-in experience, which is one of the many potential gains research has found in exploring experiences of sojourn abroad (Allen, Dristas, & Mills, 2007; Bloom & Miranda, 2015; Shiri, 2015). Another student, Daniel (5), recognises that people behave a certain way not necessarily because of their nationality, but rather individual difference. He challenges the notion that people should be expected to behave in stereotypical ways by arguing expectations around typical cultural behaviour can interfere with one's individual freedom.

    4. When I went to France for the first time, I also thought that everyone there would value and have a certain etiquette. Because I have cousins and aunts who live in Paris, I thought maybe they would also have this way of thinking that they are better and of saying that everything in Paris is right and better. But after spending two months there, living with them, I changed my own opinion [about French people and

etiquette] because they have this habit of saying anything that comes to mind. (Clara)

5. I have heard all these stereotypes many times before. People always say that the French are arrogant because they always want to do things their own way. As for the Portuguese, some people say that they're only good at construction work and nothing else. Lastly, people always say that Brazilians are the warmest people and that they're always happy. Honestly, I don't agree on these because I believe these stereotypes present people in an incorrect way. Just because someone is French does not mean they are well-mannered. Everyone is different. If I said that someone had to act a certain way, that would be wrong, because it limits the freedom we all have as human beings. (Daniel)

Some responses may show a contradictory position in which negative stereotypes are challenged, but positive ones are not. For example, in his response, John (7) states that negative traits are not unique to a particular cultural group when referring to Portuguese people being stereotypically portrayed as rude. Yet, he accepts and agrees on stereotypes toward French and Brazilian people, which may suggest that a positive trait, such as that of friendliness shared by Brazilians, need not be questioned, analogous to good manners by French people, despite the culturally subjective nature of some polite behaviour (Janney & Arndt, 1993; Kasanga & Lwanga-Lumu, 2007).

6. Yes, I've heard these stereotypes about Portuguese and Brazilian people. I agree that Brazilians are friendlier, but I don't think the Portuguese are rude. (Marcos)

7. I agree on the stereotypes about French and Brazilian people. But I disagree on the ones about the Portuguese because any nationality can have people who are rude and disrespectful. (John)

8. I had never heard these stereotypes before, but regardless, I don't agree. People from all nationalities are friendly, but I'm only saying this based on those I've met. (Carla)

Some students' responses demonstrate their awareness that stereotypes are rather common across cultures. This can be exemplified in Juliana's response (9), in which she reports she has heard a language-related stereotype associated with Brazilians, but to challenge it, she compares it to another language-related stereotype associated with another national group: "people who live in China." By doing this, Juliana questions relationships between country and language in which a language spoken in a country is erroneously automatically derived from its name, as in Brazil: Brazilian, China: Chinese, India: Indian, and so on. In here, we see an awareness on her part that stereotypes follow similar patterns and approaches (Jussim, Coleman, & Lerch, 1987).

9. I've heard people say that Brazil speaks Brazilian. They think that people who live in Brazil speak Brazilian, like how we think that people who live in China speak Chinese. But that's not the case. (Juliana)

Lastly, another student, Marta (10), identifies that stereotyping national groups can contribute to the propagation of discriminatory practices, as certain national groups are often only portrayed negatively in relation to their race, ethnicity, religion, and several other sociological aspects (Guo & Harlow, 2014; Stangor & Schaller, 2000).

10. Yes, I have heard these stereotypes before. Unfortunately, we still find people with racist attitudes who judge others based on their nationality. (Marta)

Part II: Identifying Stereotypes

Overall, through their responses, students demonstrate knowledge and awareness of stereotypes associated with their cultural groups, predominantly Portuguese, but with a smaller number of students belonging to more than only one cultural group. Within the Portuguese group, the majority of students focus on stereotypes first around Portuguese cuisine as a fish-based one, and second around an enthusiastic communication style—for some students, the latter may be seen as impolite by non-Portuguese others. However, some responses suggest that students understand that stereotypes cannot always correctly represent an entire cultural group. Other stereotypes had to do with family relationships, social behaviour, and sports.

11. I heard people say that the Portuguese like fish, and that they talk too much, but I don't think these ideas are right because not all Portuguese are the same. (Pauline)

12. I hear that Portuguese men work in construction. Also that Portuguese people like to eat fish and potatoes. (Miguel)

13. I have heard people say that the Portuguese are rude, impolite, and curse all the time. (Mariana)

14. Some common stereotypes associated with my background, which is Portuguese, are, for example, that the Portuguese are bad drivers and that there are many car accidents in Portugal. Other stereotypes about Portuguese people are that they are good at soccer, because Portuguese soccer is always on the news, and that all Portuguese men play soccer. As for the Portuguese in Toronto, the stereotype is that they like to smoke, that they get together and smoke outside their offices. Also, that wherever the Portuguese live, they barbecue sardines on the weekends and that the neighbours can recognise their Portuguese neighbours because of that strong fish smell. Many people think that all Portuguese people eat sardines and codfish. The Portuguese like to get together with family and friends, and discuss a number of topics, one of them

being soccer. I also think that the Portuguese discuss their ideas with a lot of passion and enthusiasm, but that these conversations don't always seem very diplomatic [because] they talk loud. But it's just their way of being. (Sandra)

Juliana (15) identifies a number of stereotypes associated with Portuguese people. First, she refers to negative stereotypes related to group behaviour, which she reports encountering very frequently: rudeness, impoliteness, wiliness. Second, she refers to eating "a lot of cheese" as a stereotype, which she does not challenge because it does not carry a negative connotation for her. In fact, she accepts it and inserts herself into this group, presenting it as a stereotype of accurate representation. Then, Juliana identifies stereotypes associated less nationally but more regionally, such as the one in which her interlocutors cannot identify her city of origin and at times even mistake it for a place in Spain, and another stereotype in which a regional dialect becomes the factor behind the stereotype. In her final response, Juliana ascribes the propagation of cultural stereotypes to the media as a primary source (Harrison, Tayman, Janson, & Connolly, 2010; Lee *et al.*, 2009; Winter, 2009).

> 15. In relation to my country of origin, I always hear the same thing: that we are rude, wily, and that we eat a lot of cheese. Also that we're impolite. I eat cheese everyday, which is something typically Portuguese, it's a stereotype. But the one of everyone being ill-mannered is not true. Nobody in my family is like that, but yes, I have met some who are like beasts.
>
> I always have to correct people when I say I'm Portuguese and they tell me they don't know the city [I'm from] or that it's a province in Spain, and I always have to correct them. There's a village in Portugal named Valverde. They say people from there are known stereotypically because they speak differently.
>
> There is so much on social media and the internet about other countries. There are TV shows from other countries. All this influences us to develop an image [that is] not totally correct because of the ideas that come from outside sources. We hold on to this idea that a country is a certain way just because we see things on TV or the internet. (Juliana)

In Teresa's response (16), we see that cultural stereotypes of a particular cultural group may go beyond simplistic references to food and behaviour, but may also include a reference to more sensitive ideas, such as unequal gender relations in the target culture (Talbot, 2003). In addition to identifying negative stereotypes of impolite behaviour, and of a fish-based cuisine, as other students similarly did, Teresa reports hearing that Portuguese men are "very sexist" and Portuguese women are inferior. However, Teresa challenges this stereotype by drawing on her immediate family experience in which her father and brother help her mother in the home. Teresa describes the attitude of Portuguese men toward women as a form of pride, although she reports that this is not the case all the time. Lastly, while still making reference to family, Teresa reports hearing that Portuguese men's attitudes toward women in the home tend to change negatively once they get married.

> 16. I've heard stereotypes toward Portuguese people, that they are rude, ill-mannered, and that they curse all the time and only like codfish and custard tart. I've also heard that Portuguese men are very sexist, and so the women have to do everything, women are their slaves. But actually this isn't true. Yes, Portuguese men are prouder but not always. Like in my house, my dad helps my mom and my brother helps around the house, and I hope this won't change when he gets married because I've heard that this happens a lot. (Teresa)

Lucca (17) identifies stereotypes of Italians—one of his ethnic and cultural backgrounds—at three levels: some which may be unique to Italians, some which are relatable to another cultural group, and those which are shared by a much broader cultural group. First, he refers to stereotypes he reports are characteristic of Italians: being noisy, eating pasta, and drinking. Then, he identifies stereotypes that, in his experience as an Italo-Portuguese, both Italians and Portuguese share in terms of close family relationships and feeling content. Finally, he identifies a stereotype based on the habit of smoking that encompasses a much larger group ("Europeans") to insert Italians into this broad cultural group. Lucca's act of relating and comparing suggests that cultural stereotypes may overlap according to the student's self-identification in terms of their cultural identities.

> 17. With respect to Italians, stereotypes are that they are very noisy. Also, that they like to eat pasta, drink, and smoke, like many Europeans do. And that like the Portuguese, they enjoy being with family, grandparents, grandchildren, nieces and nephews. They are family-focused and content. (Lucca)

The activity also sought to explore students' stereotypes of Canadians as the students lived in Toronto. Generally, students referred to stereotypes of polite behaviour, as in Canadians being helpful, nice, apologetic, honest, and kind people. However, Clara's response (18) suggests an awareness that these stereotypes exist, but that they may not represent all Canadians. Moreover, despite York University, Toronto, and Canada as a whole being spaces where various cultural, ethnic, and linguistic groups can be found, the stereotypes identified by the students presented Canadians as one singular group, through simplistic inter-related images, such as the cold weather and hockey (Robidoux, 2002). Because some students were also Canadian in nationality, or identified themselves as such, they included themselves in their references to Canadians, as John's response (22) reveals.

18. I think that Canadians are friendly and kind, but I don't think all of them are. (Clara)

19. Canadians are very polite, and they like to say "sorry." (Marcos)

20. I hear that all Canadians like Tim Horton's, live in igloos, like hockey, and like to apologise. (Miguel)

21. Stereotypes associated with Canadians are that they are very caring and always want to help other people. (Daniel)

22. As for stereotypes about Canadians, it's that we're friendly and honest in what we say. (John)

Part III: Reflecting on Stereotypes

All students agreed that people held preconceived ideas of them before getting to know them. A closer look at the responses points to four possible major factors which, individually or in conjunction, play a role in informing others' development of preconceived ideas toward the students: physical look, dress code, facial communication, and national background. In connection to students' physical looks, students report that others tend to assume their nationalities based on one or more physical aspect they have, such as skin colour and hair length. Camila (25) and Carla (26) demonstrate an understanding that physical appearance is often an early factor which influences the images people develop of others. Camila goes one step further and explains that not only stereotypes are difficult to change, but that, for some, the opportunity to get to know someone personally may not be sufficient to help alter their preconceived ideas of that same person.

23. When I visit Portugal, people ask me if I'm Mexican because of my skin colour and long hair. (Paulina)

24. As for myself, many people tell me that I'm always happy and content, and they're right about that. I'm also the type of person who reflects a lot on what I should and should not be doing. People also think that I'm Arabic, and not Italian or Portuguese. I don't know why. Must be the beard. (Lucca)

25. I think it's normal to have an opinion about others before you get to know them, but these opinions aren't easily changed even after two people become more acquainted with each other. The reason for stereotypes at first is the physical look, in my opinion. (Camila)

26. Before meeting me, people think I'm Hispanic. But I don't mind it because I think it's very natural for someone to assume before really knowing. (Carla)

For other students, preconceived opinions are formed on the basis of more than just one factor. While the majority of students do not go into detail in describing the way they dress, they do identify dress code as a possible factor. In this sense, the students note that their choice of clothing is perceived to communicate a message to others that is supposedly reflective of their personality or mood. The same can be said about students' facial communication. For example, Clara (27) reports that she may be perceived as a serious person because of her choice of clothing or because at times she does not look happy. Similarly, John (29) reports that his choice of clothing and facial communication may play the same role in informing people's perception of him. Here, we find an awareness on the part of students that intended or unintended presentation of the self through social behaviour can communicate incorrect ideas (Anderson *et al.,* 2002; Burgoon, Guerrero, & Floyd, 2016).

27. I do feel as though people sometimes have a preconceived opinion of me before they actually meet me. I think many people may think that I'm a very serious person, and that I'm strange. It could be from the way I dress, or because sometimes I look bored or sad, but after they get to know me, I think their opinions change. (Clara)

28. Yes, I do think people have a preconceived opinion of me before they meet me, which is normal. The reason for this could some physical aspect or the way I dress. (Marcos)

29. I do think people have a preconceived opinion of me before meeting me. The majority of people think that I am—how do we say this—arrogant or rude, but I'm not. I'm not sure why people think of me that way. Maybe it's the way I dress or because I'm not always smiling. That's what I think. (John)

Nationality is another common factor which can evoke stereotypes of the other. But first, Juliana (30) reports that most people she meets do not know Portugal even exists. Then she explains that by presenting herself as Portuguese, those who do know about the country tend to think of her in stereotypically negative ways. Plus, she reports that people tend to judge her based on her northern Portuguese dialect. However, to challenge these preconceived ideas of her based on her nationality, she highlights positive experiences she has had: good academic performance and more than one job. Juliana's experience reinforces the notion that stereotypes may not only be inaccurate, but also detrimental. As for Marta (31), because of her skin colour, she becomes a "candidate" to a number of possible nationalities. She reports that when others know she is Portuguese, cultural images around cuisine, music, and sports tend to surface.

30. People who only know others by their nationality have stereotypes. The majority of people I meet have never heard of Portugal, and the ones who have think that I'm wily, impolite, and that I speak strange just because I'm from the northern part of the country. But this is completely untrue because I'm doing well in school, I work three jobs,

and I'm not rude. Totally different from what people imagine or expect when I say that I'm Portuguese. (Juliana)

31. Sometimes people have a preconceived opinion of me, maybe because of my physical appearance, like my skin colour and dark hair. They presume that I'm Spanish, Italian, or Portuguese. Normally when they do know I'm Portuguese, they think of a culture that includes good food, good wine, soccer, and fado. (Marta)

Daniel's response (32) illustrates a number of associations between nationality and stereotypes. First, by referring to himself as a member of a large linguistic and cultural community, which is not a nationality per se (Latin American), but nonetheless carries common cultural images (Dávila, 2012), especially in connection to the Spanish language, he is expected to be a good dancer and a romantic person. While he rejects the former but accepts the latter, Daniel still understands that these are preconceived ideas of him. Moreover, Daniel reports that he has been most commonly stereotyped as someone from Mexico, and sometimes as an illegal resident of Canada (see Timberlake & Williams, 2012), despite being a Canadian citizen. In his experience, he has not been successful in changing these images, even when having an opportunity to clarify these to his listeners, which is then not taken seriously. From being Canadian, Daniel also refers to stereotypical images of Canadians. Lastly, he explains that his choice of professional clothing can sometimes communicate an inaccurate image of him to others as someone who is "always serious."

32. I do think that people have a preconceived opinion of me for a number of reasons. The first reason is the fact that I'm Latin-American. So people think that I can dance salsa and tango, but in reality I'm the worst dancer. Because I speak Spanish, women think that I'm romantic and that's true although they think that before they get to know me. Lastly, I tend to dress professionally because for me it's imperative to have the respect of my professors. By the way I dress, I show that I'm serious, but the problem is that some people think that I'm always serious. But I do like to tell jokes. But I don't understand how people can think in such stereotypical ways. The most incorrect and common association people have of me is that I'm illegal, and that I'm Mexican, and when I correct them, they don't believe me and think I'm joking. I'm [also] Canadian, so then I [must] play hockey, eat maple syrup, live in an igloo, and have a beaver as a pet. (Daniel)

Jane (33) suggests that preconceived ideas which others may have of her may be based on her outfits, physiognomy, and nationality. She explains that the more comfortable clothes she prefers to wear are tied to a certain opinion others could have of her. Also, like Marta, Jane mentions that her nationality could be assumed to be any one among many possibilities because of her physical look—more specifically her brown hair and eyes—

although she confines these only to European nationalities, despite brown hair and eyes being common physical features in all parts of the world. Finally, to explain why people assume that she may be stereotypically a religious person, she draws on a nationality-related stereotype of Portuguese people as being religious.

> 33. People have a preconceived opinion of me because we always have opinions about others. I think it might be related to the way I dress because I like to wear skirts, dresses—I like clothes that are very comfortable—and so I think people have an opinion of me based on this. Also, when people look at me, they see my brown eyes and hair. From that they know I'm from Europe, my grandparents and parents come from Europe: Italy, France, and Portugal, but people always think I'm Italian. Lastly, people also have an opinion about my religion because the Portuguese are very religious. (Jane)

Mariana (34) identifies both physical features and facial communication as factors influencing others' preconceived opinions of her. Because of her height, Mariana reports that others perceive her as physically weak. Additionally, she reports that her low voice makes her come across as delicate and childlike. She explains that this frequent reference to her young look does not usually bother her, but can be offensive in certain contexts. Lastly, Mariana reports that the way she looks at people can communicate a certain idea about her that demotivates them to want to speak to her, making her seem unapproachable.

> 34. People do have preconceived opinions of me, almost always because of my height, voice, and the look in my eyes. In relation to my height, they say I'm not strong and that I can't harm anyone because I'm not tall enough. My voice, they say I have a very low voice and that I might be [treated like] a doll, pampered, and that I might be, like, fourteen years old or so. I'm eighteen and in university, but they would never give me more than fourteen or fifteen years old. For me, this is a compliment but it can be unpleasant to hear depending on how people use it. The way I look [at people], people have said they hesitate to speak with me because sometimes I have a mean look, so they prefer to stay away, which I find strange because yes, I can be a little bit unpleasant, but before anything I try to be friendly and polite. (Mariana)

Conclusion

This chapter discussed cultural stereotypes from the perspective of students of Portuguese as a foreign and heritage language during an in-class activity. In the activity, a pre-designed conversation of a cross-cultural nature was used to illustrate the relationship between nationality and cultural stereotypes. From there, students' relationships with stereotypes were explored through a series of questions in which students were asked to identify, relate to, and reflect on stereotypes: those they held toward others, and those they thought others held toward them, with a focus on those directed toward their *national* and *cultural* identities. From this process, a number of stereotypes emerged.

Activities aimed at exploring stereotypes in the foreign language classroom present great potential for critical reflection and discussion. In the context of this class, students generally demonstrated a critical understanding of stereotypes and stereotyping: the ways in which they may be formed and propagated, and in which they can portray the other typically inaccurately and damagingly. Often, the students challenged stereotypes after identifying them. One reason for this might be related to students' dual position: they not only identified, but also received, the very same stereotypes, considering their direct or indirect association with the target culture, most notably through family relationships.

Therefore, activities focused on challenging cultural stereotypes may be more effective if they can be designed to position students, to the extent that is possible, as recipients of one or more aspect of the cultural images which they identify. While this could be challenging in classes where host and target cultural practices present more differences than similarities, as a point of departure, students can be asked to reflect first on preconceived ideas others may have of them. As the last part of the activity showed, in discussing these preconceived ideas, stereotypes related to nationality emerged naturally. The instructor can then use this opportunity to introduce the necessary follow-up activities that help connect preconceived ideas of others and of ourselves, such as those characterised by religion, gender, behaviour, and dress code, to issues of nationality, culture, ethnicity, and race.

Nonetheless, as the research discussed previously in this chapter has emphasised, stereotypes are hard to reduce and change. An analysis of the students' responses supports this finding on the basis that even when students challenged cultural stereotypes directed at them, they normally did so by drawing on other stereotypes as a response. Moreover, students did not question cultural stereotypes that were perceived as positive images, especially those marked by polite behaviour. Finally, in any instance, the instructor plays an important role in helping promote an awareness in the students that stereotypes, even when portraying a large cultural group in a positive light, are by nature used to homogenise and reduce.

Because of this, a critical approach to understanding stereotypes and stereotyping should be encouraged across all cultural images, instead of being expected only when an unfavourable image of the other (or the self) is evoked. Not questioning positive stereotypes because they may be seemingly harmless or even beneficial can directly affect our personal relationships with certain national groups by uncritically and inattentively categorising them into a dichotomy of "good and bad." This facile categorisation can saturate not only our view, but also our treatment of the particularly "bad" cultural or national group through micro and macro social practices informed by a continuous and delicate relationship that brings stereotypes together with our beliefs and attitudes toward the other.

References

Abrams, Z. (2002). Surfing to cross-cultural awareness: Using internet-mediated projects to explore cultural stereotypes. *Foreign Language Annals, 35*(2), 141-160.

Allen, H., Dristas, V., & Mills, N. (2007). Cultural learning outcomes and summer study abroad. In M. Mantero (Ed.), *Identity and second language learning: culture, inquiry, and dialogic activity in educational contexts* (pp. 189–215). Charlotte, NC: Information Age Publishing.

Alves, C., & Junior, E. (2019). O estereótipo nosso de cada dia: Uma abordagem intercultural para o ensino de PL2E. *Ensaios em Português como Segunda Língua ou Língua Estrangeira, 12*, 1-17.

Anderson, P. A., Hecht, M. L., Hoobler, G. D., & Smallwood, M. (2002). Nonverbal communication across cultures. In W. G. Gudykunst & B. Mody (Eds.), *Handbook of international and intercultural communication* (pp. 89-106). Thousand Oaks, CA: Sage.

Araújo e Sá, M., & Melo, S. (2007). Online plurilingual interaction in the development of language awareness. *Language Awareness, 16*(1), 7-14.

Beacco, J. (2007). *From linguistic diversity to plurilingual education: Guide for the development of language education policies in Europe.* Strasbourg, France: Council of Europe.

Bloom, M., & Miranda, A. (2015). Intercultural sensitivity through short-term study abroad. *Language and Intercultural Communication, 15*(4), 567-580.

Burgoon, J. K., Guerrero, L. K., & Floyd, K. (2016). *Nonverbal communication.* London, UK: Routledge.

Byram, M., & Esarte-Sarries, V. (1991). *Investigating cultural studies in foreign language teaching: A book for teachers.* Clevedon, UK: Multilingual Matters.

Cardoso, I., & Dodman, M. J. (2020). Teaching Portuguese language and Lusophone literatures at York University: Creating opportunities, reshaping paths, (re)writing our stories. In I. Cardoso, A. Rato, & V. Tavares (Eds.), *Teaching and learning Portuguese in Canada: Multidisciplinary contributions to SLA research and practice.* Princeton, NJ: Boa Vista Press.

Castro, F. (2013). Construções espacio-identitárias no cinema português: A imagem territorial do emigrante luso-brasileiro nas comédias de Lisboa. *Avanca,* 876-884.

Coste, D., Moore, D., & Zarate, G. (2009). Plurilingual and pluricultural competence. *Studies towards a Common European Framework of Reference for Language Learning and Teaching.* Strasbourg: Council of Europe Publishing.

Creswell, J. W. (2013). *Qualitative inquiry & research design: choosing among five approaches.* Los Angeles, CA: Sage.

Dávila, A. (2012). *Latinos, Inc.: The marketing and making of a people.* Berkeley, CA: University of California Press.

Dodman, M. J., Cardoso, I., & Tavares, V. (forthcoming). Communicating and understanding the other through experiential education: Portuguese language and culture in Toronto. In M. Jeon, M. Figueredo, & F. Carra-Salsberg (Eds.), *Globally informed design and praxis in languages, literatures and linguistics curricula.* University of Toronto Press.

Flores, N. (2013). The unexamined relationship between neoliberalism and plurilingualism: A cautionary tale. *TESOL Quarterly, 47*(3), 500-520.

Guo, L., & Harlow, S. (2014). User-generated racism: An analysis of stereotypes of African Americans, Latinos, and Asians in YouTube videos. *Howard Journal of Communications, 25*(3), 281-302.

Harrison, C., Tayman, K., Janson, N., & Connolly, C. (2010). Stereotypes of Black male athletes on the Internet. *Journal for the Study of Sports and Athletes in Education, 4*(2), 155-172.

Ho, S. T. K. (2009). Addressing culture in EFL classrooms: The challenge of shifting from a traditional to an intercultural stance. *Electronic Journal of Foreign Language Teaching, 6*(1), 63-76.

Hughes, P. C., & Baldwin, J. R. (2002). Communication and stereotypical impressions. *Howard Journal of Communication, 13*(2), 113-128.

Itakura, H. (2004). Changing cultural stereotypes through e-mail assisted foreign language learning. *System, 32,* 37-51.

Janney, R. W., & Arndt, H. (1993). Universality and relativity in cross-cultural politeness research: A historical perspective. *Multilingua-Journal of Cross-Cultural and Interlanguage Communication, 12*(1), 13-50.

Jussim, L., Coleman, L. M., & Lerch, L. (1987). The nature of stereotypes: A comparison and integration of three theories. *Journal of Personality and Social Psychology, 52*(3), 536-456.

Kasanga, L. A., & Lwanga-Lumu, J. C. (2007). Cross-cultural linguistic realization of politeness: A study of apologies in English and

Setswana. *Journal of Politeness Research, Language, Behaviour, Culture, 3*(1), 65-92.

Knowles, V. (2016). *Strangers at our gates: Canadian immigration and immigration policy, 1540–2015*. Toronto, ON: Dundurn Press.

Kramsch, C. (1993). *Context and culture in language teaching*. Oxford: Oxford University Press.

Langenhove, L. V., & Harré, R. (1994). Cultural stereotypes and positioning theory. *Journal for the Theory of Social Behaviour, 24*(4), 359-372.

Lee, M. J., Bichard, S. L., Irey, M. S., Walt, H. M., & Carlson, A. J. (2009). Television viewing and ethnic stereotypes: Do college students form stereotypical perceptions of ethnic groups as a result of heavy television consumption?. *The Howard Journal of Communications, 20*(1), 95-110.

Lippmann, W. (1922). *Public opinion*. New York, NY: Harcourt Brace.

Lyons, A., & Kashima, Y. (2003). How are stereotypes maintained through communication? The influence of stereotypes sharedness. *Journal of Personality and Social Psychology, 85*(6), 989-1005.

Machado, I. (2018). Ressentimentos e estereótipos: ensaio sobre as representações a respeito do português no Brasil (século XIX). *Topoi, 19*(37), 125-143.

Matsumoto, D. (2002). *The new Japan: Debunking seven cultural stereotypes*. Yarmouth, Maine: Intercultural Press.

Oliveira, F., Cabecinhas, R., & Ferin, I. (2011). Retratos da mulher brasileira nas revistas portuguesas. *VII ENECULT-Encontros de Estudos Multidisciplinares em Cultura*, 1-15. Salvador, Bahina: Universidade Federal da Bahia.

Pais, J. M. (2017). As piadas como denunciadoras de conflitos identitários. *IX Congresso Português de Sociologia*, 1-13. Faro, Portugal: Associação Portuguesa de Sociologia.

Pavlenko, A. (Ed.) (2006). *Bilingual minds: emotional experience, expression, and representation*. Clevedon, UK: Multilingual Matters.

Peng, S. Y. (2003). *Culture and conflict management in foreign-invested enterprises in China: An intercultural perspective*. Berne: Peter Lang.

Peng, S. Y. (2010). Impact of stereotypes on intercultural communication: a Chinese perspective. *Asia Pacific Education Review, 11*(2), 243-252.

Robidoux, M. A. (2002). Imagining a Canadian identity through sport: A historical interpretation of lacrosse and hockey. *Journal of American Folklore, 115*(456), 209-225.

Rowland, R. (2001). Manuéis e Joaquins: A cultural brasileira e os portugueses. *Etnográfica, 1*, 157-172.

Rüschoff, B. (1999). Construction of knowledge as the basis of foreign language learning. In B. Mißler & U. Multhaup (Eds.), *The construction of knowledge, learner autonomy and related issues*. Tübingen, Germany: Stauffenberg Verlag.

Shiri, S. (2015). The homestay in intensive language study abroad: Social networks, language socialization, and developing intercultural competence. *Foreign Language Annals, 48*(1), 5-25.

Stangor, C., & Schaller, M. (2000). Stereotypes as individual and collective representations. In C. Stangor (Ed.), *Stereotypes and prejudice: Essential readings. Key readings in Psychology* (pp. 64-82). Philadelphia, PA: Psychology Press/Taylor & Francis.

Statistics Canada. (2017). Immigration and ethnocultural diversity: Key results from the 2016 Census. Retrieved June 1, 2018, from https://www150.statcan.gc.ca/n1/daily-quotidien/171025/dq171025b-eng.htm.

Statistics Canada. (2017). Census in brief: Linguistic diversity and multilingualism in Canadian homes. Retrieved February 24, 2019, from: https://www12.statcan.gc.ca/census-recensement/2016/as-sa/98-200-x/2016010/98-200-x2016010-eng.cfm.

Statistics Canada. (2017). Immigrant population in Canada, 2016 Census of population. Retrieved February 24, 2019, from: https://www150.statcan.gc.ca/n1/pub/11-627-m/11-627-m2017028-eng.htm.

Talbot, M. (2003). Gender stereotypes: reproduction and challenge. In J. Holmes and M. Meyerhoff (Eds.), *The handbook of language and gender* (pp. 468-86). Oxford: Blackwell.

Timberlake, J. M., & Williams, R. H. (2012). Stereotypes of US immigrants from four global regions. *Social Science Quarterly, 93*(4), 867-890.

Ting-Toomey, S., & Chung, L. C. (2005). *Understanding intercultural communication*. New York, NY: Oxford University Press.

Vitorio, B. S. (2007). *Imigração brasileira em Portugal: Identidade e perspetivas*. São Paulo, SP: Editora Universitária Leopoldianum.

Winter, C. 2009. *Branding Finland on the internet: Images and stereotypes in Finland's tourism marketing*, Master Thesis, Jyväskylä: University of Jyväskylä.

BOAVISTA PRESS 2020

www.ingramcontent.com/pod-product-compliance
Lightning Source LLC
Chambersburg PA
CBHW071418160426
43195CB00013B/1734